D1565653

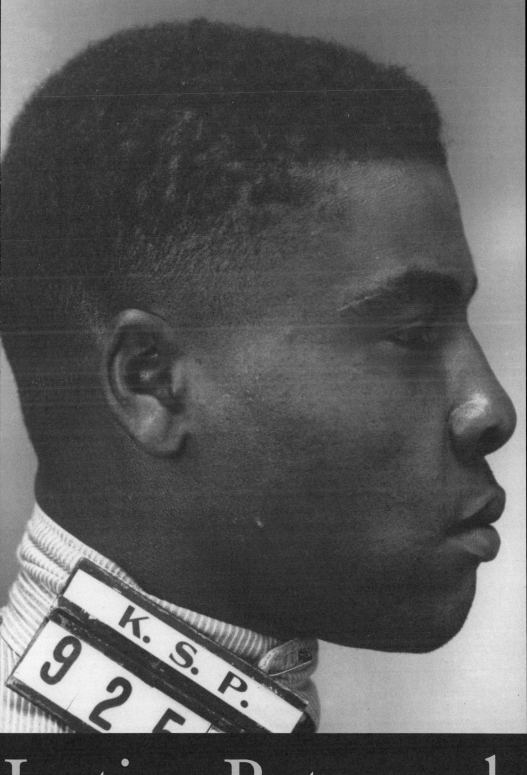

Justice Betrayed

UNIVERSITY OF NEW MEXICO PRESS

ALBUQUERQUE

Justice
betrayed

A Double Killing in Old Santa Fe

RALPH MELNICK

Library of Congress Cataloging-in-Publication Data:

Melnick, Ralph.

Justice betrayed : a double killing

in old Santa Fe / Ralph Melnick.—

1st ed.

p. cm.

Includes bibliographical references and index.

ISBN 0-8263-2901-2

1. Murder—New Mexico—Santa Fe—Case studies.

I. Title.

HV6534.S335 M445 2002

364.15'23'0978956—dc21

2002003834

For Oliver Smalls and Curtis Turner
Who brought me closer

Contents

List of Illustrations

List of
Illustrations
(continued)

With Thanks

As so many others have noted, no work of research is possible without the kind assistance of those who keep the records for us all. Because of the subject of this book and the possible ill will that may be engendered toward certain individuals because of the conclusions that I alone am responsible for, I wish only to offer a blanket "thank you" to the various archivists and court clerks and librarians who assisted me at various stages. Nor should I fail to mention a dear friend in Santa Fe who laboriously photocopied court records for me, once I had located them. He knows who he is and, I hope, how grateful I am for his invaluable assistance.

Indeed, it is the warmth of his friendship, and of all those I have met in Santa Fe over these last number of years, that I wish to acknowledge. The search for truth, however unpleasant, can only be liberating. It is because I feel so deeply for their city that I trust that my work will be received with the caring spirit in which it was undertaken.

And as always, the strength to keep on with my work is rooted in my loving family, who seem to have a boundless amount of love and affection to share—my parents, Evelyn and Lester; my siblings, Michael, William, Don, and Barbara, and their spouses and children; and most certainly, Joshua and Ross, my extraordinary sons, who cheered me all through the months of searching for an editor willing to take on so unpleasant and sensitive an issue. But as before, it is Rachel, with whom I share each moment, who deserves my profoundest thanks for showing the nurturing and patience and love asked of all who live with a writer.

Lastly my thanks go, as they have repeatedly in the past, to my intrepid decipherer and typist, Deborah Tomasi, whose keen eye has caught the errors of a quick hand, even unto these final words.

There is only one person at the
ceremony who is not guilty of murder.
George Orwell, on capital punishment

A Chance Encounter

It was my long search for the now forgotten sculptor of Pueblo Indians, George Blodgett, that first brought me to the corner of Griffin and Mackenzie in the heart of old Santa Fe, New Mexico, and to the studio his wife, Hazel Hyde, had built for him shortly after they wed in the fall of 1931. By itself an imposing structure, the studio had become in time but one part of an interconnected complex of buildings surrounded by high adobe walls and adorned with two interior *placitas,* elements of a neo-Spanish colonial style of architecture first imposed upon the town by a handful of politically well-connected and commercially minded Anglos in the years leading up to the Great War.

Their early attempt to remake this quiet little corner of the old Southwest unwittingly set in motion forces of growth and change that have continued to transform the City of Holy Faith for nearly a century now. Yet much of what author Mary Austin said of her adopted home in that same year of 1931 could still be sensed as I made my way to Blodgett's studio that day so many decades later. Awed by her surroundings, Austin wrote in her essay "Life at Santa Fe" that "from any appreciable point within the city limits," she could "look out [and] see beyond the town, over and around it into sheer desertness." "My house stands close to the foot of Cinco Pintores Hill," she continued, "and the road past it leads up a narrow winding lane which disappears over the top, from which one has a wide prospect of bushy junipers across rolling open lands that drop away to the west and rise on the east in pointed, sparsely planted hills of piñon pine. Below me lies the little town of perhaps ten thousand inhabitants, huddled in the meager valley of the Santa Fe River; and on beyond that, rising abruptly on the north, tawny

FIGURE I. Jaramillo home and Blodgett studio.

Photo by T. Harmon Parkhurst, courtesy Museum of New Mexico, neg. no. 69249.

barren hills go on indefinitely to the high far mountains of Jemez, ethereally blue."

And so, "in spite of the increasing clutter of automobiles" brought in by the growing tourist trade and of the uncertain future they heralded, she stayed on, continuing to find in this "attractive town, touched with the quaintness of an alien sort of life," the spiritual center she had searched for earlier as a refuge from a crueler world. For all around her still were "burro loads of wood going by, scions of Spanish colonial families loitering in the plaza, pretty señoritas tripping, Indians bright with blankets and silver and turquoise, . . . [and] the black shawled women coming and going about the cathedral."

As I wandered through the mazelike compound over which Blodgett's immense peeling white studio still loomed like a weathered apparition and thought of Austin's romantic vision of the peaceful little town in which it had been built so long ago, my host asked if I knew anything of the young woman from a prominent old Spanish family who had been brutally raped and murdered in one of its front apartments. Though today a part of this same complex, her home had once stood separate and apart from the others, tenuously clinging to an ancient identity in a changing world. A black man of uncertain origin had been executed for the crime, my guide told me, though she recalled hearing the whispered mention of a deathbed confession by an unidentified, highly placed government official, a rumor that had, from time to time, cast an element of doubt over the verdict and threatened to scandalize the memory of those involved.

Regrettably, the woman who now owned the walled-in compound could add little else to these scattered bits of folklore. But I knew from experience that memory, however suspect, often retains some element of fact, and though many of the details had evidently strayed, I sensed that something profoundly disturbing remained hidden.

There was, of course, the real possibility that the accused had committed the crime for which he had been killed. But it was the era of Jim Crow, a time when blacks who managed to evade the lynch mob's noose could rarely hope for an acquittal in the courts.

At first merely curious, I stayed well beyond my initial encounter with this story of old Santa Fe, and as I dug ever deeper, I discovered that what had happened in that distant time and place sharply mirrored so much of what we see around us still—racial and class prejudice, political corruption, media-induced hysteria, and a level of moral indifference that allows a community to sanction the killing of another while remaining without either a statute or a name for the crime of conspiring to send an innocent man to his death.

It seemed to me then, as it does now, that the young white woman and her alleged black assailant have left us with a legacy by which we can measure how far we have come in our search for justice. It is ours for the taking, if we will.

In Pursuit

A T four-thirty on the morning of November 16, 1931, the telephone in District Attorney John J. Kenney's Santa Fe home rang with news of Tom Johnson's capture. "We've picked up your man," Albuquerque's police chief, R. C. Charlton, shouted into the phone, his clipped voice filled with excitement. Sixty miles closer to the Mexican border, his office was the first to be called as the net spread outward from the crime scene shortly after midnight. Johnson's clothes were "bloodstained from head to toe," Charlton added, and when captured by Officer Zumwalt outside the Pekin Café, he was carrying a knife whose narrow, four-and-a-half-inch blade was suspiciously dotted with something red.[1]

By 6:00 A.M., a posse from Santa Fe had reached Albuquerque. Detective H. C. Martin had quickly assembled the group after receiving a call from Kenney. Sheriff Jesus Baca and Police Chief Tom Stewart were the first to be contacted, and they in turn had rousted Deputy Ike Alarid and Officer Oliver Holmes from their beds.

"I know what you're after, you damn detective," Johnson yelled as Martin and the others burst into the interrogation room at police headquarters. "You want to send me to the electric chair!"

"Exactly that," Martin shouted back[2] as Charlton grabbed Johnson,

FIGURE 2. Angelina Jaramillo, as a senior at Loretto Academy, 1931.
Courtesy Museum of New Mexico, neg. no. 167845.

stood him up, and removed his handcuffs so that Martin could pull off his striped, blood-splattered coveralls. There was more dried blood on his hands, and his shoes were stained red. In a matter of minutes Johnson stood there, stripped and naked.

Without further prompting, Johnson admitted to beating Oscar Churchill that night in the garage where they both worked and then leaving him for dead. It was all in self-defense, he insisted. The blood, he tried to explain, was from their struggle. They had fought over a two-dollar loan that Churchill demanded he immediately repay, and when he failed to revive Churchill, he fled in panic, taking the cash receipts from the register and a Buick parked out back.

But he knew nothing of the murder of a young woman named Angelina Jaramillo. Over and over again during the next several hours, Johnson denied any involvement in this other crime. And when his interrogators pressed on, repeating the same accusation over and over and over again, Johnson finally cracked. "You'd do anything to hang a man!"[3] he screamed, his rage directed straight at Martin.

Johnson's willingness to speak of his struggle with Churchill worried his captors. As a multiple offender, he faced the possibility of life imprisonment if convicted of assault. Why, then, had he been so willing to talk? they wondered. Was he using one crime as an alibi for another? Frustrated and exhausted, they stopped the interrogation and prepared their quarry for the trip back to Santa Fe, where he would be charged with the murder. There was little reason not to charge him. The "negro" was surely guilty.[4]

Many hours had now passed since Martin had first arrived at the Jaramillo home after being summoned by Sheriff Baca. Just past midnight, a neighbor, Mrs. J. F. Clark, had been awakened by Angelina's eleven-year-old cousin, Marie, as she screamed and pounded on her back door. The young girl had fled in search of help after being stirred from a deep sleep by the shouts of the victim's mother, Cleofas. As Clark ran back to the Jaramillo house with Marie at her side, her husband phoned the police.[5]

Baca, Alarid, Stewart, and Holmes were at the house within minutes of the call.[6] After a quick survey of the crime scene, Martin concluded to himself that Johnson was responsible for the murder. Martin had not yet heard about the incident at the garage, but Johnson, a Negro drifter with a criminal record, had recently been freed from the state penitentiary in Santa Fe after serving four years on a charge of burglary. Though little evidence had yet been recovered, Martin felt certain of his choice.[7]

Kenney, and then Drs. Ward H. Livingston and D. B. Williams, were next to arrive. There was a gash on Cleofas's head that appeared to have been caused by a blow from the heavy glass vase that was now scattered in small pieces throughout the house. The two physicians had been called in to attend to the mother's needs, but at Kenney's request, they would stay on a while longer and examine her daughter's body as well. A stab wound to the left temple from a thin knife was the apparent cause of

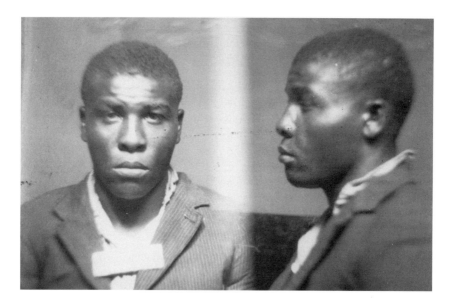

FIGURE 3. Tom Johnson at the time of his return to Santa Fe, 1931.

Department of Corrections, State Records Center & Archives, Santa Fe, New Mexico, no. 5931.

Angelina's death, they reported. She had also been raped, they continued, shocking the others with their discovery.[8]

Martin quickly turned to Kenney and asked that he go with him to the Plaza Café. Over several cups of hot coffee, he shared his thoughts with Kenney and urged him to seek Johnson's immediate capture.[9] As they stepped outside the café, the two were quickly intercepted by Baca. "We've got another murder on our hands!" he excitedly told them. "The night watchman at Andrew's Garage has been slugged!"

In need of gas for the long night ahead, Baca had stopped to fill his automobile's tank but had found the garage closed. Suspicious, he telephoned its owner, Alfred Muller, and asked that he come down to the garage and unlock the door. Finding signs of a struggle, they searched the area thoroughly and soon discovered the bloodied body of the night attendant, Oscar Churchill, lying gagged and bound under a pile of blankets. Though still alive, he was not expected to survive what appeared to be a fatal wound to the head.

Muller checked the cash register and discovered that $34.60 had been taken. A moment later, he saw that a Buick was also missing. When Martin learned that Johnson was employed at the garage and was suspected by Baca of this assault, he added his earlier claim to the discussion. There was little opposition from the others as he tied the two incidents together.[10]

Within minutes, an alarm was sent ringing throughout the state and into neighboring southern Colorado and Texas. Armed with descriptions of Johnson and the Buick, the manhunt began. A few blocks away on Sandoval Street, Baca and his deputies searched Johnson's room. The place had been hastily packed up and abandoned, its single bulb still dimly lit as they entered. He was clearly in flight.[11]

But the chase was now over. With Johnson in hand, the posse prepared themselves for the trip ahead, however uncertain they were of what might be waiting for them along the road back to Santa Fe. News of Johnson's capture had spread rapidly throughout the town's tight-knit Spanish community, and several mobs were already forming by the time Martin, Baca, and the others telephoned from Albuquerque to ask Judge Miguel Antonio Otero, Jr., for permission to confine Johnson in the state penitentiary. It was an unprecedented move, but the county jail, an aging giant ironically sitting across from the garage where Johnson worked, was certain to prove vulnerable if the menacing crowd gathering outside the building should choose to storm it.[12] The state penitentiary, a massive stone structure completed nearly a half century earlier on a tract of land that was then still a full mile beyond the city's southern boundary, would require a far larger crowd to breach its walls.

Opened with a "gala housewarming" attended by a who's who of prominent New Mexicans, the fortresslike building had once offered a progressive program of rehabilitation that served as a national model. But vocational training, classroom education, and a library had each been abandoned over the last several years in favor of retributive imprisonment. And when in 1929 the state legislature mandated electrocution in place of hanging for those convicted of murder, it was the inmates themselves, perhaps even Johnson, who constructed the still untested electric chair and the small structure that housed it.[13] With the penitentiary's promise of greater security, Otero was quick to offer his approval.

FIGURE 4. Santa Fe jail, considered too insecure a facility to hold Johnson.

Photo by Central Photographic Studio, courtesy Museum of New Mexico, neg. no. 134571.

After first being photographed encircling their prisoner, Johnson and his captors left Albuquerque at 9:30 A.M. Rushing through the cool midmorning air at sixty miles an hour, they succeeded in surprising a group gathered alongside the Albuquerque Road near Fairview Cemetery and sped past them. As the lone car approached Santa Fe from the south, Deputy Sheriff James Baca, together with four vehicles filled with heavily armed men, provided additional protection for the final two miles.

They soon reached the state penitentiary, only to find another crowd waiting to greet them with a thunder of shouts and threats.[14] But there was, in fact, little to fear. Angelina's powerful grandfather, Julian Martinez, had already sent word to his people that there was to be no lynching. All was to be done within the law. Johnson would be held for trial and then executed, he promised. And so, when the caravan reached the prison gates at 11:00 A.M., it was allowed to enter without incident, as Martinez had wanted.[15]

FIGURE 5. Santa Fe officers as they started back from Albuquerque with the suspected killer. Left to right: Deputy Sheriff Ike Alaris, Detective H. C. Martin, the suspected murderer, Chief of Police Tom Stewart, Sheriff Jesus Baca, Patrolman Oliver Holmes.

Reproduced from *Master Detective*, "The Clue of the Lipstick" (March 1935), in the collections of the Library of Congress.

Mayor J. C. McCovey's broad response to the murder seemed to further ease the community's tensions. "In view of recent deplorable happenings, you will use every means at your command to rid Santa Fe of undesirable people if such remain in the city," he instructed the city's chief of police. "You will question suspicious characters and on failure to prove they are law abiding citizens with a visible means of support, you will take such steps as you may deem necessary in preserving the peace and safety of the citizens of Santa Fe." With his constituency so highly incensed, the mayor insisted on full compliance. "You and your entire force," he told Stewart, "will be expected to be extra diligent to this end."[16]

The press, however, needed no such instructions. "GIRL ATTACKED, KILLED; NEGRO IS HELD," the *New Mexican*'s banner headline read within hours of Angelina's murder.[17] "SLAIN GIRL STUDENT AT LORETTO, MEMBER OF OLD SPANISH FAMILY," it continued in only slightly smaller type on the very next line. "Her beauty was of the type

MEXICAN

TY OF THE HOLY FAITH, AT THE END OF THE SANTA F... AZ.

ER 16, 1931   PRICE FIVE CEN

NEGRO IS HELI

SLAIN GIRL STUDENT AT LORETTO CONFESSES

MEMBER OF OLD SPANISH FAMILY MURDER OF CHURCHII

Miss Angelina Jaramillo who was murdered last night by a negro named Thomas Johnson, was considered one of the most attractive young girls in Santa Fe. At the time of her death she was a pupil at Loretto academy.

Coming of an old and prominent Spanish family, her beauty was of the type that is characteristic of the Spanish people. Like her aunt and her mother, both of whom were noted for their beauty, she was of the "petite" type, with large brown expressive eyes, a wealth of raven black hair and a sunny smile. She had a delightful disposition and the most charming manners.

The news of her tragic death shocked countless people in and near Santa Fe today.

Miss Jaramillo was known by many Santa Feans and by her itors. She had assisted her mother and her aunt Mrs May Smith to conduct the new Spanish dining room, "La Placita" within the shadow of the Presbyterian church. It is located in the old adobe structure in which is the newly built studio of the sculptor G. W. Blodgett of Santa Fe.

The house where the crime was committed is one of the old houses of Santa Fe, charming in its Spanish design, with a grass covered and flower-bedecked placita in front of it and in the rear, as is customary.

Captured in Albuquerque
Convict Admits Killing M
Who Is Still Living

BELIEVE MAY SUCCUM

Sheriff Finds Body in Gar
Johnson Served Time
Three Prisons

FIGURE 6. Front page of the *Santa Fe New Mexican*, November 16, 1931.

that is characteristic of the Spanish people," the newspaper memorialized, and "like her aunt and her mother, both of whom were noted for their beauty, she was of the 'petite' type, with large, brown expressive eyes, a wealth of raven black hair and a sunny smile," and possessed as well of "a delightful disposition and the most charming manners."[18]

But now all of this had been taken away by "the negro" who had viciously killed "one of the most attractive young girls" in this otherwise quiet little town in the high desert country of northern New Mexico's Sangre de Cristo Mountains.[19] To the Spanish community of old Santa Fe, the brutal killing of Angelina Jaramillo was nothing less than a violation of their own sanctity. The *New Mexican*'s carefully designed comparison between victim and assailant, as stark as the news was shocking, sent a new wave of anger rippling through Santa Fe's streets. Details of the crime itself merely added feelings of loss and panic to the already overheated atmosphere.

To construct its account of the crime that Monday afternoon, the paper simply followed the prosecution's reconstruction without question. "Angelina Jaramillo, 18, was assaulted and murdered in her bed at 142 Griffin Street shortly before 12 o'clock last night," the report began. "Her mother was hit over the head with a vase and seriously injured when she surprised the assailant in the girl's room. Within an hour, Oscar Churchill, night man at Andrew's Garage, was attacked and beaten into insensibility. Mrs. Jaramillo and Churchill are both in hospital. Tom Johnson, 30, negro ex-convict is behind penitentiary bars, having confessed to attacking Churchill and charged with the three crimes. He was captured in Albuquerque and returned to Santa Fe."[20]

In what passed for balanced reporting, Johnson's repeated denial of any involvement in the rape and murder of one of Santa Fe's most promising young women had, of course, landed in the lower right-hand corner of the newspaper's two-foot-long front page. It could hardly compete against the centrally placed recounting of Angelina's virtues and the nearly page-long description of the crime, with its damning characterization of the accused. Condemned by the press, few cared to know more about the "negro" and the journey that had brought him to their desert community.

Tom Johnson's parents, Thomas and Magdalene Bishop, had married in 1900 amid the live oaks and grassy marshlands of coastal South Carolina, a land framed by dangling strands of Spanish moss and the strictures of Jim Crow. The repeal of the state's civil rights law eleven years earlier had signaled a period of relentless change for blacks as segregation quickly spread throughout the region. In Tom and Maggie's own hometown of Beaufort, Judge Christie Benet had angrily stopped the proceedings in his court one day and ordered an immediate end to the mixed seating of blacks and whites. "God Almighty never intended that the two races should be mixed," he scolded those seated before him.[21]

And so Thomas and Magdalene, like thirty-three thousand other blacks in South Carolina at this time, left their homes penniless, and went to Georgia in search of greater opportunity.[22] With them that day was their infant son, Thomas, Jr., born on the last day of September 1900.[23] If the move to Savannah meant separation from family and a life of ceaseless labor, they believed that chance good fortune might yet be theirs. But Johnson's father, a stevedore who, like so many other blacks, worked the city's docks six or seven days a week, died before the birth of his third child in 1906. Tom, Jr., had watched as exhaustion and medical neglect took his father's life,[24] leaving his mother to struggle on alone in her often desperate effort to keep her family alive. A laundress by trade,[25] there were times when taking in others' wash was not enough, times when survival meant a life fully in service, when housing her family meant the stark walls of former slave quarters down a narrow alley, behind the big house that employed her—times when being able to read and write mattered little in a harshly segregated world without opportunity, a world that, with time, saw her son grow bitter and hardened.[26]

Yet through it all, Maggie was determined to see her children have better lives. Schooling in rural Beaufort County had taught her to treasure education. Tom, Jr., Henry, and Silvena would have at least as much. For eight years, Johnson attended school until there was no more school to attend. The need for black laborers and domestics convinced white authorities that high school education was unnecessary, and so the day came when young Tom, with no classes to attend, began laboring where and when he could to help his family.

By 1916, Europe was at war and talk of American entrance into the conflict appeared more promising to Johnson than the Jim Crow atmosphere that had steadily come to envelop Savannah as well. Broad shouldered and muscular, and with the look of someone older than his years, Johnson talked his way past the gates and joined the U.S. Navy at its base in Charleston, South Carolina.[27]

But it proved to be a short stay. Within the year he found himself in trouble with the law while on leave in Columbia. There was a scuffle and an arrest. Few questions were asked, and after several weeks in the local workhouse, he was released. Discharged from the navy, he went to Savannah, but soon left for West Virginia, where he remained for the next three years.[28]

Returning home in 1920, he worked first as a laborer and then as a painter and a garage attendant. He would come to use these skills as he traveled around the country in the years ahead. Only once during his stay at home was he jailed. Arrested for disorderly conduct in May 1921, he spent thirty days at the Chatham County work farm.[29] Together with petty larceny and vagrancy, this vague charge was often used to gather together cheap labor either for public work or for hire. Once seized from the streets, the individual would be tried and judged by the city recorder, who would then impose sentences far more severe than called for by the alleged offense.[30]

Johnson stayed on in Savannah as long as he could, and then made his way north by foot, boxcar, and truck, a part of the Great Migration of blacks out of the South that had begun in 1914 and peaked in the early 1920s. Beyond unequal pay and squalid living conditions, persecution—by judicial means or the Klan—had already driven more than seventy thousand blacks out of Georgia by the time he left for Ohio. The renewed hope of change held by black veterans of the Great War had been dashed by the reality of oppression and lynching that had greeted them at home.

As flight robbed the region of its cheap labor force, financial threats, beatings, and ultimately arrests were used by the authorities to stem the flow. This was particularly the case in Savannah, where so many businesses depended on black laborers. In fact, Maggie herself may have insisted on her son's flight northward after his release from the county jail. "There is scarcely a Negro mother who does not live in dread and fear that her husband or son may come in unfriendly contact with some white person so as to bring the lynchers . . . which may result in the wiping out of her entire family," the white *Savannah News* commented not long before Johnson set out once more.[31]

As a skilled automobile mechanic, he soon found work in Dayton, Ohio, and established a home for himself there. But on September 7, 1922, Johnson was accused of petty larceny and sent to the county workhouse.[32] Released after several months' labor, he made his way back south again, only to be stopped by the police in Columbia, South Carolina, and accused of operating an automobile without its owner's permission. After another three months' imprisonment, he returned home, packed his few belongings, and bid his family farewell for the last time.[33] The "desire for freedom," Johnson would tell his jailers some years later, was driving him onward.[34]

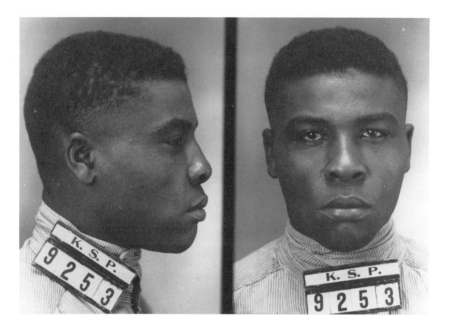

FIGURE 7. Tom Johnson at the time of his incarceration in Kansas, 1925.
Kansas Historical Society, Topeka, Kansas, neg. no. 10253.

So many blacks before him had gone to Detroit to work in its automobile factories that it seemed the ideal place for a fresh start. Years of garage work offered the hope of a better future, but on his third day in town, with his things barely unpacked, Johnson was stopped on the street, as blacks routinely were, and searched. Found to be carrying a pocketknife and charged with possession of a concealed weapon, he was given hard time in the Michigan State Penitentiary at Jackson. It was here that he first used the name Johnson, adopting this alias, he later said, so as not to further embarrass his family.

Sentenced on April 8, 1925, for a term of six months to two years,[35] he was granted an early parole. By October he was living in Kansas but once again he found it difficult to settle down. Arrested that December for theft, he broke out of jail before the case could be tried. Recaptured and charged for this secondary offense, he was sent to the Kansas State Penitentiary for a period of eleven months to two years.

Johnson was released early in the spring of 1927, and wandered through the Southwest until he came to settle in Albuquerque, where he again found work as a garage attendant. But that July, he was arrested for a series of burglaries, to which he readily confessed, and was sent to the state penitentiary in Santa Fe, from where he was once again paroled early for good behavior on July 22, 1931. Older and more settled now, Johnson had been working long hours at Andrew's Garage since then and doing all that he could to keep clear of any involvement with the police when, in mid-November, the world came crashing in upon him once more.[36]

By the afternoon of November 10, a coroner's inquest had been convened to hear the case against him. Other suspects would not be considered by the six men who had been called to the Sayre Funeral Home, nor would they entertain the possibility of his innocence. For nearly two hours, the district attorney questioned Martin, Baca, Stewart, and Livingston, pulling together a seamless narrative of facts and events to demonstrate Johnson's guilt. Kenney began by describing the crime scene, locating various incriminating objects throughout the house, and giving each a role to play in his story of the killing. Johnson's own recapitulation of the previous night's events was then reported and discounted, and his bloodstained coveralls displayed together with the alleged murder weapon, the knife recovered from him in Albuquerque. Though Cleofas had insisted that the killer wore a black-and-white-striped work shirt or jacket, Kenney maintained that she was wrong, that her assailant, in fact, was dressed in the dark-blue-and-white coveralls Johnson was wearing when captured.[37]

Aware of the problem this discrepancy might later present, Kenney quickly diverted the jurors' attention away from the coveralls and toward the knife. This latter piece of evidence, he assured them, was far more crucial to the case. But Dr. Livingston, after first reviewing his autopsy report, testified that he could not conclusively say that Johnson's knife had been used to commit the crime in question. All that could be asserted at this point was that death had been instantaneous. Pointing to the wounds on Angelina's body, he explained how a long narrow knife shaped like Johnson's had pierced the victim's left temple just to the front of her ear.[38] Left unexplained, of course, was how a left-sided wound to the head could have so readily been inflicted by someone like Johnson who was himself left-handed.

Nor could Kenney explain Cleofas's continuing insistence on not being able to identify the race of her assailant, though he had been close enough to reach for her throat. According to testimony presented by those who had spoken with her, she had been awakened around midnight by either a light or a muffled sound coming from her daughter's room and had decided to look in on her before going back to sleep. Carrying a lit candle, she made her way down the hall from the rear of the house to the front. "What's the matter, Angie, are you sick?" she was said to have called out as she pulled back the heavy drapes cloaking her daughter's bedroom. Within seconds she saw a man described by Kenney as "heavy set" standing at the foot of the bed. Startled, he lunged at her, choking and dragging her into the adjoining living room, where he was said to have smashed a heavy green vase over her head, rendering her unconscious.[39]

Uneasy with this turn in his investigation, Kenney told the jury that he planned to assist Cleofas in this matter by conducting a lineup of black prisoners for her at the state penitentiary as soon as she was released from St. Vincent's Hospital, where she was suffering from emotional paralysis.[40] It was typical in such cases that much remained to be studied, he assured them. Since an inquest was not a trial, the state need not be fully prepared to convict as yet. Another day or two would be needed before any conclusions could be drawn from photographs of fingerprints found on the victim's iron bed, on a windowsill in an adjacent room, and on several pieces of the shattered vase. Their origin was still to be determined, he further advised those hearing the case, though there was little chance of their belonging to anyone other than the accused.

Kenney felt equally certain that the murderer's point of entry was through a small window that led into an area of the house to the left of Angelina's room, though a large, heavy typewriter had been found on the sill undisturbed.[41] Neither was there any doubt that the assailant's motive had not been robbery, Kenney further asserted. Angelina's necklace was still clasped around her neck when she arrived at the funeral home. Indeed, nothing of value was missing from the house, though Johnson had previously been imprisoned for robbery and not for a crime of violence.

Nor was Johnson's repeated assertion that he was unfamiliar with the murdered young woman to be considered, Kenney argued. Instead, two police officers were brought forward and testified that he had been seen loitering in her neighborhood on several previous occasions. Even more damning, Kenney insisted, was the fact that Angelina's uncle, Robert Smith, had recently begun working at Andrew's Garage, where Johnson was also employed, and that she had often stopped in to see Smith on her way home from school. How, then, could Johnson possibly hope to have a jury believe that he had never met the victim?[42]

Little time was needed by the jury before rendering its decision. It was their finding that "the woman child, of the age of 18 years, found dead within the County of Santa Fe, came to her death as a result of a stab wound . . . having first been criminally assaulted," and that "the circumstantial evidence in the case points very strongly to the guilt of Thomas Johnson, the colored man under arrest for said crime."[43]

With the coroner's inquest adjourned, Kenney rushed out to bring news of the jury's findings to an anxiously waiting press. The investigation was, of course, still ongoing, he told them, and so the accused's next court date would have to wait until this work was completed. But there was no question that the evidence, while still being gathered, would demonstrate his guilt. The findings of several fingerprint experts would be received within the next two or three days, Kenney informed those hungrily anticipating his report. "We will also await the possibility that when Mrs. Jaramillo is able she may be able to give testimony regarding the clothing worn by the slayer." Still troubled by differences over this crucial bit of evidence, he nevertheless reassured the reporters gathered before him that "the state believes it is on the right track" and was "advancing its case with deliberation to insure that justice takes its course, as contemplated by the law."[44]

"I have no doubt of the guilt of Johnson," Kenney confidently repeated to those who rushed back to his office the next morning. The case against Johnson was, in fact, "closed." Though evidence was still being gathered, none was critical. Even the fingerprints under analysis at the state penitentiary's lab would merely strengthen an already convincing case. Furthermore, a witness, as yet unnamed, had come forward and would testify that Johnson had been seen walking along Griffin Street not long before the time of the murder. "Every step will be taken to insure prompt justice in this case,"[45] Kenney told the press as he concluded his remarks that day.

With Judge Otero fully involved in the process, Kenney could be certain of this. But since court was not in session now, a special term would have to be called. And because there were no funds available for this unscheduled opening, a member of the state board of finance would have to be asked for an advance on the coming year's budget. The case was too important to wait until March, he insisted. By the afternoon, Otero's request had already been granted.[46]

An Enchanted Land

L IKE the black-shawled women of Mary Austin's vision, Angelina and her mother had attended Sunday mass and then returned home for their noontime meal that last day before her murder. When they finished, Angelina turned to her mother and, with a "touch of sadness . . . so different from her usual cheerful self," asked for permission to play the piano, though her grandmother's recent death had dictated that it remain silent for a respectful period of time. According to the memoir she wrote many years later, Cleofas reminded her daughter that "the Spanish people are very strict about observing mourning. Some might hear it and think we had no feeling." But Angelina's continued pleadings, and her despondent mood over the last several months, ultimately forced her mother to relent.

At first hesitant, Angelina sat herself in front of the piano and began to run her fingers listlessly over the keyboard, only to get up a few moments later and leave the room. "How strange she was acting," Cleofas thought. It was so unlike her daughter not to perform her usual repertoire of music and song.[1] Angelina soon returned to the sitting room and began to read. But as the day wore on and her restlessness continued, Cleofas insisted that she put her book away and go out in the fresh air.

Over the previous few months, Angelina had made a habit of visiting her family at her grandfather's house at 125 Grant Street on her way back from school each day. Around the corner from the Jaramillo home, Julian Martinez shared his house with his son, Benjamin, his daughter, Mae (Salome) Smith, and their families. That last Friday, while standing in the doorway to her aunt's room, Angelina had commented to Mae that she felt "so queer!" But when her aunt asked what she meant by this, Angelina responded, "I don't know," and bolted from the house. Later that day, Mae recounted the incident for her sister, Cleofas, and remarked that Angelina seemed "very pale and sad."

Now, with her daughter's mood still unimproved two days later, Cleofas pushed her to go out for a Sunday afternoon walk. "Yes, I am going to see the girls at the convent," Angelina remarked wistfully, referring to those of her classmates who were boarding at the school run by the Sisters of Loretto. She would walk across town and visit with them for a while, she repeated for emphasis.[2]

Cleofas stopped in at her father's house later that day and, while there, received a telephone call from Angelina. "Mumsy, the Clarks have invited me to go to Lamy with them," she told her mother. Mr. Clark was a railroad engineer, and Lamy was the nearest Santa Fe Railroad station. The large new powerful engine and well-appointed Pullman cars, one of which had recently been named for her father, had proved too enticing for Angelina to let pass without a look. Though hesitant, Cleofas relented a second time, but only after exacting a promise from her daughter that she would return in time to prepare dinner. "You rest and I shall be back to fix it," Angelina assured her mother without hesitation.[3]

But six o'clock passed, and then seven, "and no Angie," Cleofas later recalled. Unable to wait any longer, she put supper together with her housekeeper's assistance. "We had just seated ourselves at the table when Angie 'blew in' out of breath—just like a 'cyclone,' I used to tell her." More animated than she had been for some time, Angelina went on and on about what she had seen. "Let me tell you, Mumsy," she began her long narrative, and when she finished, she promised Cleofas that "as soon as I finish school, I am going to work, save money for one year and, then, we shall travel; work again and travel."[4]

With her eighteenth birthday now behind her, Angelina looked forward to completing her last year of school and going to Hollywood to become a dancer. Cleofas listened attentively as her daughter spoke of her dreams, but was as uncertain as ever as to how she should respond—for Cleofas never quite understood how her daughter's life had changed during these adolescent years. Though mother and daughter were both deeply rooted in the same world of privilege that had been built out of vast landholdings granted to their ancestors by the king of Spain, Angelina, like others of her generation, had begun to openly challenge its traditions. But to Cleofas, this new world was alien and something to be opposed. "As a descendant of the Spanish pioneers, I have watched with regret the passing of the old Spanish customs and the rapid adoption of the modern Anglo customs by the new generation," she would later remark in her memoir.[5]

This invasive Anglo culture had come with the defeat of Mexico and the region's annexation by the United States in 1848. The religious faith, tightly woven families, and tiny villages of Cleofas's tradition-bound youth, had more recently fallen under increased pressure for change. Equally worrisome were the postwar economic depression and the recent Crash of 1929 that were now endangering her family's position of political and social prominence. Despite sizable real estate holdings within Santa Fe and to the north, they seemed to be losing their hold on this world. And so it seemed necessary to Cleofas that she take up the banner of her people, however late in the struggle, however much it conflicted with her own daughter's need for separation and an independent life.

For Cleofas, the past remained an almost mythical time when "children, fed with simple food raised on their lands, and housed in neat little whitewashed houses with large sunny yards, were healthy and happy . . . quiet and respectful," and not yet "spoiled by too much liberty." "People's lives radiated between church and home," she repeatedly told her daughter. "Mothers stayed home taking care of their children, satisfied to live on their husbands' earnings. They were not buying new clothes all the time, nor visiting beauty shops. No one was ever late for church, although some of them lived two and three miles distant and rode in slow wagons or even walked. How nice it would be if people now would live thus!" she declared openly and often.[6]

But for Angelina, the past was but a place to visit. Though warm and familiar, it could not satisfy her need to dream of a future far beyond her mother's world. In this, as in so much else, she took after her father, Cleofas lamented. "A delicate brunette . . . with her father's bright sparkle in her unusually big, black eyes . . . nature had endowed her with my family's looks but with the Jaramillos' lively, volatile temperament, easily aroused, but generous, kind and affectionate."[7]

It was the Jaramillo family's wealth and position as one of the Southwest's largest landowners, with holdings estimated at half a million acres, that had already opened many doors for Venceslao when, at the age of twenty-two, he asked his cousin Cleofas, a shy and cloistered young woman three years his junior, to marry him. Their "unexpected romance" had begun with a chance encounter at a wedding in the small northern village of Abiquiu.[8] Cleofas would later comment how, after a steady stream of notes and small gifts, sent with her father's permission, "this genteel young man had become my ideal suitor and had changed my mind from my becoming a nun or remaining an old spinster."[9]

Though intrafamily marriages were banned by canonical law, dispensations could be obtained from the church by those who inhabited Venceslao and Cleofas's world of privilege.[10] Yet in spite of their wealth and position, she hoped to have a simple early morning wedding ceremony in the village chapel of Arroyo Hondo, with a small breakfast gathering of relatives and friends at her home afterward, as was her people's tradition. But it was not to be.

Four decades later, Cleofas's brother, Reyes Martinez, recalled how the events of July 27, 1898, had all too quickly taken on far greater social and political significance. "The ceremonies of this prominent couple lasted several days. The bridegroom rented the whole Barron Hotel in Taos for the use of the guests. He brought from Denver a famous negro chef. He engaged the band of Don Pancho, from Santa Fe, for the occasion."

But it was Governor Miguel A. Otero's presence that most radically altered the occasion for her. Together with a "brilliant display of fireworks, the reception given the Governor was celebrated by a parade of most of the populace of Taos, who rode out the eve before the wedding as far as Ranchos de Taos in flag-bedecked carriages and horses and on

FIGURE 8. Venceslao Jaramillo and Cleofas Martinez
at the time of their wedding, 1898.

Photo by Schumacher, courtesy Museum of New Mexico, neg. no. 67224.

foot to meet him." Serving as Venceslao's best man, the governor, together
with his wife, the bridal couple, and "other prominent personages,
occupied a stage at the head of the spacious banquet hall." Interest
seemed to move away from the bride and groom as "speeches were made
by the Governor and other speakers during the dining which lasted well
into the late afternoon."[11]

Cleofas never fully recovered from the trauma. And in the years
ahead, as she moved farther away from her small village and came in
contact with the Anglo world her husband appeared to value so highly,
she withdrew even further. A half century later, she spoke of how, "in my

FIGURE 9. Venceslao Jaramillo (far right) as a member of the
staff of territorial governor M. A. Otero (second from right).

Courtesy Museum of New Mexico, neg. no. 52884.

timidity, I encased myself in a quiet reserve before an English-speaking
gathering. Not having enough practice in speaking their language fluently,
nor being yet schooled in their social ways, I was afraid to make a
mistake." And though she felt as if she had "profited by [her] quiet
observation," she feared "giving people the impression of being stupid."

In the end, Cleofas chose to remain apart, forever a spectator in her
husband's universe of political contacts and social obligations. Yet she
thought herself a failure for not being more helpful to him[12] and
attempted to compensate by remaining "scrupulously faithful" to her
responsibilities at home as he went out in pursuit of other goals.[13]

But nothing could replace the comforting world out of which she had
fallen, and when she returned periodically to her village in later years,
images from an earlier, simpler time spent among the people of her "little
valley of the Arroyo Hondo River" came flooding back. "Hemmed in by
high mountains and hills, sheltered from the contamination of the outside

world, the inhabitants lived peacefully, preserving the customs and traditions of their ancestors," she lamented repeatedly.[14] "I had lived so happily among these people for whom I had an inherent love. I went with them, through their happy feast days and religious ceremonies, kneeling on the ground, answering their hymns and prayers, with the same faith and fervor as theirs. Oh, time, turn back and let me live again, just for a minute, those happy days!"[15]

Schooled in Denver, Venceslao had served on Governor Otero's territorial military staff shortly after returning to his family's hacienda in El Rito[16] and, by age twenty, also held a seat in the legislature.[17] A tireless supporter of statehood and a coauthor of the territory's proposed constitution, Venceslao stood among those honored for their efforts when New Mexico became the country's forty-seventh state on January 6, 1912.[18] In the years that followed, he went on to become chairman of the state's Republican Party and one of the region's leading businessmen, with interests extending northward from Santa Fe to Denver.[19] There was even talk of a seat in the U.S. Senate, but on May 30, 1920, tuberculosis, aggravated by years of excessive work and frequent travel, took his life.[20]

Death soon revealed how unsteady Venceslao's vast financial empire had become during the recent postwar economic decline. Widowed and in debt, her life of ease and comfort now gone forever, Cleofas turned to her daughter for support, placing an impossible burden on her six-year-old shoulders and causing her, at times, to wish that she, rather than her brother, had died in infancy. "He would be bigger and could help you," she would tell Cleofas, who thought of her "poor girl's life [as] mapped out for sacrifice."[21] But as the years passed, Angelina managed to grow into "a young lady, reserved but pleasure-loving," as her mother would characterize her some time later.[22]

How different Cleofas had been as an adolescent, refusing to adopt "any new fad my girl friends had" or to wear clothing that was deemed improper.[23] And when she and her friends danced in their youth, it was "smooth waltzes and swinging quadrilles" from which they derived pleasure, "before jazz music turned us into tap dancers."[24] "Any open gaiety on the part of the women or girls was met with disapproval by the husbands and fathers,"[25] she noted approvingly,[26] commenting further that a sense of "spiritual dignity and respect" had been required at all times.[27]

But the old ways were vanishing now, together with the "quiet reserve" she so deeply valued. Her daughter's generation, "finding the strangers' customs new and attractive, began to adopt them and to forget their own. Modern music, songs and dances [had] replaced the soft, musical melodies and graceful folk dances" of her own youth, and the rules of etiquette that had determined the nature of each relationship between a boy and a girl seemed no longer to be applied. Cleofas later recorded that she had "found it hard to get accustomed to the new ways" and had proudly resisted wherever she could.[28]

How unacceptable to her, then, was the first boy with whom Angelina at the age of sixteen had developed what Cleofas characterized as "more than just a friendship." The boy's father was a simple building contractor, at work on an addition to the Spanish-American Normal School that Venceslao had helped establish in 1909 in El Rito, the village to which Angelina and Cleofas returned each summer after his death. Worse, still, was the boy's parents' shameful decision to divorce.[29]

Cleofas had hoped the relationship would end when she and her daughter returned to Santa Fe in the fall. But the young man would not be discouraged and, in his pursuit of her daughter, had further violated traditional patterns of courtship and propriety by corresponding and exchanging photographs with Angelina without first seeking Cleofas's permission. "You do not want your picture flying around the country in the hands of a boy we know nothing about, except that his father left his mother," Cleofas argued. And when Angelina returned home from school one afternoon and discovered that her mother had removed his picture from her dresser, she flew into a rage, protesting that Cleofas disliked him because he was poor. No, Cleofas insisted, "character, education and refinement have always counted more than money."[30]

Angelina never forgave her mother, nor ever again shared her deepest feelings with her. "In a few days the storm blew away," Cleofas recorded, "but we were not the same. Angie grew cooler. I missed her kiss on her leaving for school and on going to bed." Yet Cleofas was "too proud to apologize," as she later admitted.

That fall, Angelina was sent to a boarding school in Albuquerque run by the sisters. It would prove to be Angelina's happiest year. Free of her mother's critical eye, she gravitated toward the school's dance teacher,

Beulah Kahnt, and as their fondness for each other deepened, Angelina visited her home with increasing frequency. In May, Angelina's skillful participation in a dance recital at Albuquerque's Kimo Theater received special attention in the *New Mexican*. But when Kahnt asked Angelina to go with her to Hollywood that summer to visit her sister, a professional dancer, Cleofas withheld her permission. "I was opposed to Angie's becoming a dancer and changed their plans," she later noted.[31]

There was little discussion of the matter beyond her suggestion to Angelina that she ask a few friends to spend some time with them in El Rito, under Cleofas's watchful eye. But Cleofas could not be everywhere, and when Angelina commented to her, following a dance performance at the city's Fiesta, that "the boys are calling me the queen," she angrily told her daughter not to be "such a proud señorita."[32] Even a family friend's wedding that summer gave Cleofas cause for concern when Angelina returned home and excitedly reported that "everybody was so nice!"—especially the bride's brother.

Troubled by her attractive daughter's unmet needs and unsure of how best to deal with them, Cleofas decided rather precipitously not to send Angelina back to Albuquerque for a second year, using Venceslao's still unsettled estate as the reason. With characteristic resignation, Angelina returned to the rigorous curriculum and strict disciplinary code of Loretto Academy. It was her final year of school, and so she decided to make the best of things as they were. But however hard she worked at hiding her emotions, she just could not mask her sadness.

"How disappointed Angie was," Cleofas later recalled, still believing that her daughter simply missed her former teacher, Sister Florian, and her good friend Margaret. "Such a sweet girl, full of pure, innocent wit," so unlike those others against whom Cleofas repeatedly warned her daughter, girls "who are just in their teens [but] look old already . . . [from] going out at night, smoking, drinking and dancing."[33]

Yet as the weeks passed, Cleofas grew vaguely uncomfortable with her decision to keep Angelina at home. "For some unexplainable reason, I did not like to see Angie on the streets so much that year, going and coming from school."[34] She would later recall how trying it was "to have [Angelina] come late from school. . . . She had so many excuses—choir, plays, music—all required practice."[35] Cleofas, of course, suspected that

FIGURE 10. Loretto Academy, where Angelina Jaramillo was a student.
Courtesy Museum of New Mexico, neg. no. 12169.

her daughter was involved in a new relationship, and when a friend remarked that "Angie is so different this year," she decided to keep an even closer watch over her.[36]

Angelina soon found herself working after school in the Spanish tearoom that her aunt Mae had established that fall.[37] Though eighteen years separated Cleofas from her sister, a common background of family and schooling had recently brought them closer to each other. Placing her daughter in Mae's care appeared to be a safer alternative than allowing her the freedom of an unstructured afternoon. And while Angelina found it easier to relate to Mae, there was still sufficient distance between aunt and niece to ensure proper supervision and guidance. Though Mae was not at all pleased with this role, she had little choice but to accept the assignment. After a bad marriage had ended in divorce, she needed whatever help she could get in her struggle to make ends meet.

Mae's former husband, Robert Alexander Smith, had come to Santa

Fe in 1917 from Montreal, Canada, where he had been born to Alexander Gould Smith, a brass finisher, and his wife, Mary Ann MacDonald, on June 5, 1896.[38] Within two years of his arrival in New Mexico, he had wed "one of Santa Fe's most attractive girls." A traditional marriage breakfast had been held in Mae's parents' Grant Street home, where her brother, Ben Martinez, the state's deputy treasurer, had witnessed their marriage license and served as Smith's best man. The groom "has made many friends here," the *New Mexican* informed its readers on July 5, 1919. "They will wish him and his bride much happiness."[39] But Smith had married above his station and Mae below hers, and so they lived away from the center of town at 359 Garcia Street, a small dirt street off Canyon Road, itself still unpaved.

In time, Smith's increasing use of alcohol and questionable activities with other women left him unemployed and his wife with ample grounds for a plea of abandonment as grounds for a divorce. According to the complaint filed against him on August 20, 1929, Smith had "failed to support and maintain . . . their said children according to his means and station in life . . . owing to the fact that he is addicted to the excessive use of intoxicants." The Martinez family, embarrassed by this turn of events, offered him an arrangement that would allow them to avoid any publicity while he accrued certain benefits for himself. In exchange for his agreement not to contest the complaint or the proposed terms of settlement—full custody of their children and ownership of their house and it contents for Mae, and monthly support from him in the amount of one hundred dollars[40]—he would be allowed to remain in the house with his former wife and their children and to live under her father's protection.[41]

Social prominence and a long political association with the local newspaper's owner, U.S. Senator Bronson Cutting (who had recently funded the addition to Venceslao's school in El Rito),[42] had made this deception possible. While other Santa Fe divorces were routinely published in the *New Mexican,* notice of theirs would never appear on its pages. As desired by the family, all hint of scandal had been avoided.

Smith's habits, of course, continued largely unchanged, and though he again found work—first at the Santa Fe Motor Company, a Chevrolet dealership down the street from Angelina's school, and then at Andrew's

Garage, two blocks from her home[43]—he still failed to meet his financial obligation to Mae and their children. The economic fallout of the Crash of 1929 merely exacerbated the situation. Having no other choice, Mae rented out their house on Garcia Street to another family[44] and moved together with her children and Smith into the larger Martinez home around the corner from Angelina and her mother.[45]

But as her father's fortunes declined, Mae was forced to open her tearoom on the *placita* of her sister's home. Reluctantly agreeing to employ her niece, she repeatedly complained to Cleofas that Angelina's work was inadequate. "I would not hurt her feelings by telling her," Cleofas recalled. "To rush home, set tables, help prepare some of the food and serve tables for three hours" after a long day of classes seemed to Cleofas work enough for any eighteen-year-old. Nor did she take her sister's complaints all that seriously, noting that "It has always been that way—my family taking for granted all I have ever done for them."[46]

Angelina was, of course, pleased that she was now earning her own money and made her first purchase a birthday gift for her mother, before buying a pair of pants for herself that Cleofas had previously disapproved of. Over the past year, the matter of clothing had become a source of increasing friction between them. "I am the only one who wears long stockings," Angelina had protested the previous spring. "We were divided in our opinions as to style," Cleofas later remarked concerning the pants Angelina had purchased with her first earnings that fall. "I wanting the full-cuff style and she the tight-fitting leg. She won, and I had to admit to myself that she really looked cute in them,"[47] though she could not bring herself to tell this to Angelina at the time.

Growing ever more assertive, Angelina now made a strong effort to resume her dancing and invited Miss Kahnt to spend a night at the Jaramillo house. After first winning Cleofas's approval, she brought her former instructor to Loretto Academy and succeeded in arranging for a dance class to be held there once a week. Cleofas, however, grew concerned several weeks later when a neighbor reported seeing Angelina dancing in her room without first closing the window shades. There were reports of a Peeping Tom in the area, and a man's footprints, found near the neighbor's windows, had continued onto the Jaramillos' property.[48]

Since moving into the house at 142 Griffin Street following

FIGURE 11. Jaramillo home, the rear bedroom
occupied by Cleofas Jaramillo and Marie Gonzales.

Photo by T. Harmon Parkhurst, courtesy Museum of New Mexico, neg. no. 69236.

Venceslao's death, Cleofas and Angelina had shared the rear bedroom. But when a young cousin of eleven, Marie Gonzales, came to live with them for the new school year, Cleofas moved to a front room, leaving Angelina and Marie to share the larger space. The cousin's restless sleep, however, soon proved too disturbing for Angelina, and after repeated and impatient pleading, Cleofas exchanged places with her daughter.

Cleofas's mother objected to this unsupervised arrangement, but Cleofas told her that Angelina needed "a room in which to keep her nice things and for her girl friends when they visit." Once the warmer weather returned, she planned to convert the back porch into a sleeping space for her daughter. "We shall be close together" again, Cleofas promised her mother. But Angelina hoped otherwise and redecorated her new room. "I shall fix it lovely," she announced with pride, for here, at last, was a chance to shape a place in the world that was wholly her own.[49]

Not surprisingly, Angelina's initial exhilaration soon collapsed under the weight of her still restricted life at home and at school. Though her eighteenth birthday that October should have been a day of joyful celebration, she simply could not overcome the deeper sadness into which she had again descended. Returning home from school and finding preparations for her party still incomplete, "she picked up the cake ingredients and went to my mother's and asked my sister, in a crying fit, to help her make the cake," Cleofas recalled. There was so much to do, and Cleofas had decided to leave the cake for last. Everything was, of course, ready for her guests when they arrived that evening, "the table fixed very pretty with flowers and candles," but Angelina's eyes remained "red . . . and sad. She was not her happy self, which she had always been at her parties."[50]

And so, when Cleofas saw how depressed Angelina was that last Sunday, she allowed her to visit with friends for the afternoon, only to grow concerned when Angelina did not return home as promised. Cleofas was, of course, relieved to see her daughter arrive home later that evening. Newly energized, she talked incessantly throughout dinner and then quickly finished her schoolwork. Retreating to the privacy of her room, she soon reemerged dressed in a new pair of silk pajamas that were to be worn only when visiting. Cleofas reminded her of this, but Angelina merely responded with a whimsical look and once again left the room. Cleofas decided not to pursue the matter, fearing that she might again upset her daughter.

Years later, Cleofas would retrace those final troubling moments when she saw Angelina alive for the last time. "After supper we again sat around the dining table, the girls preparing their lessons and I reading until bed-time; then we picked up our books and each went to her own room. Angie came back tying the belt on her robe. She leaned against the radiator in front of the bathroom door. I was washing my hands, and looked up at her, noting that she was wearing the new silk pajamas which her aunt had just sent her from Denver. I said, 'There you are, wearing your best, which you should be saving for visiting.'" Angelina looked down at them for a moment, and, "with a queer, little smile, turned and went back to her room without a word—not even her customary goodnight. I was surprised, but thought I had vexed her, and went to bed."[51]

It was routine for Cleofas each evening to place a key in the front door lock from inside so that it could not be picked while they slept. By November 15, the windows, too, would normally have been locked. But Cleofas had hired someone to clean them on Friday and had shut all but the one in the dressing room at the front of the house, next to Angelina's bedroom. Angelina had been asked to secure it but appeared to have forgotten. Still, the large potted cactus and the heavy typewriter resting on the sill of a window visible from the street should have discouraged any would-be intruder, or so Cleofas thought as she looked back on her daughter's brutal murder many years later.[52]

"I slept soundly until a flash of bright light on my eyes awakened me," she continued her carefully measured reconstruction of those horrifying moments. "'Angie!' I called, opening my eyes but seeing nothing but darkness. That seemed so strange. Had not someone just lit the light in the kitchen?" she recalled asking herself. "I lit the candle on the little table by my bed, slipped on my slippers, took the candle and stepped into the kitchen. Finding the dining room door still swinging," she realized that someone had just gone through it.[53]

"Slowly I pushed the door open, [but] seeing no one, I placed the candle on the table and, then, noticed the light in Angie's room. Cautiously I walked through the living room, [and] held back the portiere, which someone had drawn over the opening between that room and her bedroom." Suddenly, "a horrified scream escaped me as I saw before me, standing by Angie's bed the broad shoulders of a man in a black and white shirt. Startled by my scream, his shoulders gave a quick shrug. I imagine he sprang at me and caught me by the throat, for my throat later felt sore all night. Fortunately, as I screamed, my eyes closed in a faint and I was spared the terrible fright of seeing his face, which like those black and white stripes, would have been impressed upon my mind, making me shudder every time I see a dark face."[54]

Cleofas remained unconscious for only a brief time. "The next thing I saw, as my eyes opened for just a second, was the corner of the dining room wall. . . . I screamed in a horrible voice, 'Marie!' and knew nothing more. I had fallen in a faint by the dining room table."[55]

"How long I lay there I don't know. As I began coming to, I felt something rough on my cheek, and felt around with my hand, wondering

FIGURE 12. Jaramillo home, the living room through which
Cleofas Jaramillo passed on the way to her daughter's bedroom.

Photo by T. Harmon Parkhurst, courtesy Museum of New Mexico, neg. no. 69250.

why I was lying on the rug at my bedside. Then, like a flash, there came to me the thought of what I had seen in my daughter's room, and I sprang up and ran to her room. From the opening I turned back, horrified at the ghastly sight which met my glance. There was my daughter stretched across the bed, her face covered with a pillow. Mute with fright, I ran back to my room."[56]

"Hurry! My daughter!" Cleofas cried out as she saw Sheriff Baca and Deputy Alarid approach the house. As one of the men ran to Angelina's room, the other took Cleofas by the arm and guided her back to her bed. There he sat holding Cleofas until her brother, Ben, and sister, Mae, arrived. But neither one could calm their sister.

It was then that Cleofas's neighbor, Mrs. Clark, appeared in the bedroom doorway with Marie standing at her side, too traumatized to be on her own. "What doctor shall I call?" Clark asked Cleofas, who, out of grief and confusion, angrily confronted her neighbor in response. "Why didn't you come sooner," she shot back, wishing to believe that her daughter had still been alive when she saw her lying on her bed. Clark remained silent and left the room. And Cleofas never forgave her.[57]

Dr. Livingston, the family's physician, soon arrived and quickly determined that Cleofas was in need of hospitalization. The wound on her head was not at all serious and could easily be attended to, but her emotional state was too tenuous to allow her to remain in the house or to go home with her family. "Wrap her up and take her to the hospital," he ordered. "My car is out front." At St. Vincent's Hospital, Ben and those who had helped place his sister in Livingston's vehicle carried her into the building and put her to bed.

Throughout the night, Cleofas suffered from nausea and a choking sensation, and repeatedly gasped for air as she attempted to swallow the water that was offered to her.[58] By daybreak, she was emotionally exhausted and unable to move. Mae had remained through the night and in the morning was relieved by her sister's oldest friend, Marguerite. Later in the day, Cleofas's three brothers arrived from Taos and joined several good friends from El Rito who had preceded them. It was a silent vigil. There was nothing to be said as Cleofas cried unceasingly.

Marguerite kept watch the second night and into the next day until Cleofas's brothers returned. "Mr. Sayre says he will come in the morning and take you to see Angelina, if you wish," Marguerite told her. "Yes, you had better see her," Cleofas's brother Tom urged his sister. "She looks so beautiful. I have already prayed to her." But Cleofas remained fearful and asked only that Tom stay with her, telling her friend to go home and rest.[59]

Cleofas spent the night in prayer and by morning felt ready to see her daughter for the last time. "You may tell Mr. Sayre to come for me," she told Marguerite when she arrived. But Livingston was deeply concerned that his patient's emotional state was far too fragile to allow her to leave the hospital. Only after Cleofas's family argued that she needed to see her daughter peacefully at rest did he grant permission for her brief visit to the Martinez house, where Angelina lay in her casket.

Still unable to walk, Cleofas was wheeled on a cot into an ambulance and then driven to 125 Grant Street. For fifteen minutes she lay next to her daughter's coffin, the living room so filled with flowers that it resembled a "floral shop," she later commented. "You have many friends," the funeral director told her in an attempt to offer comfort where none could be found. "For a moment I looked down at my dear Angie," Cleofas would recall. "Yes, she looked sweet and so natural, as if in a happy dream. She was dressed in the pale pink chiffon dress, all of which I had made by hand for her for the junior-senior banquet." But Cleofas knew that Angelina would never again enjoy such occasions. "As I looked down at her pale hands, I realized that she was not just asleep, but that she was now leaving me, and that this was my last look at my dear one." She continued to peer over the edge until she grew faint and was taken back to St. Vincent's.[60]

Soon after Cleofas left the house, Angelina's body was brought to the flower-filled Cathedral of St. Francis, across from the courthouse where Johnson was to be tried. Every seat was filled. Friends and relatives from throughout the region and beyond had come to pay their respects. The entire student body of Loretto Academy tearfully said good-bye as the school's choir accompanied Father Leonard in celebrating the funeral mass. Carried into the cathedral by eight of her classmates dressed in white caps and gowns, Angelina was later borne on their shoulders as the crowd of mourners accompanied her to the Rosario Cemetery, along the northern reach of the city. There, amidst a stand of stately trees and protected by the shadow of a small, elegant adobe chapel, she was laid to rest in the Martinez family plot beside her grandmother, whose funeral she had attended less than a month before.[61]

In the City of Holy Faith

THE search for evidence in the case against Johnson had continued unabated throughout these first crucial days, though little new was found in the Jaramillo house beyond what had turned up during its initial search. Several as yet unidentified fingerprints, together with fragments from a shattered vase, two broken matches, and a washer said to be of a type occasionally used for automobiles seemed hardly enough for a conviction, however confident the prosecution felt. More evidence and other witnesses would be needed to strengthen the case against Johnson.

George Kyle's name had first been mentioned by Johnson himself while still in Albuquerque. They had been in prison together and were now living near each other in an area close to the Jaramillo home. "You dirty ___," Johnson had shouted at Detective Martin after being relentlessly questioned by him. "You're just like George Kyle; you'd do anything to hang a man!" It was later said by the prosecution that within hours of Johnson's return to Santa Fe, Kyle had approached Martin, anxious to tell his story. He spoke of seeing the accused standing about 250 feet from the victim's residence at around ten-thirty on the night of the murder. "I asked him what he was doing in that part of town at that time of night," Kyle told Martin, "and he answered that he was working near there."

Since then, a second witness had come forward, a woman who reported seeing Johnson in the same neighborhood, albeit a few days before Angelina's murder. With her story in hand, Kenney went straight to the newspaper, certain that he could rely on the cooperation of the press to help secure Johnson's conviction. "NEGRO WAS LOOKING FOR 'ANGELINA'" the *New Mexican*'s Wednesday headline proclaimed throughout the city. He was said to have knocked at an as yet unidentified woman's door the previous Thursday and Friday evenings and to have asked, in Spanish, if she knew where Angelina lived, though on both nights, he had been unable to supply a last name when questioned by her. Concern for the prisoner's security had prevented Johnson from being removed from the prison for a lineup, Kenney explained, and so Sheriff Baca had brought the woman to his cell. "That's the man," she assured Baca. "Go closer; take a good look," he urged her in response. But she had refused, claiming that her "good eye-sight" made a closer look unnecessary. The sheriff was satisfied and later commented to reporters that Johnson, who spoke some Spanish and understood their conversation, had "turned a shade lighter . . . [as] he stood staring at her fixedly through the bars of his cell door."

Johnson later tried to explain to Kenney that he had been looking for someone named Alexander, and because the two men barely knew each other, he had not known his address, but only that he lived somewhere in the area. He had knocked on the woman's door asking for Alexander, and not for Angelina, he insisted. Perhaps the woman, upset by the sight of a black stranger at her door, had confused the two names when she later heard that "a negro" was accused of killing Angelina.[1]

But there was no reason for Kenney to consider this possibility. As reported to the *New Mexican* that Wednesday, a police officer had seen "the negro . . . on the street here at 7 P.M." that evening. Johnson's claim of not having returned to Santa Fe from Albuquerque until 9:00 P.M. that Sunday night was clearly a lie.[2]

Johnson, of course, continued to insist that he had hitched a ride to Albuquerque earlier that day to see his former landlady, whom he had heard was quite ill. But when he arrived at her home, he found that she was no longer there. Unable to find out where she had gone, he began to look for a ride back to Santa Fe. It had taken him until nine to return, and after walking a mile from where he had been dropped off, he had made Tony Rael's pool hall, situated a few blocks from both his rooming house and the Jaramillo home, his first stop in town.

But Kenney now had all that he needed to move forward with an arraignment. Previously held over only for questioning, the case against Johnson had grown strong enough during these first forty-eight hours to allow for one to be scheduled. "The case is coming along fine," the prosecution told the press, feeling even more confident than before. Johnson's prints, on file at the state penitentiary's lab, were at that very moment being compared by inmate technicians to those found at the crime scene. A conclusion was promised by late that afternoon. Should they fail to match, Kenney assured the press, there was enough other evidence to win an easy conviction, and more to come.[3]

Yet when the prison lab inconclusively completed its analysis later that day, photographs of both sets of prints were rushed to Frank Powers, an expert working with the El Paso, Texas, Police Department.[4] The *New Mexican,* of course, decided not to mention this unexpected development, nor to say anything about Churchill's slightly improved condition that Wednesday. Only the *Albuquerque Journal* reported both. Churchill was, in fact, now conscious, though he as yet had no recollection of his fight with Johnson.[5]

The *New Mexican* waited until the next afternoon to report only that Churchill was "very much better" and that Cleofas, too, was improving, though both continued to offer no further details. The paper did, however, break its silence concerning the fingerprints of "Thomas Johnson, negro," and mentioned that an "identification expert" in El Paso, having found the photographs to be "unsatisfactory," had requested that the originals be sent to him immediately.[6]

The next edition of the *New Mexican* reported that Johnson had been served with the warrant and that a preliminary hearing was scheduled for two o'clock the following afternoon in the warden's office. It had been thought to keep the date and time secret for fear of a violent response from the townspeople while the prisoner was being moved to the courthouse. But Judge Otero's decision to hold the hearing at the prison had now eliminated that concern.[7]

"Tom Johnson, negro ex-convict, continued to protest his innocence of the murder of little Angelina Jaramillo," the *New Mexican* went on to report that day. Constant grilling had not shaken his resolve. "I am not guilty of that," he had repeatedly insisted as Sheriff Baca "read the warrant to him through the bars of his cell." But again, Johnson's refusal to confess to the crime was of no real concern. Kenney's willingness to go forward without Powers's fingerprint report in hand, the *New Mexican* confidently assured its readers, was clear "evidence that the prosecution has finished marshaling its evidence against the alleged slayer."[8]

By the afternoon of the hearing, the court had found an attorney to handle Johnson's defense. At the age of seventy-four, Jacob H. Crist was nearing the end of a long career in the law that had included nearly one hundred murder trials either as a prosecutor, a defense attorney, or a judge, a dozen of which were considered famous by the standards of their day. Yet while serving as Santa Fe's district attorney in the 1890s, he himself had knowingly assisted in the wrongful conviction and execution of two defendants from whom he had financially profited through the acquisition of their land and mines.[9] What role his involvement in these earlier cases now played in his decision to accept Johnson as a client and to attempt a vigorous fight against Kenney's prosecution remains open to speculation. But at his age, repentance could no longer be postponed.

Born in Pennsylvania and educated at its state college, Crist had taught school for a short time before lighting out for the New Mexico Territory in 1884. Active in Democratic politics soon after his arrival, he founded a weekly newspaper in Santa Fe and, while practicing law, became involved in a series of mining and land investments, some of which may have tainted his legal work.[10] Together with his wife, Adele Mayne, the daughter of British explorer and writer Sir Richard Francis Burton, he had once owned vast tracts of land near Taos.[11] But financial reverses had now forced him back into the practice of law in spite of his advancing age.[12]

The preliminary hearing was still in progress when the *New Mexican* hit the streets that day. A second edition would appear late that afternoon, a rare occurrence in the small town of Santa Fe. It was reported that with the advice of counsel, Johnson had refused to waive his right to this preliminary procedure, though he himself would not take the stand at this time. Instead, a plea of innocent would be entered. Crist, having just barely met his client and as yet without any ideas for a defense, planned to listen attentively to the prosecution's case.

News that Churchill's memory of Johnson's assault had returned was reported as well. But however much this promised to add to the prosecution's case, testimony from "the dead girl's mother," along with several other "startling developments" promised by the prosecution for later that day,[13] would prove to be key elements in the upcoming trial, the paper noted.

As promised, Kenney introduced previously undisclosed evidence at the hearing. Following the coroner's inquest, Dr. Dwight W. Rife, a criminologist trained at a well-respected lab in Chicago, had been asked to scrape the underside of Angelina's nails for any particles of potential evidence and then to do the same with Johnson's.[14] Rife now reported that with the use of a microscope, the "tiny caramel colored refractory particles" of lipstick found on both the victim and the accused were identical. A single short brown hair and some "brown pigmented epithelium" were also discovered under Angelina's nails, though under cross-examination, it was acknowledged that no effort had yet been made to identify the origin of either. Crist further countered Rife's testimony by asking him if the particular lipstick in question was not, in fact, in general use, to which Rife answered yes.[15] But it seemed not to matter.

Angelina's aunt Mae had been the first to speak of this lipstick at the hearing. As she took the stand, those who had gathered in the warden's office suddenly "shed their expression of boredom," the *New Mexican* reporter observed. "They sensed that a disclosure was coming." Mae testified that until that final Sunday afternoon, when Angelina stopped by the Martinez house, she had never before seen her niece wearing any makeup. It was, she assumed, the first time.[16] Mae was particularly struck by the lipstick's garish appearance, a bright red that clashed with the coloring Angelina had applied to her cheeks. "I tried to get her to rub it off because she had it on too thick, and because it was a shade different from the rouge and not becoming," she explained under oath.[17]

Having recaptured his audience's attention with her testimony and that of Dr. Rife, Kenney then called to the stand several eyewitnesses he had withheld until just such a moment as this. Their task was to definitively place Johnson in the general area of the Jaramillo home both during the night of the murder and at an earlier time. George Kyle repeated the story he gave several days earlier at the coroner's inquest, that he had known Johnson from their time together in the state penitentiary and that he had questioned Johnson as to why he was out along Griffin Street at ten-thirty on a Sunday evening and standing only eighty yards from the lighted windows of Angelina's house. Kyle claimed to be accompanying his wife's friend to her home at that time, though he declined to give her name.

Nor was Dorothy Linney of 234 Griffin asked to identify the "negro man" whom she again swore had passed her on a "quite dark" street as she walked to the post office at 9:00 P.M. that night.[18] There was no need to. It was enough merely to imply that the "negro man" was Johnson.

Similar problems with other testimony that day proved to be of no greater consequence to the court. Oliver Holmes, the police officer who earlier claimed to have rousted Johnson at 7:00 P.M. that evening, now gave the location of their encounter at some distance from the crime scene, while another witness, city inspector Alex Barnes, testified only that he had confronted Johnson near the Jaramillo home two and a half months earlier, on the night of September 5. He had asked Johnson why he was loitering near Mackenzie and Griffin, to which Johnson had replied that he was looking for a friend. Moments later, Johnson's knife was introduced as the weapon allegedly used to murder Angelina. A small dot of what was said to be the victim's blood appeared on the blade, though neither the nature of the "drop" nor its origin was ever substantiated.[19] But such inconsistencies and oversights seemed not to matter as implication was easily substituted for evidence.

More damaging still was Kenney's promise of Cleofas's future testimony regarding the clothing worn by her assailant. Though she had previously spoken of him as a man wearing a striped shirt, it now appeared that she was prepared to accept Kenney's description of the garment in question.[20]

Unfortunately, Johnson's own story, as related by Crist that afternoon, appeared to further unravel when placed beside the testimony of the two individuals with whom he admitted interacting that evening. Contrary to his claim of not returning to Santa Fe until 9:00 P.M., Tony Rael insisted that Johnson had spent the half hour between 8:30 and 9:00 P.M. with him, while Eliseo Quintana, whom Johnson said he had visited after leaving Rael's pool hall, now testified that the accused had appeared at his door at seven-thirty that night asking to borrow four dollars.[21]

Crist tried to counter this testimony as best he could, arguing in his summation that Johnson's account, related to him by his client just prior to the hearing, had, in fact, been corroborated by the prosecution's own witnesses, albeit with some slight variations in the times recalled by his client. Consequently, he himself was now more certain of Johnson's truthfulness than before. If he were not, he would have asked to be excused from the case, he told the jury. "I am glad to say that the story related here by the officers is the same story which Johnson told me. I have asked questions in cross examination here expressly intended to gain verification of Johnson's story to me." It was clear, however, that he would need more time "to assure that this man's defense is competently presented." The defense's own expert witnesses would have to undertake their own analysis of the "scientific data," he insisted, though with little or no funds available to him, the search for such a person promised to be a lengthy one. Judge Otero, however, remained unconvinced and, in response, reconfirmed Johnson's previously announced trial date of December 1.[22]

"Negro Seen Near Jaramillo House" the *New Mexican*'s late edition told the news-hungry townspeople soon after the hearing ended at 4:00 P.M. "Tom Johnson, negro ex-convict," was to be held without bail and tried in district court before Judge Otero, Jr. Crist's unhappiness with the judge's plan to open the court for a special term in just ten days was reported as well. The prosecution had been working on its case for some time, he noted. Yet there seemed little reason to seek a postponement. The court was certain to deny any such motion.

Throughout the afternoon, Johnson had sat staring straight ahead. Rarely had he looked over at Kenney or at any of the witnesses. Dressed in faded blue prison overalls, he was described by the *New Mexican* as seated "erect with folded arms in prison fashion." "No change of expression fleeted over his face at any time," the newspaper added to its carefully drawn portrait of this cold-blooded Negro killer. Only once did it offer its readers a different image of the alleged rapist and murderer. At the very end of its report, the paper mentioned that when the hearing

FIGURE 13. District Judge Miguel Otero, Jr., and his wife.
Judge Otero presided at the trial for Angelina's murder.

Reproduced from *Master Detective*, "The Clue of the Lipstick"
(March 1935), in the collections of the Library of Congress.

ended, Johnson turned to Sheriff Baca and, in a low voice, asked him to please retrieve the scapular and rosary he had left behind in his Sandoval Street room and to bring them to him at the prison.[23]

At a news conference the next morning, Kenney happily told the press that the "identification of fingerprints taken from the bedroom of Angelina Jaramillo as those of Thomas Johnson, alleged slayer of the girl, clinches the case." Despite the lack of concern he had previously exhibited, he was noticeably relieved. "The district attorney's office is delighted with the accumulation of evidence. . . . Now we can relax a little." Frank Powers's report had arrived from El Paso only a few hours after the preliminary hearing had ended and had "materially strengthened" the case. The fingerprints were "undoubtedly those of Johnson," Powers concluded. One of the seven sets of prints said to have been taken from Angelina's bedroom matched those on file at the penitentiary.[24]

Kenney was equally pleased to report that Cleofas had left the hospital that morning and was now resting at her father's home on Grant Street.[25] Though still not in any condition to take the witness stand, Kenney felt certain that she would be well enough to appear at the upcoming trial.

"After five days I was longing to be with my family," Cleofas would later recall. "The doctor said I could be taken home. My brother, Ben, and my sister came for me, taking me and placing me in a bed by my father's bed. For more than a week I lay there, too weak and disheartened to care to live. I tried to pray, but my heart was too grieved." Overcome by "shock and desolation," the days passed slowly until, in time, her "heart grew more resigned"[26] to the reality of what had happened. It would be Kenney's good fortune that she began to heal just as her testimony was needed.

Following this Saturday morning press conference, Kenney filed a revised "Criminal Information" with the district court. Eliminating the charges of rape, assault with intent to kill, and larceny, he now focused his attention on the sole charge of first-degree murder. Johnson, it stated, had "unlawfully, willfully, feloniously, maliciously, purposely, and of his deliberate and premeditated express malice . . . attacked Angelina Jaramillo, a woman child . . . and with a sharp instrument . . . stab[bed] her . . . just above and toward the front of the left ear . . . inflicting upon the body of her . . . one mortal wound, of which said mortal wound, she, the said Angelina Jaramillo, then and there instantly died."[27]

On Monday, November 23, Judge Otero issued a warrant authorizing Sheriff Baca to bring Johnson before the district court on December 1, 1931, "to answer to [this] Criminal Information for First Degree Murder." Two additional days would pass before he was actually served the warrant, further reducing the time available to Crist to prepare his client's defense against the thirty-seven prosecution witnesses named in the warrant. To Crist, this situation appeared even more hopeless than before.[28]

The following Saturday, November 28, Crist informed the press that he would make a final decision about filing for a change of venue after he met with Johnson that afternoon. Snowed in at Tierra Amarilla for the past three days, he had not seen his client since the preliminary hearing a week earlier. For the moment, he was certain only that Johnson would take the stand in his own defense. "I want him to tell his story to the 12 men chosen as the jury, so they can look him over and pass on the veracity of his story," Crist asserted.[29] With no defense witnesses as yet identified, there simply was no other choice but to have him take this risk.

The Negro Crime

THERE was now little doubt left in the community that Johnson was guilty as charged. He had twice been judged culpable in court proceedings and had been repeatedly convicted by the press. Only his employer, Al Muller, had come forward with anything positive to say about him, though he, too, emphasized from the beginning that the crime deserved everyone's condemnation and that the perpetrator had to be dealt with swiftly. Still, Muller felt compelled to mention in Johnson's favor that "the work he did was the hardest, dirtiest work in the garage" and that whatever the task, "his work was in every way satisfactory." Johnson had reported each day as expected and "was courteous in every way to the people with whom he came into contact," Muller further noted. "Every customer for whom he worked was thoroughly satisfied." So much so, in fact, that "a number of them refused to have work done by anyone except Johnson."[1]

Muller's kind words were, of course, carefully buried in a small article in the center of the *New Mexican*. To have done otherwise would have violated the newspaper's position on the case. At every turn, Johnson's name had been dropped from its headlines, and, to retain his usefulness as a symbol, his photograph had yet to be shown. Each racially charged reference to "the negro"—"the negro gaining entrance to the house through a window," Cleofas "knocked unconscious by a heavy glass vase with which the negro hit her," "the negro had worked" at Andrew's garage, "the Negro's victim [Churchill] had lost a great deal of blood," a package on which "the negro" had pillowed his head "was stained red with blood," the inability of Cleofas in a darkened room to see whether "the man who sprang at her from beside her daughter's body was a negro"[2]—served only to further inflame the already volatile situation and to imprint ever more indelibly on the public's mind the particularly outrageous nature of the assault and of the threat it represented to their community's well-being. From the beginning, E. Dana Johnson, editor of the *New Mexican,* had seized on the opportunity presented by the crime and had spoken unequivocally of "the indescribably sickening shock of having the Negro Crime committed at her own doors, under circumstances which almost numb the average person with horror." The need to rid Santa Fe of any possibility of its repetition, he declared, was unmistakable.[3]

Dana (as he was known about town) had come to New Mexico from West Virginia in 1902, at the age of twenty-three. Though rooted in his New England ancestry (including Jonathan Edwards, the eighteenth-century theologian of the Great Awakening) and claiming descent from a sheriff of Nottingham (perhaps even "the country politico with whom Robin Hood had such a merry time," he once wrote in an autobiographical sketch[4]), he soon became "a native New Mexican in every sense." As one of his colleagues later noted, "Whatever concerned New Mexico concerned him—vitally, intimately, personally."[5] A supporter of progressive causes, including Venceslao's egalitarian state constitution, Dana became a close personal friend and ally of Bronson Cutting, who, as owner of the *New Mexican,* had appointed him its editor in 1913.[6]

An "Old Santa Fe Nut" by his own account, he had made a "hobby of old Spanish customs"[7] and, according to local poet and cultural leader Alice Corbin Henderson, had "supported every cause and movement that tended to keep New Mexico, and Santa Fe its ancient capital, a symbol of the races that made it." For decades he worked "to preserve its essential character and integrity . . . as it is, and was, and as he wanted it to

FIGURE 14. E. Dana Johnson, editor of the *Santa Fe New Mexican.*
Photo by De Castro, courtesy Museum of New Mexico, neg. no. 55998.

remain."[8] "No one born here cared more for its traditions nor worked harder to preserve the beauty and character of the city," wrote another of Dana's admirers. Nothing "that touched the character of the city he loved best escaped him."[9] As a leader in "all the civic and social groups," he had watched over "the successive changes" that befell the "tri-racial [Indian, Spanish, and Anglo] social scene" and had "waged many a fight" to keep things as he wished them to be.[10]

Perhaps he felt so passionately about keeping the city free of blacks because change, to the land and to the culture he had loved for nearly thirty years, was already becoming obvious and irreversible. "Even the population is changing," a member of Dana's staff at the *New Mexican* would later write in his obituary. "From now on, had he lived and continued to be the civic monitor of Old Santa Fe, his fight probably would have been just one reversal after another."[11]

But in 1931, this fight, however frustrated by the realities gathering around him, did not yet seem lost. And so, with characteristic determination, he moved "relentless[ly] for the sake of a cause,"[12] using the *New Mexican* as his primary weapon. For news was not something merely "to be dished out," he believed, "but . . . interpreted, correlated, and integrated for understanding, use and betterment of conditions,"[13] especially in Santa Fe. "We believe the first time [for the Negro Crime] will be the last," he insisted. To secure the townspeople's safety, measures would have to be instituted for the "barring in future of Negroes from this town, save for its old timers, a thing possible here because Santa Fe is yet a small town."

The assault, in fact, had raised the still larger issue of worsening race relations across the country, Dana maintained. It was a problem he had hoped Santa Fe could avoid. "For 300 years we have escaped this particular social problem," but it had finally come to town, in spite of his best efforts. "Some months ago the *New Mexican* warned that this community, which has inherited no black and white problem, should not allow itself by negligence and indifference, to acquire one." Though previously ignored, Dana was now certain that "no further warning will be needed as to the necessity of stamping it out in infancy. . . . The inconceivably frightful thing of last night . . . [has] scared [*sic*] the soul of the community like a branding iron."

Nor could there be any doubt that "the city, chamber of commerce, police and sheriff's office must establish a perpetual community rule that Negroes are not desired here," he insisted. Prohibit them from settling in Santa Fe and they would commit their particular species of crime elsewhere. The logic of his proposal was clear, as was its corollary, that temporary residence had to be denied them as well. Whether on their own or as servants to Anglos[14] seeking refuge in Santa Fe from an increasingly chaotic America, they could not be allowed to enter. In short, "They do not belong here, they bring a racial conflict even more intense than elsewhere. The thing to do is to keep them out. It can be done peaceably, officially, in an orderly manner, and especially with wide publicity."[15] Dana hoped that his editorial would signal the beginning of this process.

Five years earlier, a traveler to New Mexico had commented that blacks "are as sparse as rose bushes upon the prairies."[16] The federal census of 1930 confirmed this observation, counting barely 3,000 among a statewide population of 423,000.[17] In Santa Fe, blacks constituted only 0.007 percent of the city's population.[18] Yet their relative absence from the area mattered little to those for whom even a marginal presence was too much, particularly in an era of economic depression.

Color consciousness had first been used in colonial New Mexico to separate subjugated Indians from their Spanish rulers, though in each generation the degree of blood mixing between Indian and Hispanic had increased. Far less attention, however, was paid to the small number of blacks and their descendants, free or slave, during this early period.[19] In time, most blacks simply vanished into the general population, first as mulattos (of recognized African descent) and then as part of the far larger grouping identified merely as mestizos (of mixed Spanish-Indian ancestry).

Yet while these racial boundaries were never wholly fixed, and under the weight of external pressures and shifting class distinctions were continuously being redefined, there were some, particularly among the dominant families of Angelina's world, who nonetheless grew more insistent on doing so—for as power slipped into the hands of the lighter-complected Anglos, and the old ways that Cleofas fought so hard to preserve slowly weakened, the issue of race only grew stronger, encouraging them to lay claim to being of pure Spanish descent. Surely the existing order of rank and dominance had to be maintained before it, too, was lost forever.[20] Even the Hispanic poor supported these distinctions, for they, too, while often darker than their *patrones,* benefited from a social reconstruction of race in which those of a still darker complexion occupied an ever lower social position.[21]

So pervasive had this changing attitude toward race become that Cleofas's own childhood image of herself had been affected as color came to play a role even within her own family. Though her brother, Reyes Martinez, could tell a WPA field worker gathering the region's folklore in 1937 that "many of the first families that settled in northern New Mexico

FIGURE 15. Cleofas Jaramillo at about the age of her
daughter, Angelina, at the time of her murder, ca. 1900.

Courtesy Museum of New Mexico, neg. no. 9927.

were of pure Spanish stock,"[22] Cleofas forever remained troubled by the
shadows that had been cast on her own racial purity. "I, not being so fair
and blue-eyed as some of my brothers and cousins, was considered the
ugly, thin, pale duckling," she recalled in later years. Only her position as
the lone daughter among seven children, until Mae's birth, had protected
her from even greater scorn.[23]

Yet however troubled by her coloring, Cleofas knew that she
belonged to "the crowd of white people."[24] There was no questioning this

fact. And when in her youth "the very first colored man ever seen within the memory of old-timers" passed through her village, she, like her neighbors, young and old, ran out into the square to see this strange sight. For there, "riding a white horse and driving a bunch of what seemed to be thorough-bred race horses,"[25] was a hapless black man who had suddenly and fearfully found himself confronting the villagers' ridicule. "There were dark complexioned people in Arroyo Hondo," Cleofas's brother Reyes later reported, "but none near the deep shade of black of this man. He was one of the darkest specimens of his race."

Frightened at first by the villagers' silence and then by their mocking laughter, the man tried to ease his way out of town with a few songs. "Raising his hat well above his forehead and facing his curious audience, he sang in a clear voice, with earnestness, a plantation song of his native south. At first, his listeners laughed heartily at him; his appearance, as he sang, seemed funny to them; then, little by little, they were enraptured by the melody of his voice, till soon they stood in silent ecstasy of his song." With a total lack of self-consciousness, Reyes recalled more than forty years later that the man "left a lasting impression in their minds of what a colored man really is, not only in appearance, but in ability as an entertainer, which is characteristic of his race, as well."[26]

Other stories collected throughout New Mexico by the WPA in the years following Johnson's arrest expressed similar attitudes, tales just as unselfconsciously told, of "the old darling we called 'Nigger Dick,'" who could be counted on to "watch and trim those trees" that provided shade for the family that owned the land or of "'Nigger George,' one of the most highly respected citizens of the colored race" because of his "faithful service" as a cowboy—and of the "Negro nurse" Lorenza, purchased from the Comanches at the age of seven, who "people from far and near came to see" as the first black brought into that area of the territory, and whose "soft, thick lips" had made her a "very pleasant" experience for the young child placed in her care.[27]

Like the country it found itself a part of, the Spanish community of New Mexico, after first being well served by its egalitarian state constitution, came to find the Anglos' system of racially based disabilities equally useful to themselves as well.[28] "Race distinctions do not appear to be decreasing," a national study reported in 1910. On the contrary, "distinctions heretofore existing only in custom tend to crystallize into law."[29] In 1923, the New Mexico legislature chose to follow this pattern. Breaking its own legal tradition, it established "separate schools for colored pupils." Reaffirmed in 1925 and again in 1929, two years before Johnson's arrest, the new law assured the state's citizenry "that separate rooms [will] be provided for the teaching of pupils of African descent."[30]

Nor was there any greater desire among the Anglos to live alongside these blacks. Even so progressive a person as Elizabeth White shared this sentiment. A woman of wealth and privilege and a guiding force in Santa Fe's cultural life since coming west from New York following her work as a nurse in the Great War, she had long championed the Pueblo Indians' struggle against the assimilation being imposed on them by the federal government. But in April 1930, she amended the deed to her estate by stating unequivocally "that no conveyance shall be made or granted of said premises, or any part thereof, to any person or persons of African or Oriental descent."[31]

It is not surprising, then, that mention was rarely made of those blacks who had lived in New Mexico for generations as farmers or ranchers, businessmen or lawyers, teachers or homemakers. Their individual lives and accomplishments went largely unnoticed, as did that of a young black man whose contest-winning essay at Santa Fe's high school in the spring of 1931 was deemed unfit for inclusion in the *New Mexican*.[32]

And so, when Johnson was arrested several months later for the rape and murder of a young white woman, there was no end to the pronouncements of his guilt by the Anglo-controlled *New Mexican,* or to the Spanish community's willingness to accept its pretrial verdict. On this issue, if little else, both groups could agree. For who could doubt Johnson's involvement in a crime that so perfectly fit what was known about the black male?[33] Characterized as violent liars and rapists, thieves and murderers, capable of little more than animal-like behavior and said to be hateful toward all whites, there was scant reason to doubt his guilt,[34] particularly after four previous incarcerations. What greater proof was needed than the conviction several months earlier in Scottsboro, Alabama, of nine boys charged with raping two white women? If they could commit such heinous acts, why not an adult twice their age?

A few white readers of the *New Mexican,* however, were outraged by Dana's editorial demand for the banning of all blacks from Santa Fe. Shortly after it appeared, Katherine Gay, "astonished at the conclusions which you draw from . . . Santa Fe's shocking tragedies of Sunday night," chided its author, insisting that "no race is to be judged by its criminals." Though she could not leap to Johnson's defense, she asserted that "the crimes . . . if proved against him, are Johnson's crimes and his only, not the crimes of the Negro race. It has yet to be proven . . . that the crime of rape is peculiar to the African race." In New York, where the largest black population of any city in the country resided, this same charge was, in fact, more commonly leveled against "a certain untutored class of immigrants from the South of Europe. To debar self-respecting, law-abiding Negroes from Santa Fe because one Negro convict has added to his list of crimes," Gay argued, was "as rational as if Chicago had held its finest Jewish citizens punishable for the deeds of the depraved Loeb and Leopold"[35] (whose murder of an adolescent younger than themselves had been committed with the belief that superior intelligence would allow them to escape detection).

Gay, however, suffered no illusion that the *New Mexican* would publish her letter. The next day she wrote to the New York office of Walter White, head of the National Association for the Advancement of Colored People (NAACP). It was the NAACP that had recently come to the aid of the Scottsboro Boys. Recalling that their mutual friend, Paul Robeson, had previously introduced them to each other, Gay informed White of "the crisis we now have on our hands." With perhaps no more than a dozen black residents in Santa Fe, she feared that the NAACP might not think its intervention important. But she had found the enclosed editorial so "shocking and stupid" that it required her "written . . . protest to the paper," and, she hoped, White's own response. For while the paper's owner "has shown himself rather more liberal than otherwise in his attitude toward Federal censorship and toward Soviet Russia," his editor, a Virginian, was "a man with a very limited and conventional point of view" and someone who, she believed, would not print her letter.[36]

She was, of course, right. The decision had already been reached not to grant her space in the *New Mexican.* In its place, a more conciliatory

FIGURE 16. Walter White, NAACP official, ca. 1930s.

Photo by Underwood and Underwood Studios, Courtesy of Photographs
and Prints Division, Schomburg Center for Research in Black Culture,
The New York Public Library, Astor, Lenox, and Tilden Foundations,
no. SC-CN-79-0224.

response, penned anonymously by the newspaper's owner, was being
prepared for publication the following day. A native New Yorker whose
wealthy Long Island family were intimate friends of the Teddy
Roosevelts, Bronson Cutting had come to Santa Fe in 1910 to recover
from the tuberculosis that had interrupted his senior year at Harvard
University. Like Dana, he, too, quickly involved himself in the city's
business and civic affairs. Buying its newspaper in 1913, he won
appointment to the U.S. Senate when a midterm vacancy arose in 1927.[37]
Though fashioning himself a progressive Republican, he had grown

increasingly dependent on the more conservative Spanish members of his party to counter the growing Democratic influence within the state. Home from the Senate for the Thanksgiving holiday, Cutting now found himself having to defend an editorial stance supported by the very families positioned at the center of his political base, though he knew it was otherwise untenable.

Anonymously signed "An Old Subscriber," Cutting began his letter to the *New Mexican* by gently asking if, "as a citizen of Santa Fe," he might "respectfully protest against the policy advocated" in its editorial the previous day. While personally troubled by the paper's approach, he hoped that others would understand how "the most revolting crime ever perpetrated in this community has stirred us all to a depth which makes it hard for us to reason in a normal way." Still, it was the press's responsibility under such circumstances "to use its powers and its intelligence to curb the blind reactions of horror and prejudice." "Guilt," Cutting reminded his readers, "is personal not racial." The fact that "the criminal in this case is a negro" did "not justify an implied indictment of the negro race," nor a call for new laws barring all blacks from the city. Both were clear violations of "the fundamental principles of American fair play." The tolerance previously shown by all of Santa Fe's citizens had been a credit to the city. He hoped it would continue.[38]

Cutting's attempt to prevent any further criticism of his friend or of his newspaper, however, failed. The next morning, the *Albuquerque Journal* unfavorably compared the "unwise advice" of Cutting's editor to the "most commendable attitude" displayed by other Santa Feans, despite "the violence and nature of the crime perpetrated." Theirs was a reaction contrary to what the "Old Subscriber" had judged to be natural. Moreover, "the general condemnation justly heaped on the accused negro" had not led to "mob violence, as would have been the case in several states in the union." How disturbing then to find the *New Mexican* "attempt[ing] to incite a racial conflict." This truly was not "the spirit of a free America," the *Journal* concluded.[39]

"Let Us Modify It," Dana wrote in self-defense later that day, denying any previous intent to cause violence or to level a blanket condemnation against "the entire negro race for the act of one depraved member." "The *New Mexican* did none of these," he protested. It was all a misunderstanding. If his writing had confused some readers, it was "perhaps beclouded slightly by a harrowing situation," what the "Old Subscriber" had correctly identified as "extenuating circumstances." But the egregious opinions ascribed to him were, in truth, not his. Had he not "specifically mentioned the 'beloved and respected [black] citizens of Santa Fe,'" men like Bill Andrews, "one of our oldest and beloved amigos"? he protested. There could be little doubt, then, "that the editor is far from being racially prejudiced or intolerant." Rather than bar all blacks, it was merely the *New Mexican*'s "hope that fortune and vigilance [would] keep Santa Fe free from an influx of actual or potential criminals of any race."[40]

But if some found Dana's remarks too extreme or imprudently forthright, the editor of Raton's newspaper thought them "unquestionably timely and proper" and their author "well within his rights in the matter, since he was looking toward the future peace and tranquility of his people, which is what editors were created for." It was, he stated without hesitation, a "remarkable editorial" and one that reflected a serious problem shared by other communities as well. "The truth of the matter is that Santa Fe is not the only town that has been grossly lax in the matter of permitting unbridled incoming of Negroes." Many others had been equally remiss and had experienced "a constant problem in the worthless and 'bad' Negroes." While admittedly "the good negro is a useful member of the community scheme of things . . . it is hard to tell which is good and which is bad at first sight. The safer plan," he argued, as Dana initially had, "is to keep them all out." And if Dana neglected to mention the "means of such exclusion or expulsion," there really was no need to. "Everybody knows them, and if it is the sense of the community, they are easily and efficiently employed."[41]

To some, like Katherine Gay, it seemed only a matter of time before such action would be taken. By now, she had received a response from Walter White, copies of which had been sent to the *New Mexican* and to Cutting, whom White had met some months earlier at the Progressive Conference in Washington, D.C. A separate note from the association's director of publicity was sent to Gay as well, praising her efforts and promising to investigate the situation, though no time frame was mentioned. The letter to the newspaper was a "good attack," he told her; the association would certainly "follow it up."[42]

White's response to the *New Mexican,* additional copies of which were forwarded to Santa Fe's mayor and to its chamber of commerce, condemned "the shocking attitude of mind revealed in [its] editorial. . . . For an editor to seek to discredit an entire race in the way you do and ask its exclusion from a community because of a single instance of crime, one which you yourself say is unique in the community," was, he argued, clear "evidence of a backwardness and narrow-minded prejudice which we sincerely hope your community will repudiate." It was White's fear that the citizens of Santa Fe would give credence to what was "neither humanly generous nor . . . in accord with the dictates of true patriotism." The "menace of a serious race problem" might well result from such thoughts and thereby threaten the very well-being of those whom "you yourself admit . . . are law-abiding, orderly, and even 'much-beloved' colored citizens in your community."[43]

Unaware of Cutting's ownership of the *New Mexican,* White sent a copy of both Dana's editorial and of his own reply to the senator's Washington office, "believing that such an expression cannot possibly meet with your approval."[44] Cutting's secretary acknowledged receipt of White's material two days later, on November 21, and promised to bring it to the senator's attention "at the first opportunity."[45]

Cutting would use his absence from Washington to excuse his delayed response to White's appeal, waiting until December 10, several days after his return to the capital and two days after Johnson's trial had been concluded, to finally respond. Stressing that he agreed with White's critique of the *New Mexican* and that he had, in fact, sent a letter of his own stating his objection to its editorial position, he nonetheless wished to draw White's attention, "in extenuation," to the brutal nature of what Johnson had done. "I hope you will remember that the particular crime was almost unheard of in our friendly and somewhat pastoral community, and that the particular crime was in its details by far the most horrible I have ever heard of anywhere. You will realize that under the circumstances the first shock was terrific, and that it was difficult for the average citizen to keep his head."[46]

A week and a half earlier, on the eve of the trial, Senator Cutting—a close friend to Sheriff Baca and a mentor to Judge Otero, whose legal education he had paid for[47]—had written his mother of the pleasant

FIGURE 17. Senator Bronson Cutting in conference with
President-elect Franklin Delano Roosevelt, 1932.

Courtesy Museum of New Mexico, neg. no. 138126.

Thanksgiving he had enjoyed at the "Indian Village" that Ernest Seton
had created some eight miles south of Santa Fe. It seemed to him a
pleasant enough way to celebrate the holiday, seeing how an Anglo had
reconstructed Navajo life in an effort to instruct other whites on what
they might do to live more natural and spiritual lives. Both Cutting and
his mother had attended Seton's lectures during Cutting's early years in
New Mexico, and so he felt that she would find his story interesting,
though, as he commented, the village "is quaint but seems a little
artificial."

But it was now time to return to Washington, Cutting told his mother. Though nothing in the Senate compelled him to return, his work in Santa Fe was done. As he noted, "There is no longer the slightest doubt about the guilt of the negro whom Jesus arrested, as the government expert positively identifies his finger prints both on the bedpost and on the vase with which he knocked out the old lady. Of course the moral case was overwhelming before, but it is a comfort to be certain, because of course the Judge would have sent him to the chair in any event."[48]

Not of One's Peers

"REGARDLESS OF HOW MANY OF US FEEL PERSONALLY," Otero instructed Baca, "it's up to us to see that the man gets a fair trial." There were to be no irregularities, nor any appearance of impropriety. As sheriff, it was Baca's responsibility to make sure that the proceedings concluded without incident. His first task would be to gather prospective jurors from around the county and to lead them into the courtroom at 8:00 A.M. on Friday, December 4, one hour before the trial was scheduled to begin.

Though originally scheduled for the first of the month, Otero realized that three additional days would be needed before all of the interested parties could be brought together. Johnson's attorney was now due to return from Colorado by Thursday, while Detective Powers was still motoring in from El Paso. Not content with merely sending his damning report, he wanted to proudly display his findings. Kenney was, of course, only too happy to comply with his request.

Nor had Kenney objected when Crist insisted that a jury be brought in from outside Santa Fe. Even the *New Mexican* had admitted that "town dwellers may be prejudiced." On balance, it seemed a rather practical suggestion. "If any Santa Feans are drawn they are likely to be challenged by the defense, putting the county to the expense of drawing another venire," Kenney noted with concern for his constituents. The whole business would take no more than two days, he thought, and a decision would be reached by the jury no later than Saturday evening. Any potential cause for delay was, therefore, to be avoided. Besides, given the mostly Spanish population of rural Santa Fe County, the jury was certain to favor the prosecution even more than if the ethnically mixed townspeople were included.

Kenney must have exchanged glances with Otero as the judge spun the drum from which the list of potential jurors was to be drawn. The machinery creaked along "as though the oil, if there was any, had been congealed by the coldness of the courtroom," the *New Mexican* commented that Tuesday afternoon, the first of December. Of the twenty-three names drawn for the panel, all but two were identifiably Spanish, as were the additional dozen alternates selected.[1] Otero then subpoenaed the prosecution's thirty-eight witnesses,[2] none of whom Crist would be able to interview prior to the trial.

With the stage now set and the players chosen, there was little to do but wait for the next act in this scripted drama to begin and for the final scene to be played out. Few surprises were expected. As Otero commented to the press that Tuesday, there was every reason to feel confident that "the negro ex-convict" would be quickly and properly dealt with. And so, for the next two days, the *New Mexican* lay silent.

When the paper spoke again on the day the trial began, it painted Johnson as a difficult prisoner, indifferent to the process by which he was certain to be sent to his death. An anonymous former employee of the state penitentiary had told the *New Mexican* that "Johnson was always fighting with the other prisoners" and that he had "'taking' ways, always stealing everything he could get his hands on." Consequently, he had been "thrown into the 'hole.'" "Records show that the negro served a week in solitary confinement on bread and water," the paper noted, without ever asking if Johnson, with a long record of early release for good behavior, had acted in self-defense against the largely Spanish prison population among whom he had been placed.[3]

At five o'clock that Friday morning, the entire sheriff's department, together with all of Santa Fe's police force, accompanied Johnson from the prison to the courthouse.[4] The streets of the city were still empty, the lines waiting to enter the courtroom not yet forming. For more than three hours, Johnson sat pensively in an area adjacent to where his fate would be determined. And as he sat there, the court slowly filled, until it could seat no more. Others stood four deep around the periphery of the room, while outside an overflow crowd spilled into the hallway and beyond.

In the past, women were rarely seen in court as spectators, but this was a special case, and when several of the morning's visitors gave up their seats for the noon recess, they, too, joined in the wild rush for a chance to sit through the afternoon session. Like the men, they were willing "to pass up lunch for the privilege" and to be searched for weapons before entering the courthouse—a sign of the heightened emotions that filled the air that day, the *New Mexican* observed.[5]

So agitated had the crowded courthouse become, even before Johnson was led in that first morning, that Judge Otero was compelled to forcefully address those who had gathered. "Don't make it necessary for me to send somebody to jail for contempt of court for doing something you know you should not do," he cautioned his audience. "We don't want any demonstrations here of any kind." Instead, there was to be "perfect order and quiet at all times." The aisles were to be kept clear, and those standing in the rear were not to "shuffle around on [their] feet, changing position." To help keep order, a large number of "special deputies" had been brought in and scattered through the crowd, he further warned.[6]

Having concluded his remarks, Otero ordered the bailiff to bring in the prisoner. It was now 9:16 A.M.[7] After nearly three weeks of interrogation and imprisonment, Johnson, fearing what appeared inevitable, sat down in a state of despondency. The press, of course, redrew his hopeless expression into one of arrogant indifference and framed his portrait with the same widely accepted racial imagery it had used unsparingly over the last several weeks. "Johnson was in a dark blue civilian suit and a new set of handcuffs glinted on his wrists," the report began. "The soft collar of his shirt was open. He exhibited no more interest than a spectator in the proceedings. His thick, black wooly hair was standing up in little conical clumps—a modified Topsy style."[8]

Only in the final paragraph of the page's four-column recapitulation of the day's proceedings did the reporter relate how Johnson had asked to go to the rest room before the court was called to order that morning, but had retreated in fear when he "saw the mob outside."[9] When Johnson's attorney arrived at the courthouse shortly after nine, he, too, was forced to alter his route and to enter the courtroom through the judge's chambers.[10] Minutes later he watched as his heavily guarded client was led in, the first time they had seen each other since the preliminary hearing nearly two weeks earlier.

Though Crist had spent little time preparing for what the *Albuquerque Journal* the next morning identified as "Santa Fe's Most Sensational Murder,"[11] he was nonetheless determined to free his client. Fighting to secure the best possible jury, Crist reminded the court before the selection process began that barely twenty-four hours had passed since the panel of jurors had been served on the accused.[12] By noon, only seven of the first fifteen potential jurors remained. Five had been excused by peremptory challenge and three others because they were already convinced of Johnson's guilt. Of the seven remaining, six were Spanish.

Kenney's examination of the fifteen had been brief, his primary concern being their possible objection to capital punishment. But Crist spent far more time with each one, pointedly reminding the court that with such "great public interest" in the case, they had more than likely been exposed to opinions that were detrimental to his client. Though news normally took a week or longer to reach the more rural areas of the county, talk of this particular crime had spread quickly.

Under Crist's persistent questioning, each, in turn, acknowledged having some degree of familiarity with Angelina's murder and Johnson's arrest. It became clear as well that Kenney's claim to the press that he had a "complete case" against the accused had prejudiced all of the potential jurors. When the first of these finally admitted to having a "fixed opinion about the case," laughter broke out in the courtroom, forcing Otero to again demand silence from the crowd. There would be no mockery made of the proceedings in his court, he angrily told those who had come to see that justice was done.

Within an hour after the lunch recess had ended, jury selection was complete. Of the five additional members chosen, all were Spanish.[13] At 2:45 P.M., the twelve were sworn in. Instructed not to discuss the case, nor to reach any conclusions before all of the evidence had been heard, they were now ready for the trial to begin.[14]

Aware that the district attorney's case against Johnson was largely circumstantial, Crist had filed a pretrial request that a fuller definition of this type of evidence be given to the jury. But Otero had refused to allow it.[15] And when Crist now objected to the amount of detail contained in Kenney's opening statement, Otero overruled him, leaving everyone present with a clear sense of the difficulty of the task that lay ahead for the defense.[16]

H. W. Livingston, the Jaramillo family's physician, was the first witness to be called by the state. Throughout the testimony that followed, Crist raised one objection after another, and nearly as often, Otero ruled against him. Crist would then note his exception to the ruling, hoping to create as many possibilities for a successful appeal as he could. It was a pattern the two men would repeat throughout the trial. And so, when Kenney asked for a description of the several wounds he had found on Angelina's body, Crist once again interrupted, protesting that Johnson was being tried for the sole crime of murder. Multiple wounds "would indicate the commission of another crime," he argued. "I ask that the testimony of this witness be confined to the wound on the body which in his opinion, professional opinion, was the cause of death." Overruled by the court, Crist once more noted his exception.

"There was one wound in her left temple" that had been caused by a "sharp instrument . . . approximately half an inch in length," Livingston began again. The weapon had "slipped in without meeting obstruction for a distance of about two and a half inches," though there were bruises around this wound and the skull had been fractured just below it. In addition, "several minor bruises on the back, shoulders and hips" were also discovered, and "a large amount of bleeding from the vagina" had occurred.

Rising to his feet, Crist insisted that any further "examination of the condition of the body be refused." The sole focus of the witness's testimony should be the one wound that was "sufficient to cause death," he reminded the court. Anything more would prejudice the case against his client by indicating a second crime. But once again he was overruled, and once again he noted his exception.

Encouraged by the court's favorable response, Livingston began to embellish on his testimony and, without Kenney's prompting, added that his "examination of the vagina showed various lacerations—recent lacerations." With visible anger, Crist leapt to his feet and insisted that "the same objection I have made heretofore to this line of questioning" be entered into the record. Unexpectedly, the court now agreed with him, only to reverse itself moments later when Crist objected to Kenney's asking whether these same lacerations were the result of a "criminal assault" (rape).

Pleased with Otero's decision, Kenney then prodded Livingston to go further. Had the profuse vaginal bleeding caused the victim's death? he wondered.

"I think the fractured skull was the cause of death," Livingston replied, "with the loss of blood and shock from the other being a contributory cause. There is possibly a question as to whether she might not have died as a result," Livingston continued, only to be abruptly cut off in midsentence by the defense.

"Just a minute, I object to any testimony by this witness that is in the nature of speculation," Crist protested more angrily than before.

Otero again surprised everyone in the courtroom by concurring with the defense's objection. "The last portion of the answer of this witness" was to be disregarded "in arriving at your verdict," he advised the jury, who by now were confused as to exactly what part of this testimony was admissible and what it was they were not to consider.

Concerned that the expert medical testimony of his first witness had become muddled, Kenney asked Livingston if the stab wound to Angelina's left temple had been fatal.

"Yes," was all that he said in response.[17]

It was now Crist's turn to pursue the doctor's speculations under cross-examination. Pressured by Crist, Livingston finally conceded that Angelina was menstruating at the time of her murder and that the amount of vaginal bleeding caused by the criminal assault could, therefore, not be determined. However excessive the bleeding, as evidenced by the soaked bedclothes and mattress and by the pool of blood beneath the bed, there was no way of measuring the specific amount caused by either. Nor had a chemical analysis of the fluids found ever been conducted, Livingston acknowledged. In fact, he had neglected to even measure the total volume of blood lost, so that the vaginal bleeding, he further conceded to Crist, could itself not be put forth as either a cause of, or a contributing factor to, Angelina's death.

With this admission wrung from the witness and with Livingston's repetition of the earlier claim that "the wound to the temple was sufficient to cause death," Crist again moved to have "all of the testimony of this witness with reference to the flow of blood from the vagina" stricken from the record. Overruled by Otero, Crist simply noted his exception and returned to his seat.[18]

Under redirect examination, Kenney showed Livingston a double-edged knife and asked "if the stab wound in the temple . . . might have been inflicted with a weapon of that type or kind?"

"Yes," he answered matter-of-factly.[19]

Crist quickly threw himself between the prosecutor and his witness and asked if the object in question wasn't "of a class of knives which is very common, especially in use around the kitchen as a paring knife?"

"Sure, there is a resemblance," Livingston agreed, before admitting under further questioning from Crist that he had neither accurately measured the wound nor "endeavor[ed] by any examination or any experiment to determine the kind of knife that had made the fatal wound in the temple." In fact, he had not autopsied the interior of Angelina's skull to determine the precise cause of her death. Instead he had relied upon "the nature of the wound" to reach his conclusion. It was because "the skull immediately under this wound was fractured and pushed into the brain" that the knife could so easily enter "without meeting obstruction," Livingston tried to explain.[20]

Kenney was more than happy now to move on to his next witness and asked Detective Martin to describe the crime scene, both the physical layout of the house and any particular objects within it that were relevant to the case.

"A great number of broken glass" fragments had been found scattered throughout the bedroom, the living room, and the hallway, Martin noted. Making certain "not to place my finger in any portion of them in case that the intruder may have left his fingerprints," they had been carefully retrieved and delivered to Warden Ed Swope at the state penitentiary and to Mr. Brunk, the prison's fingerprint expert, for analysis.

It seemed the appropriate moment now for the court to be shown the glass fragments, and as Kenney brought them out, Johnson leaned forward to get a better look. It was as if he were seeing them for the first time, the *New Mexican*'s reporter noted with surprise.[21]

Martin, however, felt emboldened by their presence and suddenly volunteered that in addition to these pieces of glass, several broken and unbroken matches had been found in Angelina's bed and in a trail that led from the bed to the door of the room.

But rather than attempt to establish their relevance to the crime, Kenney turned his witness's attention toward Johnson's struggle with Oscar Churchill and his subsequent flight to Albuquerque.

Establishing the sequence and times for each event that night, Martin related how, together with Sheriff Baca, Deputy Alarid, Police Chief Stewart, and Patrolman Holmes, he had found the defendant in police custody in Albuquerque, covered in "splotches of blood from head to foot," including his shoes and his hands.

Kenney next introduced the coveralls Johnson had been wearing when arrested, as well as the corduroy pants, the two shirts, and the underwear that had also been removed from him that night, and then pointed to what he claimed were bloodstains on each of the garments.[22]

Johnson once again leaned across the defendant's table and looked carefully at the clothing stripped from him on the night of his arrest.[23] After a few moments, he settled back in his chair and waited for Kenney to continue.

Having established that the prisoner had been found with blood-splattered clothing and hands, Kenney now brought his witness back to a discussion of the knife that had been found in Johnson's pocket.

Martin noted that Johnson had identified the knife as the one he used in repairing tires at Andrew's Garage and that he had further admitted to washing it at some point during the previous evening. There was, however, a small red spot still on its blade, and when asked about it while still in Albuquerque, Johnson had claimed that it might have come from his fight with Churchill.

Several minutes of cross-examination by Crist then followed, during which he attempted to undercut Martin's assumption that the glass fragments contained fingerprints belonging to the defendant. "Have you made anything like a careful or critical examination so that your knowledge is based on something substantial?" he asked.

"There was nothing else broken in the house similar to that glass or that vase, and I am satisfied in my own mind that this piece is a part of this vase," Martin responded.[24]

It was 5:15 P.M. by the time Martin finished testifying, at which point Judge Otero called for a ten-minute recess. When the proceedings resumed, Kenney announced that Martin had "stood to one side" in order to allow the next witness to step forward.[25] "Not quite five feet tall, slender, wearing a black cloth hat with half veil, black coat with black fur collar, and black shoes and stockings, Mrs. Jaramillo, holding a small white handkerchief to her face, was escorted through the crowded courtroom to the witness stand. She did not even glance at the shackled negro," the *Albuquerque Journal* reported the next morning. During the questioning that followed, she spoke "in a voice so low [that] she could not be heard more than a few feet from the jury box, [forcing] the spectators [to] lean forward to hear her words."[26]

Cleofas had dreaded this moment and would later recall "the awful court trial of the accused." Her only previous visit to the courthouse had left her with the happy memory of an evening during her courtship with Venceslao when he surprised her with tickets for *The Bohemian Girl*, a play that was performed in this very room.[27] But the memory was now darkened forever by the sadness that had brought her back to this site of an earlier joy. "I was summoned to appear as a witness and my cousin, Blanch, came and took my sister and me to the courthouse. District Attorney Kenney led me by the arm to the witness chair," she recounted years later in her memoir, still thankful for his kindness. There were, however, "some people" who had advised her to say that she had seen the face of the defendant on that terrible night. But she had refused to do so, she added without identifying who it was that had approached her. "A man's life was at stake; I could not lie," she insisted. Whatever testimony she would give had to be the truth.[28]

The hour had already grown late, but Kenney wanted to leave his jury with fresh images of the victim's tiny, grieving mother as they retired for the evening. A few moments would be all that was needed. "Will you please state to the jury what occurred so far as you saw," he began, gently and carefully guiding her through the testimony that followed.

"I was sleeping in the bed room when a bright light hit my eyes and woke me up, and thinking it was my daughter, I called out her name." When there was no response, she "jumped out of bed . . . lit a candle" and walked into Angelina's room. "Before me stood a man right by her bed side, and I gave a scream and I guess I fainted because I don't remember anything more after that."

Asked for a physical description of the man, she described him as being of medium height and having broad shoulders that "went up" in response to her scream. The "brightly lighted" room had allowed her to see that he was wearing a "striped suit, black and white," which she agreed "does look like" the "coveralls, striped in dark blue and white," that were now being shown to her by the prosecution.

Crist rose up and objected to Cleofas's inability to identify the garment with any greater certainty. "Well, I was too scared, I guess," she calmly responded. "What I know, it was dark and white and striped."[29]

Had she seen the murderer's face? Kenney asked.

"No, just his back," she emphatically responded.[30]

Crist allowed her answer to go unchallenged, but when Kenney inquired whether she herself had been wounded by Johnson, he shouted his objection in an attempt to drown out her response. And though quickly sustained by the court, it was already too late. A more vicious image of the defendant had now been laid out for the jury to consider.[31]

All that remained now in the final moments of that first day in court was to recall Martin to the stand and to allow him to complete his identification of the photographs being entered as evidence—and for Crist to add his final objections, particularly to Martin's assumption that a certain window shown in one of the photos was "where the intruder got in." The court surprisingly sustained this objection as well, allowing the defense to savor a small victory as the day's drama drew to a close.[32]

At 5:40 P.M., Otero told the jury they could retire for the evening. He reminded them of their need to "observe the instructions heretofore given you by the Court," and then ordered them to be back in the jurors' box at eight-fifteen the following morning. A rarely called Saturday session was to be held.[33] Like Kenney, Otero hoped to conclude the proceedings that next evening.

Facts Not in Evidence

AFTER the first day's crush, Judge Otero decided to limit the number of spectators in the courtroom to a maximum of two hundred. They were all to be seated upstairs, with the lower floor reserved for those participating in the trial. Many were again leaning against the rear wall of the balcony when court resumed at eight-forty that next morning, while a greater number than on Friday could not gain access to the building. As the *New Mexican* commented, "The crowds, eager to hear the trial, are said to be unparalleled in the history of the county."[1]

News from outside the region that day told of a Maryland mob that had lynched a man in the yard of a local courthouse. Hospitalized after first attempting suicide and then shot by the son of the man he had allegedly killed, the accused had been dragged from his guarded hospital bed and hung from a lamppost while two thousand cheering witnesses looked on.[2] As the courtroom's spectators waited for the second day's proceedings to begin, many sat and read their morning newspapers, with banner headlines telling of the lynching facing outward for the accused to see. But "if Johnson observed them, he gave no sign of it," the *New Mexican* would later note in its continuing effort to demonize the defendant.[3]

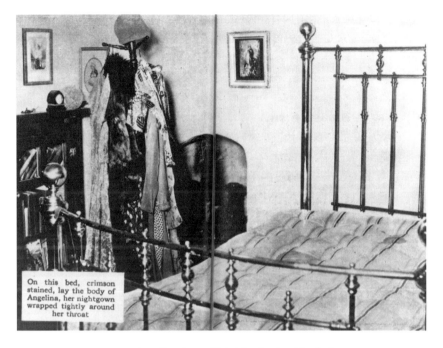

On this bed, crimson
stained, lay the body of
Angelina, her nightgown
wrapped tightly around
her throat

FIGURE 18. Angelina Jaramillo's bloodstained body lay on
this bed, her nightgown wrapped tightly around her throat.

Reproduced from *Master Detective*, "The Clue of the Lipstick"
(March 1935), in the collections of the Library of Congress.

By afternoon, the city's attention was again focused on the trial at
home. "Crist Batters Evidence of Bloodstains," the newspaper's headline
read, aptly characterizing the morning's courtroom encounter between
prosecutor and defense attorney as they battled over Martin's continuing
testimony.[4] Kenney had begun by asking him about the cosmetics
belonging to Angelina that were found in a dresser in Cleofas's room.

In response, Martin told the court that having gone back to the
Jaramillo house for a second look the day after the murder, he had
discovered Ben Martinez, Marie Gonzales, and Marie's father already
searching for evidence. It was Marie who had led him to the appropriate
drawer, he further noted.

Crist remained silent until Kenney attempted to introduce Angelina's powder, rouge, and lipstick as evidence. There was "no proof whatever that this was the lipstick used by the deceased," Crist argued. As such, it was "irrelevant and immaterial."

Kenney promised that he would soon establish its materiality, but agreed to withdraw his request until that time. Instead, he asked Martin to describe the state in which he had found Angelina's body.

"She was lying flat on her back with her head on the left side," he responded.

"And the blood, where was the blood?" Kenney continued, as if to quickly recapture the mood of the previous day.

"There was a pool of blood on the pillow and also a pool of blood under the buttocks," Martin noted as graphically as he could.

"This blood was underneath her?" Kenney emphasized for the jury's benefit.

"Yes, sir," Martin responded with sadness and a nod as he looked over to Kenney.[5]

Crist would spend the next three hours cross-examining Martin, ending all hope of a Saturday verdict. Referring to the open window in the alcove adjacent to Angelina's room that was alleged to be the murderer's point of entry, Crist asked Martin if he had examined it or the sill for fingerprints on the night of the murder. Given its position close to the ground and its small opening of just two feet, was it not fair to assume that someone using it to enter the house would have had to grab onto the frame at some point?

But Martin had not looked for fingerprints that night. And when he returned to the house the next day, there were none to be found near the window. Neither were there any identifiable footprints on the gravel path that led from Griffin Street to the window, Martin was forced to acknowledge.

"You were therefore unable to determine either from foot prints, marks on the path, or from finger prints on the window sill, or window, whether the person who had committed the crime which you found inside had entered that house through that window or not?" Crist summarized for the jury.

Though Martin had been willing to speculate the previous day that the killer had used this point of access, he could now do little more than nod in agreement. Worse, still, for the prosecution's case was his further testimony that no other windows in the house had been open when he arrived shortly after the murder had been committed.[6]

The two doors to the house, however, were open, Martin confirmed under further questioning, but like the open window, fingerprints were again not looked for until the following day.

"Well," responded Crist, "if you didn't make an examination at that time, any examination you may have made subsequent would be practically useless because of the use to which the doors were put in opening and shutting."

Again Martin could not disagree.[7]

With no clear basis now left for establishing precisely how the killer had entered the Jaramillo house, the jury was free to infer what it chose to—even, perhaps, that the murderer was known to his victim and that she had opened the door nearest her bedroom for him, or so Crist hoped they would conclude.

Crist continued to press Martin on the matter of fingerprints and, after a heated exchange, established that no fingerprints, bloody or otherwise, had been found in the room after a thorough search, except for those on the brass bed's footrail and the vase fragments previously mentioned.

Martin, sensing that he had been outflanked by the defense, tried to recover by noting that a number of prints had been found "on the neck of the vase" as well, though he couldn't say how many. "I didn't work on that neck myself personally," he admitted when pressed further. Nor did he know the outcome of the "comparison" that had been made by others, he added.[8]

From this critical line of questioning and the doubts he had raised concerning the answers given by Martin, Crist then moved on to the heart of his morning's cross-examination of the witness, the bloodstained clothing he had removed from Johnson while they were still at police headquarters in Albuquerque. Throughout the day, Johnson had been seen whispering to his attorney, but never as much as now.[9] The importance of this testimony could not be overstated, and so when Martin proudly stated, "Yes, sir; the ones I took off myself," Crist repeated his boast. "Took them off yourself," he noted mockingly before asking Martin to discuss the blood spots "just in the neighborhood of that part of the pantaloons that immediately cover the privates of an individual."

Though at first reluctant to openly discuss such matters, Martin ultimately acknowledged that while blood was present in that general area of the coveralls Johnson had worn over his corduroy pants, no blood had been found in that area of the pants themselves.[10] There were, however, "four or five spots" on that part "of those trunks which immediately cover the privates," he countered. But when asked if they had been tested to see if, indeed, they were spots of blood, Kenney quickly interrupted. Rather than allow Martin to respond, he asked him to simply mark those spots by drawing a circle around each one.

Crist decided not to pursue the point any further, but instead moved on with similar questions regarding the two shirts Johnson had been wearing when captured. Martin pointed to several spots on the inner shirt, but Crist again asked if they had been tested.

"No, sir; personally I didn't," the witness acknowledged as reluctantly as before.

Having gained the upper hand, Crist then questioned whether these spots, in fact, even existed.

"If you put it to the light you can see it," the detective said of one.

"They are infinitesimal spots aren't they?" Crist argued.

"Some are small," Martin conceded.[11]

It was then that Crist, believing he had demonstrated a major fallacy in the case against his client, attempted a fatal strike at Martin's credibility. Hammering away at the prosecution's chief investigator, he pushed again and again in an effort to force Martin to admit that the clothing removed from Johnson showed no signs of his having committed the rape that preceded the murder for which he was being tried. "You would hardly consider them as evidence of a man having raped a woman?" Crist insisted.

"I would say they are," Martin responded.

"You would say they are," Crist countered, "and you would say those are the only blood spots he would get in committing rape on a woman when she was menstruating and flowing freely from the vagina from lacerations of the vagina? You call that evidence of having committed the rape?"

Kenney at first watched in silence as Crist attempted to dismantle his case by demanding simple yes and no answers to a series of questions, cutting the witness off whenever he tried to expand his responses with detailed explanations. But when Crist questioned the detective's professional competence, Kenney grew visibly angry. Crist was in midsentence, asking Martin, "Is that the class of judgment," when Kenney jumped to his feet and shouted, "Wait a minute; you are arguing with the witness."

But the court wished to hear Martin's answer as well. "Go ahead and answer," Otero insisted, overruling the prosecution's objections to Crist's manner of attack.

"I couldn't say if he had his shorts on or not, Mr. Crist," Martin was compelled to respond.

It was the opening Crist had been looking for. "You heard all of the evidence so far in the case?" he asked.

"Yes, sir," Martin replied.

"Have you heard any that he was undressed in any way?" Crist inquired.

"No, sir," the prosecution's witness reluctantly answered.

"Assuming that he was not undressed," Crist continued, "would you call that blood stain there and these two little ones there, and these infinitesimal ones which you point out that you can see when you hold it up to the light, would you call those evidence that a man was guilty of committing rape on a woman who was menstruating, and who was bleeding freely according to the Doctor from lacerations in the vagina? Now, is it your judgment those are evidence on his clothing of having committed the rape?"

Martin could do little else now but insist, "The blood stain doesn't come from any other part, in my judgment."

But "a man in the act of committing a rape on a woman would smudge his clothes with blood in large splotches," Crist rebutted. "Don't you know that as a fact?"

"I cannot say," Martin shot back. "I never saw it."[12]

If the stains on Martin's clothing were, indeed, blood, might they not be evidence of his fight with Churchill? Crist argued in return.

"No, sir; I wouldn't say they are," Martin answered argumentatively.

"That is your judgment?" Crist asked Martin quizzically.

"Yes, sir," he responded.

"I want the jury to know the value of your judgment and that is why I am asking you, Mr. Martin," Crist stated openly, hoping thereby to raise further doubts about the witness's competence at reaching any conclusions based on the evidence before him. "Now, I want your judgment on this," he went on. "So far as the evidence that you have heard shows, this defendant was dressed. Now, what is there on those pantaloons that would show in any respect that this defendant had committed a rape on Angelina while she was menstruating and while she was flowing blood freely from lacerations of the vagina? Point them out to the jury."

"There is no blood in this part, Mr. Crist," Martin observed, confirming the defense's prior assessment of his ability to analyze the material before him.

"Now, unless he was undressed, where would those pantaloons be on him when he was in the act of committing rape? Right where I hold them, wouldn't they?" Crist asked.

"Yes, sir," Martin had to admit.

"And after he was through committing the act of rape on a woman flowing the blood she was flowing according to the Doctor, and restored his pants to their usual place, what would his clothes show?" Crist continued.

"Should show blood, Mr. Crist," the detective confirmed.

"Yes, but do the shirts show blood at the place where he restored them to the usual place inside his pantaloons after he was through committing the act of rape?" Crist insisted on knowing.

"They show splotches," Martin responded in an attempt to salvage his testimony. And "some are smears," he added. "If you examine [them] carefully. Exactly what he did after, I don't know," he had to conclude. "I wasn't present."

And neither was the jury. But it was their task to discern the truth in the matter and Crist's job to assist them, all the while praying that they might exercise fairness and common sense. "Now, was there any evidence of blood stain any where on the shirt which would cover a man's privates after he had restored his privates to their usual place and covered them there with his shirt?"

Martin hesitated to answer, but at the urging of the court, said, "Yes, sir, right here."

"And you call that evidence of a man having committed rape?" Crist countered, demanding that Martin mark the spot with a pencil so that the jury could themselves examine the place he was referring to.[13]

"Now, you know as a matter of experience, Mr. Martin, that men usually wear their privates inside their underclothing?" Crist asked with a touch of sarcasm as he lifted the final article of Johnson's clothing.

"Yes, sir," Martin answered.

"Look at the inside of these trunks," Crist demanded, his impatience with the witness now quite visible, "and point out to the jury what appear to you to be any evidences that the wearer of them had had connection with a woman who was menstruating and who was flowing freely from lacerations of the vagina, and then restored his privates to their usual place."

"All this part," Martin countered, pointing to a dozen "splotches."

"Fly specks?" Crist asked.

"I don't know what you might call fly specks," Martin began his response, only to have Kenney interrupt, claiming that all of this had been covered before.

Otero, however, wanted Crist to proceed, yet when he attempted to define "fly speck," Kenney burst in again, and soon all three were shouting at once. As the arguing subsided, Crist asked one last time, "Is it your judgment, Mr. Martin, that after having had an act of intercourse with a woman in the bloody condition in which the doctor testified she was, that he could restore his privates to their usual place inside these trunks without leaving on the edge of that opening some evidence of blood on his private parts?"

Martin was about to answer Crist's question when Kenney once again threw himself into the fray, angrily noting that "counsel on yesterday objected to conclusions of this witness, and is now asking the witness for a conclusion and has done it half a dozen times."

"The purpose of this line of cross examination, if the court please, is to show the animus of . . . [someone] employed presumably to work up the case," Crist quickly retorted.

Ordered by the court to answer Crist's question, Martin finally responded: "Yes, he could have done it."

Crist requested that the trunks be given to the jury for them to examine its "vent,"[14] and while it was being passed among them, he raised the far more troubling issue of the physical examination given to Johnson while still in Albuquerque.

"I wasn't present," Martin responded, hoping to avoid the issue.

Crist, of course, knew this to be true, but persisted with his questioning nonetheless. Kenney, hoping to move quickly beyond this damaging revelation, interrupted his witness's testimony and offered to share the doctor's analysis with the defense. Crist scanned the report and immediately asked that Dr. Loren Elliott be brought from Albuquerque to appear in court later that day.[15] Though he had planned to have Martin relate the physician's findings, he now realized that the report might have greater impact if presented by Elliott himself. Following a brief discussion at the bench, Otero agreed to have Elliott summoned to court by three o'clock that afternoon.[16]

In the meantime, Crist returned to the broken vase and the fragments Martin had recovered, handing him the small graniteware dishpan into which he had originally placed them. Of the more than fifty pieces he was asked to count, two were of special importance, Martin noted, the neck and a part of the base. "I picked up both pieces in the living room" adjacent to Angelina's bedroom, he explained. They had been lying on opposite sides from each other, while the other, smaller fragments were scattered between them and into the two adjoining areas of the house.

Further probing by Crist, however, soon revealed that these fragments had been far removed from the path the accused was said to have used as he fled from the bedroom. And because the pieces had been so widely scattered, Martin was forced to admit, under further questioning by Crist, that he had no idea where he had found the one small fragment that was alleged to have the one identified fingerprint on it.[17]

Might he then not be wrong about the blood found on Johnson's hands and clothing as well? Bringing Martin back to the scene in Andrew's Garage and hoping that he would corroborate Johnson's account of the incident, Crist asked, "Any blood immediately around or under [Churchill's] body?"

"Yes, sir. There was quite a bit," Martin told the jury.

How far away from where he was lying could blood be found? Crist inquired further.

"Eighteen feet," he responded.

And was there evidence that Churchill had been dragged that distance? the defense continued.

"Yes," Martin acknowledged. "There was blood underneath the sofa and from there on right alongside the sofa you could see where something has been dragged and the same time was bleeding over to the place where the body was resting when we got there, behind the desk."

What, then, of the blood that was found on Johnson's hands when he arrived in Albuquerque? Crist wanted to know.

"There was blood on the top of both hands," Martin answered. "In the left hand between those two fingers there were more blood than there was on the back of the hands, and what I saw on the top of the finger nails and the fingers had more blood than any other part of his hands."

Was this true for both the right and the left?

"Yes."

And on both palms? Crist added.

"There also," Martin noted, "but not as much as between the fingers." It appeared to him that Johnson had attempted to wipe rather than wash his hands clean.[18]

And what of the stain on Johnson's knife, Crist asked next. "You testified that the defendant told you that he didn't know how the stain got on the knife," he reminded Martin in much the same tone that had dominated his earlier interrogation regarding Johnson's clothing. "Isn't it a fact, Mr. Martin, that the defendant there told you in the presence of others that the stain got on the knife probably after he had the trouble with Churchill," Crist asked, holding up Johnson's coveralls as he approached his reluctant witness, "and that when he had started or was about to start for Albuquerque, he took that little knife from this little pocket along the side of the leg, where he was in the habit of carrying it, and put it in his hip pocket, and that is how the little stain, red stain, got on the knife or might have gotten on it? . . . Didn't he tell you that in Albuquerque?"

But Martin withstood Crist's pressure and denied that Johnson had said this "in my presence."

And so Crist came at him another way, slowly demonstrating Martin's desire to skirt the truth. Hadn't Johnson told him of his "difficulty with Churchill in the garage"?

Yes, he had, Martin answered.

"I said his story, Mr. Martin," Crist responded, referring to his previous question with evident frustration.

The court, too, now seemed to be growing impatient with the detective. Perhaps it was the unnecessary delay in the proceeding or his too obvious attempt to deny the truth. Whatever the reason, Otero at this point began to insist on an answer each time Martin hesitated or tried to spar with the defense.

Yes, Johnson "had assaulted Churchill with a hammer . . . as a part of the difficulty that he said he had with Churchill," Martin was forced to admit, and had "knocked Churchill out with the hammer so that Churchill became unconscious." In fact, Johnson had been far too open with his interrogators and "told us I killed poor—," Martin began to add, until Crist stopped him abruptly. But there was no damming the torrent once it had started, and so Crist withdrew his objection and let Martin go on for a few minutes longer. Johnson had talked of dragging Churchill to the area behind the counter, though the admission had not come "of his own accord. We questioned him," Martin smugly told the jury. Repeated questioning had wrung an admission from Johnson that he had tied Churchill's hands. "First he denied it, then admitted it, then he added I killed poor Oscar."[19]

Crist probed deeper and asked Martin if he had, on returning to Santa Fe, "found some of the things [Johnson] told you to be true."

Martin again hesitated until the court demanded an answer, and only then responded with an unconvincing, "No."

"You mean none of the things he told you were true?" Otero asked in a quandary.

"Yes, sir," Martin insisted, forcing Crist to walk him through Johnson's account, point by point, until he secured an affirmative response to each.

"Isn't it a fact, Mr. Martin," Crist asked in order to reemphasize his client's truthfulness, "that with reference to what he told you in Albuquerque, you found in so far as your investigation went that in substance what he said about his movements in Santa Fe was true."

"Yes," Martin responded with great reluctance.

Crist wanted the jury to fully appreciate the importance of this admission, and so he rephrased the question as a statement. "The main facts in substance of what he told you in Albuquerque you found to be true," he began, at which point Otero, his patience with all parties now reaching a breaking point after two hours of nonstop questioning, interjected, "He answers yes." In response, Crist said that he wanted "to explain the question," but the judge allowed only one more detail in Johnson's story to be explored before declaring a ten-minute recess at 11:08 A.M.

Nineteen minutes later the questioning resumed. "Isn't it a fact, Mr. Martin, that in the presence of others, at the time of your talk with the defendant, that you prodded him two or three times in the stomach with an instrument of some sort, billy or black jack or otherwise, that you bumped his head against the wall and otherwise treated him with violence?" Crist inquired. "Now yes or no," he insisted. "Isn't it a fact that you did these things?"

"I hit him," Martin admitted, but claimed to have done so only twice, and with his hands.

"You did lay violent hands on the defendant?" Crist repeated.

"Yes, sir; I did," Martin acknowledged a second time.

Satisfied with this final stroke to the unflattering portrait he had drawn of the prosecution's chief investigator, Crist looked over at the jury and sat down.

Kenney, of course, could not let this last matter remain as Crist had left it. "Explain the circumstances under which you happened to strike the defendant," he countered.

"When he made a pass at Chief Stewart or menacing to hit Chief Stewart, I hit him in the head or face with my right hand, then I hit him again with my left hand in the stomach," Martin answered.

"I object to that," Crist angrily shouted, his voice ringing throughout the courtroom. "The only theory upon which this assault on the defendant can be justified is that of self defense."

Hoping to avoid another prolonged confrontation between the two attorneys, Otero quickly stepped in and asked them to approach the bench and to argue their positions before him. Crist ultimately prevailed, forcing Kenney to help Martin change his story. "At the moment you struck this defendant, did you believe that you, yourself, were in any danger?" he asked.

"Yes, sir," Martin willingly agreed.[20]

It was now 12:10 P.M. Crist had drilled away at Martin all morning long. "That is all," he told Otero, surprising everyone present. But in fact, there was still one clarification left to be made before he was finally done with Martin, and when the trial resumed at 1:35 that afternoon, he dramatically asked that Martin be recalled to the stand. With a refreshed, more alert jury in front of him, he began. "Mr. Martin, there is one question I overlooked asking you when you were on the stand before. When you were talking with the defendant in Albuquerque about the occurrences in Santa Fe, did you ask him, or was anything said about the murder of Angelina Jaramillo?"

"We questioned him about it; yes, sir," Martin responded.

"Did he deny it?" Crist inquired.

"Yes, sir; he did," Martin replied curtly.

"Did he at any time when you were questioning him admit that he had anything to do with the killing of Angelina Jaramillo?" Crist asked again.

"He denied it," Martin replied, showing his annoyance.

"But he did tell you about the difficulty and the assault on Churchill?" Crist emphasized.

"Yes, sir; he did," Martin responded coldly, and was then excused by the defense.[21]

Of Your Own Knowledge

THE lead detective in the case had proved to be less of a help to the prosecution than anticipated, and so when Crist finished with him a second time, Kenney was relieved to call his next witness, Foster Sayre, "embalmer and undertaker," as he identified himself to the courtroom. Kenney began by questioning him about the wounds on Angelina's body and about the downward flow of blood from her head, but made no direct mention of the vaginal bleeding he had so unsuccessfully attempted to relate to Johnson's bloodstained clothing. Instead he asked Sayre if he was present when the "debris" was scraped from beneath the victim's nails. Sayre acknowledged that while he did not perform the procedure himself, he was there to supervise his assistant in doing so.

When was it exactly that the material had been collected? Crist asked in cross-examining the witness.

Angelina's body had been removed from her home at 1:00 A.M., Sayre noted, but the area under her nails had not been scraped until later that afternoon. The debris was then given to Detective Martin, he added in a markedly clinical manner.

With no further questions from the defense, Sayre stepped down and Sheriff Baca was called to the witness stand. Asked by Kenney to recall the "story told you at Albuquerque" by Johnson concerning "his whereabouts on Sunday," Baca recounted Johnson's "claim" (a term Crist successfully objected to) that he had hitchhiked to Albuquerque to see "Grandma," as he called his former landlady. Not finding her at home, he made his way back to Santa Fe, arriving in town at about 9:00 P.M. After first stopping at Eliseo Quintana's house to ask for a loan of four dollars, he had gone to Tony Rael's pool hall, where he gambled away the money. He then dropped by to talk with Churchill, who was working late that evening at the garage next door, after which he returned to his room at the corner of Water and Sandoval Streets to get some dinner. Having finished his meal, he went back to the garage, fought with Churchill, robbed the cash register, and then stole a Buick. Parking the car outside his rooming house, he ran in, gathered up some clothing, and fled to Albuquerque.

Crist countered by establishing the fact that Johnson had given this account prior to learning that Churchill was still alive but asked if these initial "statements about his movements [that Sunday] were all voluntary on his part."

No "persuasion" was needed, Baca reluctantly told the courtroom.

And did the defendant ever admit to Angelina's murder when subsequently questioned about it? Crist probed.

No, "he denied it," Baca responded.

"Was he positive and emphatic in his denial?" Crist added.

"Yes, sir," Baca answered, acknowledging further that Johnson had said nothing in connection with her death "that would indicate a confession or an admission of the murder," as Crist had carefully worded the question put to him.[1]

Crist hoped to demonstrate to the jury that Johnson was a truthful man who in the past had always accepted responsibility for whatever he had done, and that if he now denied any involvement in Angelina's death, even after being struck by those interrogating him, he deserved to be believed.[2] To underscore this point, Crist walked Baca back through several key elements in Johnson's account of his movements that Sunday and then asked, "Mr. Baca, when you came back to Santa Fe, did you investigate the truth of what Mr. Johnson had told you at Albuquerque?"

"I did," he responded.

"You found that he told you the truth?" Crist repeated for emphasis.

"Yes, sir," Baca reluctantly conceded.[3]

Kenney was now left with the task of undoing this portrait of Johnson as a man willing to accept the consequences of what he had done. Had the defendant claimed, while still in Albuquerque, not to have been near the Jaramillo house the night of the murder? he asked Baca.

"Yes, sir," he eagerly responded. Johnson, however, did admit to being in the vicinity on other occasions, Baca added, "going down to Alexander's on Johnson Street to get a drink" from time to time.

"Did he definitely deny having been down there that Sunday night?" Kenney stressed in a final effort to discredit Crist's assertion.

"Yes, sir," Baca was again quick to respond before stepping down.[4]

Officer Holmes had been patrolling the area near the Jaramillo house on the night of the murder and, when next called to the stand, claimed to have seen Johnson at the corner of Elina and San Francisco Streets sometime between seven and seven-thirty. Holmes acknowledged under further questioning that Johnson was someone whom he had "observed as [he] saw him here in town" from time to time. That evening, Johnson had been walking west, away from the area in question and toward the home of Eliseo Quintana, Holmes noted, as if there were no difficulties of direction and time in his testimony. For on the face of it, his account appeared to give the lie to Johnson's earlier claim of not being in the area that Sunday.

Kenney next asked Holmes what he had found in Johnson's boardinghouse room. Nothing "noticeable" had shown up during the search conducted before going to retrieve Johnson in Albuquerque, he reported. But on Tuesday, when he returned to the boardinghouse with Police Chief Stewart, they "found what appeared to be a piece of stocking" in Johnson's stove. Kenney offered it as evidence, but Crist countered by asking how it had come into the prosecution's possession. Kenney responded that it had passed from Holmes to Deputy Alarid and then to him.

"I don't want to be technical about these things," Crist claimed as he probed further, but he wanted to know from Holmes directly who it was that had handed it to Kenney.

Alarid, in fact, had not given it directly to Kenney, Holmes now admitted, but to Baca, who later, in Holmes's presence, had "placed it in the custody of the District Attorney."

"Is this the identical thing you found there in that stove?" Kenney asked, showing him the "burnt remnant."

"Yes, sir," Holmes answered unequivocally.

But Crist, confident that he had now established the possibility that this evidence might well have been compromised by the succession of hands into which it had fallen,[5] did not respond. Instead he moved on with his cross-examination and asked Holmes where, precisely, the corner of Elina and San Francisco Streets was in relation to Quintana's house.

On the way toward it and three blocks west of the Denver & Rio Grande Railroad track that crossed San Francisco Street, Holmes replied, unaware that he had inadvertently offered the defense proof that Johnson had, in fact, been moving farther from the center of town and therefore away from where Angelina lived. But when Crist questioned him further about this, Holmes proved unable, or unwilling, to say which way he himself was going, let alone the defendant.

And how close to the corner was Johnson as the patrol car turned onto San Francisco from Elina? Crist asked Holmes, whose entire testimony now appeared suspect.

About a dozen feet, he thought.

And the nature of this turn? Crist inquired.

The widest possible in order to avoid a hole in the pavement, Holmes responded.

Would not so wide a turn, with headlights beaming to the opposite side of the street, have made it difficult to get a good look at a man standing so close to the corner? Crist asked, more as a statement than as a question. And rather than wait for an answer, he immediately began his next line of inquiry, asking Holmes why Johnson had been targeted for such careful scrutiny. "Had you occasion to arrest him at any time for any offense that caused you to watch him?" he wanted the jury to know.

"No," Holmes admitted, but there were suspicions of wrongdoing, he added. "We had information from the night officer about him prowling around that part of the city."

"But you had no information from the night officers, or any other source, that he had committed any offense of any kind?" Crist asked in trying to pin the officer down to a precise accusation, if one existed.

"No," Holmes acknowledged circuitously. "The only thing we had to do, somebody peeping in windows, peeping toms, and the officers had apparently been in that part of the city, and the only person I had ever met was Johnson, that is at that time of the morning when called in the morning, and that is what made me have him under suspicion."[6]

Satisfied that the jury understood that his client had not been seen doing anything improper, Crist turned back to the matter of the initial search of Johnson's room. What exactly had been found of an incriminating nature? he asked the officer.

There were several model airplanes scattered about, Holmes noted, and "a bunch of clothes . . . two pairs of pants and the rest of them were shirts." But none of this had been taken by the police. There simply wasn't any blood to be found on any of these items. They had, of course, discovered the burnt remnant of a stocking during their second visit, he reported, but could offer no explanation as to why it had been missed earlier. Nor did any other articles of clothing appear to have been similarly disposed of according to an analysis made of the stove's contents, he acknowledged under Crist's relentless questioning.

As Holmes was excused, Eliseo Quintana came forward for the prosecution. A neighborhood grocer with whom Johnson had conducted business in the past, Quintana now told the court that Johnson had come by his house sometime between seven and seven-thirty on the night in question and had asked for a loan of four dollars. It was Johnson's plan to use this money to replace what he had taken from the cash register at Andrew's Garage, he added.[7]

Troubled by the discrepancy between the time Johnson had given for his return to Santa Fe and the earlier period being asserted by Quintana as the time of Johnson's visit to his home, Crist attempted to demonstrate that the witness could only estimate the hour of his client's arrival. But a hiss quickly rose from among the spectators, interrupting Crist's effort. Angered by the disturbance, Otero slammed his gavel on the bench and threatened to hold anyone caught repeating this disturbance in contempt.

Sensing the crowd's support for his case, Kenney leapt to his feet and, shouting above the still receding voice of the spectators, asked Quintana to reaffirm that the time was definitely "somewhere between seven and seven-thirty"—only to have Crist ultimately force Kenney's witness to admit that it was still, nonetheless, an estimate and not the precise measurement that the prosecution had hoped it would appear to be.[8]

Kenney responded to this setback by calling Tony Rael to the stand. Rael insisted that Johnson had come to his pool hall at about eight-thirty on the evening of the murder and that by 9:00 P.M. he was gone.

"You look at your watch every time anybody comes into your pool hall to see what time they come in?" Crist began his cross-examination.

No, he hadn't really taken note of the time of Johnson's arrival, nor of when he left, Rael readily admitted.

"Are you able to state how long he remained in your pool hall at any other time except that Sunday night?" Crist pushed him further.

"No, sir," Rael answered with some reluctance, though he continued to deny that Johnson had shot dice or played blackjack in his establishment that night, as the defendant had claimed. But as both games were illegal in New Mexico, Rael could hardly have acknowledged that he had.[9]

Alec Barnes, Santa Fe's city inspector, was the next to be called. "I was riding up Grant Avenue toward town," Barnes said of his first encounter with the defendant in the early morning hours of September 6. "At the corner of Johnson and Grant [about one hundred yards from the Jaramillo home], I saw someone walking slow up the street. I stopped the car, got out, and went back to see who it was . . . and asked what he was doing there." Then, "some little time afterward on that same night," he encountered the accused for the second time about fifty feet "from the front window of Angelina's room. I told him if he didn't go back to his room where he lived or get off the street that I would run him in as a suspicious character," Barnes recounted as he looked over at the jury.[10]

It had been the time of the annual Fiesta, the daylong celebration marking the Spanish conquistadores' victory over the native Indian population, a time when much of the city was on the streets throughout the night and into the early morning hours. But Barnes made no reference to these many other revelers, nor to the response Johnson had made to his question when they crossed paths two and a half months before Angelina's murder.

Crist, of course, knew how damaging Barnes's testimony could be, however distant in time his spotting of Johnson had been from the brutal

FIGURE 19. The corner of the Jaramillo home.

Reproduced from *Master Detective*, "The Clue of the Lipstick"
(March 1935), in the collections of the Library of Congress.

crime he was now being charged with. If Crist was to neutralize its effect, he would have to dispel any thought by the jury that there had been a prior reason for suspecting his client of possible wrongdoing. "Had you previous to that time had any acquaintance with Johnson at all," Crist asked Barnes in rebuttal, or "any information or instructions from your chief to keep him under observation?"

"I didn't," he answered. Nor had he even known him prior to that night.

"So that your statement to him that if he didn't go to his room you would run him in was based entirely on what you saw that night?" Crist responded.

Barnes acknowledged that it was. Johnson had committed "no overt act of any kind except so-called loitering on the street."[11]

When Crist completed his cross-examination of Barnes at about three o'clock that afternoon, he approached the bench and asked for a brief recess in order to discuss an important matter raised by his client. The spirited cross-examination of Detective Martin that morning had given Johnson some small feeling of hope, and as the day wore on, client and attorney had been seen communicating more often than before.[12] Otero looked up at the clock on the courtroom wall and granted Crist's request for a short break. With a nod of thanks, Crist turned to his client and the two men quickly resumed their animated, but inaudible discussion.

At 3:40 P.M., Barnes returned to the stand. After watching Crist and his client, Kenney thought it best to have his witness relate the contents of his conversation with Johnson during their encounter on the sixth of September, as if he had been withholding it until just such a moment as this.

"He said that he was going to see a friend," Barnes began. "Then I asked him where the friend lived and he didn't know; he said very vaguely over there, but he didn't know where it was. I asked what his friend's name was and he couldn't tell me."[13]

"Was there anybody with you in your car at the time you stopped it there on Grant Avenue near the intersection of Johnson Street?" Crist wanted to know.

There was, Barnes answered, another police officer, but he was too far away, perhaps as much as seventy-five feet from where Johnson was being questioned, though he could not recall whether the officer had remained in the car or had stepped out of it at some point.

"If you don't know, that, of course, ends the value of the testimony," Crist responded with feigned frustration, hoping that the jury would come to doubt all that Barnes had previously stated.[14]

Kenney quickly responded by calling on George Kyle, for whom Johnson had manufactured toy airplanes while both men were in the state prison at Santa Fe. Kyle testified that he had been returning home after accompanying his wife's friend back to her house on the night of the murder when he suddenly crossed paths with Johnson. "It was between ten and ten-thirty, but I couldn't say exactly," Kyle insisted. "I am positive," he added, as positive as he was that their meeting had taken place near the corner of Grant and Johnson, less than two hundred feet from the Jaramillo house. "As he came up to me he says, How do you do Kyle, and I says, Hello Johnson, what are you doing over here this time of night? His reply was I got a job over here."[15]

But in cross-examining Kyle, Crist was able to demonstrate that the time he gave for his encounter with Johnson was based not on his own knowledge, but on his wife's telephone conversation in another room. It was only after his wife had finished her call and had looked up at the clock in that other room that she had commented on the lateness of the hour and had asked him to walk their friend to her home near the capitol building, several blocks away.

"So that all you know about the time of your wife's telephone conversation is what she told you?" Crist asked.

"That is a fact, sir," Kyle responded.

With this admission, Crist immediately moved that all of the testimony regarding the time of Kyle's encounter with Johnson be struck. The judge agreed.

Asked once again by Crist if he knew, "of your own knowledge," when it was that he had left his house to take his guest home, Kyle could only say, "No." Nor could he use any of the events of that night to set the time, "just to the minute," at which he came upon Johnson walking in the neighborhood they both shared with the Jaramillos.[16] And when asked if he could see the Jaramillo house "from the point where you met Johnson that night," he was again forced to admit that he "never paid any attention" to it.[17]

But Crist had, and soon he established that if Kyle and Johnson had passed each other that night, it would have been at a point at least three hundred feet away from Angelina's house.[18] Why, then, Crist inquired, did he think that Johnson was involved in the crime?

An employee of his had come to work at about 8:00 A.M. that Monday morning and "told me about this," Kyle answered. Only then had he thought of Johnson's presence on the street late the previous night as suspicious.[19]

Was this really true, Crist probed, or had troubled business dealings with Johnson caused him to reach these conclusions and to approach the police?

There was no denying that he had been angered by the defendant, Kyle explained. Johnson had agreed to manufacture toy airplanes for his business and had been advanced four dollars to buy supplies, but when work at the garage left Johnson with no time to do this work, Kyle had to demand that the money be returned. Still, that was not the reason for his testimony, Kyle insisted.

"Did you not have some rather harsh words with him prior to and subsequent to the return of these four dollars?" Crist asked.

"I believe I would answer that yes," Kyle acknowledged.

"And at one of these harsh conversations with him, did you not say to him that you would get even with him?" Crist demanded to know.

"Positively not," Kyle responded sharply. "I couldn't get even with a man of that calibre."[20]

Angered by this unsolicited characterization of his client, Crist retaliated. "You were convicted and sentenced for murder?" he began, whereupon Kenney leapt to his feet to "object to the form of the question which is perfectly improper." "I will produce the records," Crist calmly responded."[21]

Fearing that the jury might not have understood that Kyle had indeed met Johnson near Angelina's house within hours of the murder, Otero, in the guise of attempting to help clarify this now shredded testimony, asked the witness to repeat his response without the refinements offered by the defense. "The point is you met him there," Otero emphasized.

"Yes, sir," Kyle was quick to reply.[22]

After a brief recess, Marie Gonzales, the cousin living in the Jaramillo house, was called on to testify. It was now 5:05 P.M. The *New Mexican* would later report that the "11-year-old school girl brought a change in the atmosphere of the packed room when she stepped shyly to the witness chair. There was a transformation in the attitude of the audience. There was a relaxation; the crowd felt the state was getting somewhere."

The trial, in fact, had not been going well for the prosecution. Crist had staged an unexpectedly strong defense. Given his age and the nature of his client, few had thought he would make the effort. "During the greater part of the day there had been a feeling of tenseness in the room," the *New Mexican* reported after the long day's session finally ended. It was particularly disconcerting to see the "appointed attorney for the negro" hammer away at Detective Martin, the reporter commented. "Crist had the spotlight and kept it for more than three hours and the audience, or most of it, was showing signs of uneasiness" by morning's end.

Nor had he let up after the court returned from its lunchtime recess, the *New Mexican* remarked further: "The courtroom crowd, or the majority of it, was apprehensive that Crist might be able to save the defendant. For a lawyer who wasn't getting a fat fee, Crist was proving to be conscientious. He was taking his oath as a member of the bar too seriously: he was showing himself to be too good for a lawyer who at the start was not believed to have a leg to stand upon. Instead of merely going through the motions of getting a fair trial for the client who was wished upon him, the veteran Pojoaque lawyer was putting up a battle. He was giving all he had to the defense."

Marie's ascent to the stand so late in the afternoon presented Kenney with a final chance to redeem his case before the court adjourned for the day. "The jurors beamed upon her with paternal smiles of encouragement" as she began to speak, the *New Mexican* reported, though at times, she was audible only to the translator who sat beside her.[23] She had been with Angelina at Tackert's five-and-ten when her cousin bought a package of Peter Pan face powder and a Kiss Proof lipstick, she told Kenney. So, too, was she at the Jaramillo house when Martin later came to collect the evidence. It was she who had taken Martin to the drawer in Cleofas's dresser where the articles were found. Shown the drawer's contents, she now identified several articles as those purchased by Angelina in the days just prior to her murder. The rouge, however, had been acquired at an earlier time, when her cousin had shopped on her own.[24]

Crist allowed the young girl's testimony to go forward without interruption, but when Kenney attempted to enter the powder and lipstick as evidence, he asked for a chance to first question the young witness. "Did you see Angelina put the two packages that have been shown to you in the drawer in your aunt's room?" Crist began, suspecting that she had not been present at the time. And when Marie confirmed his doubts, Crist turned to Otero and, in as gentle a voice as he could manage, asked the court to note that "there is a busted link in the chain and we object to the introduction."

Within seconds, the two attorneys were again shouting at each other, and when they had each had their say, Kenney turned to Marie and asked if anyone other than Angelina had used the lipstick.

Marie thought not.

"That still doesn't show that Angelina put the lip-stick she bought in Tackert's store in the drawer where the detective found them," Crist argued in reaction to her response.

"I will admit them," Otero ruled nonetheless.

"Exception," Crist protested as he moved back toward the witness.[25] Subjected, if less delicately now, to his further cross-examination, Marie acknowledged that she had not looked at the names of the two cosmetics at the time that Angelina had purchased them, and had only subsequently seen the lipstick's wrapper. As for the powder, she had only heard her cousin ask for it by name.

Declaring the powder to have "no material bearing," Kenney withdrew it as evidence. "I will not offer it with the lip-stick," he conceded.

Pressed further by Crist, Marie admitted that she had never seen Angelina "put these two packages in the bureau drawer in your aunt's room." Yet despite this admission, Otero refused to change his ruling, as Crist once again argued he should, but instead allowed the lipstick to remain as evidence.[26]

Angelina's aunt, Mae Martinez Smith, was then brought forward by Kenney to add strength to this ruling. "Did you see Angelina frequently during her life time?" he began.

Living "close by," they had seen each other "a good many times a day every day," Mae answered. When Angelina stopped by at some time after 4:00 P.M. that final Sunday, she noticed her wearing lipstick for the very first time. Rouge, yes, but never lipstick, "as far as I can remember now, unless what she used before was a shade that blended with her type." But that Sunday, the lipstick had been such a bright red that "I almost saw that before I saw her."[27]

Taking control of the witness, Crist helped Mae to remember that, in fact, it was not the first time that Angelina had used lipstick. "She had used lip-stick before at her home," Mae acknowledged, though "before leaving her home her mother had had her take it off. I don't believe she had ever left the house with lip-stick on her lips that I know of."

Surprised that Sunday by the lipstick, she had wanted to question her niece about it, yet had chosen not to. "I felt like saying something, but I hesitated, I didn't say a word about it," Mae recalled with remorse. It was the last time that she saw Angelina alive.

Crist empathized with the witness, but explained to her that because there was another life at stake now, he had to pursue this disturbing line of questioning one step further. "You don't know then whether the lipstick had been taken off her lips after you saw her or not?" he inquired.

She, of course, had no knowledge of this, but it seemed unlikely to her, she added.

Yet "every other time her mother required her to remove the lip-stick before she went out," Crist reminded her.

Yes, but "her mother didn't see it on her lips this time," Mae responded.

Did she know this "as a fact?" he asked.

"Well, it seems to me she was coming—," Mae began, only to have Crist abruptly cut her off and insist that she speak only of those things about which she had personal knowledge. "As a fact she had lip-stick on that day," Mae tried to continue, but Crist cut in again and dismissed her with an expression of obvious doubt.[28]

Though the hour was now quite late, Crist was anxious to have one final witness called before they adjourned. Earlier that day, Crist had asked that Dr. Loren Elliott be immediately summoned from Albuquerque so that he could appear in court that afternoon. Kenney had hoped that the doctor's written report of his examination of Johnson on the morning of his arrest would be accepted without question, but Crist had refused to allow it to pass unchallenged. And now that Elliott had made the trip, he could not be asked to return on Monday, Crist argued.

Otero conceded the point, but insisted that the witness chair be taken down from its platform and placed beside the court reporter's desk with its back turned toward the spectators. Only then would he allow Elliott to take the stand. Because of its content, his testimony was to remain inaudible to all but the judge, the two attorneys, and a craning jury.[29]

Elliott recalled arriving at the police chief's office at about four in the morning and, "at someone's request," examining Johnson's genitals. At that point, Johnson was still wearing the clothing in which he had been arrested, Elliott recalled. The examination "showed evidence of moisture as you would expect to find after sexual excitement." And that was all. Despite the vaginal lacerations and the excessive bleeding experienced by Angelina, Elliott had found neither abrasions, nor lacerations, nor any blood—"nothing, in other words, except this moist condition."

Disappointed with this assessment and desperate to end the day's proceedings at a more advantageous point, Kenney tried to twist the doctor's testimony to make it sound as if "sexual excitement" was the only possible cause for this moisture on Johnson's penis.

But Crist objected. "That is not what the doctor testified," he shouted.

"Then I would ask you this question," Kenney responded, turning again to Elliott. "Is a moist condition of the glands [*sic*] penis found after sexual excitement?"

"Yes, it is, as a rule," he answered.[30]

Unwilling to allow the jury to retire for the evening thinking that his client had indeed engaged in sexual activity during the time in which he was alleged to have raped Angelina, Crist asked Elliott if there was "any peculiar characteristic of such moisture as you would expect to find after sexual intercourse that distinguishes it positively from other classes of moisture that might be found?"

"Not other than some inflammatory condition" might produce, the doctor told the jury.

"There was nothing then in the moisture which you found at that time on his organ that would definitely and positively establish that he had had recent sexual intercourse?" Crist followed up.

"Nothing definite to establish it, no, to say positively due to that cause, no." But sexual excitement was the "commonest" cause, Elliott volunteered in an attempt to assist the prosecution.

"But it's not certain?" Crist rebutted.

"No, it is not," Elliott had to concede.

Was it possible that this moisture could still be present on a man's penis or trunks five or six hours after intercourse? Crist asked next, trying to counter every possible interpretation of the evidence being discussed.

Perhaps, the doctor answered, but it differed from individual to individual.

"Are there any other evidences to be found on the male organ after sexual intercourse that enables the experienced, trained physician to determine that there had been sexual intercourse?" Crist inquired further.

"Might be traces of semen, and might be the presence of abrasions or lacerations," but none of these conditions were present, Elliott conceded. Nor was any blood found on Johnson's penis. Only the moisture, which "is not conclusive" regarding sexual activity, he further noted.

Was there any possibility that Johnson's underwear had absorbed some of the evidence? Crist inquired, still trying to preempt whatever questions might later be raised by the jury.

"I don't see why they should," Elliott answered. Nor did he think it likely that the trunks would have caused the moisture to be secreted.

"Have these little trunks ever been submitted to you for examination?" Crist asked, only to learn that, as he suspected, lab work had once again not been ordered. Yet when Crist asked if it could therefore be concluded "that there are no evidences on these trunks of such sexual intercourse," Elliott balked.

And so Crist came at the point more directly. "Is it possible by any scientific investigation to determine whether moisture found on the male organ is moisture due to sexual intercourse or to some other cause?"

"Not unless you should perhaps get hold of some of the semen and find spermatozoa," Elliott acknowledged, "and this semen would be mixed with the normal secretions which you find from any irritation." But once again, no lab work had been ordered by the chief investigator in the case, he commented.

"Just one more question," Crist added, hoping that it would emphasize the fact that no scientific evidence of Johnson's commission of a sexual act existed. Angelina had bled profusely, yet, "You found no blood on the male organ of this defendant when you examined him?"

The doctor could do little else but repeat his earlier response to this question. "No; I did not," he admitted with obvious reluctance.[31]

As Elliott stepped down, the judge turned to Crist and asked if he had any objections to the jury going as a group to mass the following day and perhaps to a movie. *The Silent Horde*, a "soul-staggering panorama of drama" involving "one woman in a land of men," according to the studio's advertisement in the *New Mexican,* was playing at the Paris Theater.[32] Crist had no objection to either outing, he told the court, so long as the bailiffs kept the panel from having any contact with others in the community. Otero agreed with Crist and instructed its members against having any such communication. And then, at 5:55 P.M., after eight hours of mostly cross-examination, the trial was recessed until Monday.[33]

Red, Blue, White, and Green

THE Lord's day passed much as it always had in Santa Fe. Catholic churches celebrated morning mass, while non-Catholics attended their own worship services or didn't. The weather was seasonally moderate, the air clean and crisp at seven thousand feet, and, as was their custom, the townspeople spent their afternoons resting or visiting and their evenings leisurely preparing for the week ahead.

But Santa Fe was no longer as it had been a mere three weeks earlier. In the days that followed Angelina's murder, the community had been transformed by fear and anger and the gossip that engulfed it. Never again would it enjoy the tranquility and innocence that had seemed a part of its timeless heritage. The desire for revenge and rumor had changed all of that forever.

The prosecution shared this fever and had hoped to quickly satisfy the people's desire for an act of reciprocity. But the defense had not cooperated. "If they put this man to death, they have to do it legally," Crist had tried to explain to the *New Mexican*'s reporters after Saturday's proceedings had ended. "That's what I'm here for, to see that he gets all the rights the accused is entitled to under the law."[1] Yet few doubted that

FIGURE 20. County courthouse, Santa Fe, New Mexico.

Courtesy Museum of New Mexico, neg. no. 16698.

the prosecution would secure a guilty verdict, and soon, now that its list of witnesses had grown much shorter.

Unlike the two previous sessions, a few seats still remained vacant when, at 8:55 A.M. on Monday, December 7, the court was called back to order. But as the slow, quiet pace of the Sabbath reached its end that next morning, the room once again became filled beyond its capacity.[2]

Kenney planned to highlight the day's testimony by focusing on the two strongest pieces of evidence available to him—the lipstick and the fingerprints found on Cleofas's shattered vase. He would start with the first of these by calling on Dr. Dwight W. Rife as his first witness of the day. As a physician trained in Chicago by a recognized criminologist, Rife had been asked to examine the debris that had previously been removed from under Angelina's fingernails and later delivered to him by Assistant

District Attorney Earl Kenney. "I took a smear, put it on two slides, two glass slides that we use in connection with microscope work, and put a cover glass, thin cover glass over this material," he began. "With one slide I performed two tests of solubility, one with distilled water and one with normal salt solution . . . to see whether any of the material would dissolve in either of these two substances."[3]

"Now, then, let's leave that subject a minute," Kenney interjected, fearing that his jury was already drifting away. "Did you afterward obtain any other finger nail debris?" he inquired, hoping to make his witness's testimony more compelling.

Rife reported that he had himself scraped "the finger nails of Tom Johnson, this colored man," and, like the previous sample, had prepared those scrapings for "microscopic examination."[4] Of the many bits of matter found under Angelina's fingernails, two types were of particular significance, he believed, and of these, the more striking were the "brilliant light red particles," several of which proved to be "identical in appearance and refraction" to the "highly carmine colored particles" similarly found on a slide prepared from the debris that he had collected from under Johnson's nails.[5] More importantly, both were "identical in color, shape, and refraction" to a sample taken from the "tube of kiss proof lip stick" that had been delivered to his office along with Angelina's fingernail scrapings.[6]

Turning next to the "blue plant fibre . . . found in the debris from the test tube," Kenney asked Rife to describe what he had discovered.

"There was delivered to me some coveralls," he began, "blue and white striped coveralls, and I scraped some of the material off these coveralls. . . . The blue cotton fibres, the plant fibres from those coveralls are identical in appearance to the small blue fibres that were found in the material delivered to me."[7]

Exactly how much material was provided in the two samples taken from under the nails of both the victim and the defendant? Crist asked as he now began his lengthy cross-examination. "You testified that in the debris contained in the test tube you found several highly colored particles. . . . As you know Doctor, several is a rather indefinite word. Do your records show how many highly colored particles you found in the debris?"

"It would have been impossible to count them, Mr. Attorney, and I might qualify that by explaining why," Rife testily responded.

"Just answer yes or no to my question," Crist demanded in a voice intended to further rattle the witness. "My question is how many; if you don't know say so."

Frustrated, Rife turned to the court for help and asked if he could try to explain his work.

"I have no objection, doctor," Crist calmly interjected in the hope that his suddenly quiet demeanor would further thin the witness's already diminished patience. "All I am trying to do is to get down to concrete numbers and facts for the use of the jury," he slowly explained. But when Rife began with, "We will say," Crist again cut him off abruptly and insisted that he "answer the question briefly."

Rife looked back over at Otero, but found himself facing Crist on his own. "Eight or ten large particles and numerous very small particles" was all that he could add.

Were all of these, large and small, examined one at a time or "in a bunch, in a lump?" Crist continued.

"They were all examined at the same time, on a slide," Rife admitted. Worse still, none had been chemically analyzed, much as Crist had suspected.

"Have you had any experience in microscopic examination of lip-sticks prior to this time?" he then asked, drawing the jury's attention away from his client's clothing.

"Just a few times," Rife answered, though he had never worked with a "so-called kiss proof lip stick . . . especially under that trade name." Not that it should make a difference, he assured the jury. "I have examined lipsticks."

"Well now," Crist responded, if that were so, "did you find any definite marked difference between the lip-stick which you had under examination, to which you have just testified, and other lip-sticks which you had examined at other times chemically?"

"No," he responded. Nor was there a need to, since they all "follow much the same formula," he explained.

Was there, then, "practically no chemical difference between the different lip-sticks that are in common use?" Christ asked.

Fundamentally, they were "much the same," Rife conceded, all one hundred or more of them.[8]

And the stores that sold one kind, were they not "now-a-days full of all kinds of them, being in common use among our lady friends?" Crist inquired.

Yes, they were, Rife reluctantly acknowledged.[9]

But there was one difference that Crist wanted Rife to demonstrate for the jury. Asked first to apply to his hand the lipstick entered as evidence, Crist then had him wipe his hand against another object. And then against a second. And when it would not "transfer" to either of these, he asked Rife how it could possibly have been found under Johnson's fingernails?[10]

Finding himself aiding the defense, Rife insisted that while kiss-proof lipstick would not easily transfer from a person's lips to an object of wood or glass or some other material, it would nonetheless adhere to another person's finger.

This was perhaps true, Crist countered, but so, too, was the fact that this type of lipstick was "in very common use" and that without a chemical analysis between the particles found under the two individuals' fingernails and the lipstick submitted in evidence as Angelina's, it could not be determined that they were, indeed, one and the same. Why, then, had such a comparison not been made? he demanded to know.

Flustered for a second time, Rife claimed that he couldn't quite follow Crist's question.[11]

But Crist was ready to move ahead and, instead of rephrasing the question, refocused his witness's attention on the issue of Johnson's coveralls. "Now, these small blue cotton fibres, which you say you found in the debris in the test tube, did you make any special chemical examination of those small blue cotton fibres with reference to their individual manufacture and construction, or did you just notice that they were in outward appearance, color and so on, the same?"

Having once again failed to do anything with the material that could substantiate his prior conclusion, Rife argued that he "was necessarily limited just to that last. They were so small."[12]

"Aside from just common dirt" and the red particles, "was there anything else in the debris of either one of them that had any special characteristic aside from common dirt?" Crist questioned Rife further.

"That were common to both?" Rife asked, seeking clarification.

"Yes," Crist was happy to answer.

"No, I wouldn't say so," Rife concluded.

And just how many bright red particles had he found in the debris removed from under Johnson's fingernails? Crist wanted to know as he abruptly shifted back to the lipstick.

"Four or five" was all, Rife responded.

Had they been found under any particular finger or on the fingers of only one hand? Crist went on, knowing that Rife's work, both his scraping of Johnson's nails and the analysis itself, had been sloppily performed.

Rife could not say. Nor could he offer anything different concerning the debris collected from Angelina. All of the scrapings had come to him in a single test tube and were similarly undifferentiated.[13]

Neither had there been any "chemical examination of the composition of the blue fibre" found in the test tube, without which, Crist was quick to emphasize, "you are unable to say whether the blue fibre you took from these coveralls was the same composition."

Attempting to defend his work, Rife, who was earlier identified by the prosecution as an expert in microscopy, interjected: "Remember, you are dealing with microscopic quantities, fibres that cannot be seen with the naked eye."

Crist could not let the moment pass. "I understand, doctor, very well that this sort of work, professional work, is to us laymen in the nature of very fine hair splitting," he responded with cutting sarcasm.

"I object to that," Kenney shouted as he jumped to his feet.

Crist cut him off by rephrasing his comments, and within seconds, an argument broke out between the two men and continued on for a few minutes until the judge, no longer amused, put an end to this latest scuffle.

Crist then picked up the thread and began again. "Then you are unable to say, doctor, that the blue cotton fibre which you took from these coveralls was the same as the blue cotton fibre found in the debris in the test tube?"

"It was," Rife asserted. "Identical in appearance."

"In appearance," Crist repeated for emphasis before digging deeper.

"Was there anything in the appearance of either one of the two microscopic pieces of blue cotton fibre that had any distinguishing characteristic from other pieces of blue cotton fibre?" he wanted to know.

"No, of course not," Rife curtly responded.[14]

Crist was about to probe further when Judge Otero suddenly called a recess, claiming that while it was only 10:00 A.M., both sides needed time to cool down. But by 10:28, Crist was back, standing in the same place, asking his next follow-up question, as if there had been no break. The blue cotton fibres "were infinitesimal, that is, microscopic," were they not? he began once more. And because they were so small, as Rife readily agreed, the jury needed to know how "material of that kind" might become lodged under one's fingernails, Crist explained.

"By scratching a piece of cloth, [or] by the more or less continual handling of a garment," Rife responded. It was, in other words, "very usual to get those microscopic particles from a garment that had that kind of material in it."

Was there something, then, about these particular particles that would allow him to say the two sets of fibers under analysis had come from the same garment? Crist asked.

"There are many garments in existence that contain blue cotton fibre," Rife conceded, and so, no, there really was nothing to distinguish one fiber's origin from the next, "nothing except the color itself," which, he admitted, was "the same as other bright blue colors."[15]

Kenney attempted to rehabilitate Rife's testimony once Crist had completed his cross-examination, but he could regain no ground as the defense successfully raised one objection after another.

Nor did he fare any better with his next witness, Angelina's uncle, Ben Martinez, whose job at this point in the trial was to fill in the crime scene with additional graphic detail. "Did you examine the body of Angelina Jaramillo?" Kenney asked.

"Yes," her uncle responded.

And "was she gagged?" Kenney inquired further.

There was "a piece of cloth tied around her, between her mouth, and tied around her head," Martinez explained.

"Was it simply around across the mouth or was it forced into the mouth?" Crist interjected.

"Inside of the mouth," Martinez noted.

"And the mouth was open and the gag was inside of the mouth like this pencil," Crist probed further, adding a bit of dramatics to his questioning.

"Yes," Martinez answered.

What, then, happened to this cloth? Crist inquired with visible suspicion.

"I took it off and threw it on the bed," Martinez responded, his voice betraying his obvious discomfort.

"Do you know what became of it?" Crist asked in pursuit.

"No, sir," came the reply.

"You don't have it in your possession?" Crist added for emphasis, hoping that the jury might finally have begun to ask themselves whether Martinez had, in fact, recognized the cloth as belonging to someone other than the victim or the defendant.

"No," Martinez answered him with greater hesitancy than before.[16]

Martinez's revelation—that he had removed the now missing gag from the victim's mouth—had proved to be too disturbing to allow the proceedings to continue without interruption. Though less than half an hour had passed since the day's first recess, Otero called for a second break in an attempt to disrupt the defense's momentum. But he could delay the trial only so long, and after twenty minutes, the courtroom was brought back to order.

To divert the jury's attention from what they had just learned, Kenney recalled Livingston to the stand. "On the night of the 15th of November, did you wait upon Mrs. Venceslao Jaramillo?" he asked.

Yes, Livingston answered, she had been injured.

Were the fragments of glass presented to the court as evidence the same as those he had seen that night? Crist wanted to know.

"I saw pieces of a vase that resembled them," Livingston testified.

"Will you state whether or not those wounds of Mrs. Jaramillo were of a type that could have been caused by striking with this vase?" Kenney questioned the doctor.

"It was," Livingston responded with unflagging certainty.

Could he then give more detail about the vase itself? Crist asked, only to draw an immediate reaction from Kenney. The prosecution was

FIGURE 21. Cleofas Jaramillo was found lying just in front of this table, stunned by a blow to the head.

Reproduced from *Master Detective*, "The Clue of the Lipstick"
(March 1935), in the collections of the Library of Congress.

not about to have another witness's testimony shredded if it could be prevented. But after having his objections to this line of questioning overruled twice, Kenney retreated, leaving Crist to return unimpeded to his discussion of the vase.[17] "In which room were these pieces you saw?" he asked Livingston, referring to the "half a dozen, more or less," that he had already spoken about.

"As I remember, the majority of them were in Angelina's bed room," the doctor responded, though he hadn't seen any of it lying about the house. "The glass had been picked up and placed on a table before I got there," he told the jury.

How many pieces? Crist inquired again.

"Probably three to six," Livingston thought.

Were there as many pieces as were present in court? Crist asked, his face cleverly displaying a puzzled expression.

"Not on the table I have in mind," Livingston conceded. "But as I said, they were scattered over the house."

Crist pressed the issue even further and again asked if he had seen other fragments on the floor.

No longer certain of his answer, Livingston protested the question. "I was looking more after the patient than the pieces of glass," he wanted the jury to understand.

But that was exactly Crist's point. "I wouldn't expect you to have given particular attention to that," he told Livingston with feigned empathy. And because he had been preoccupied with his patient, Crist wanted to know how he could possibly speak "about a piece of glass with which a wound similar to that found on Mrs. Jaramillo could have been inflicted."[18]

Kenney could do little more than look on as Crist once again managed to raise serious doubts about the prosecution's case. He would now have to hope that his next witness would bring renewed life to his efforts. "I want to bring in a witness who is bed ridden and on a stretcher,"[19] Kenney told the court as he turned to the rear of the room and cued the bailiffs. Using all of the drama they could muster, the two court officers ceremoniously swung open the doors. With blankets raised up to his chin and his bandages cleverly removed to reveal several fresh scars on his head, Oscar Churchill was wheeled in and brought to the front of the room to lie there in full view of all who were present.[20]

With his entrance so effectively orchestrated, Churchill would now be called on to speak of his encounter with the defendant on the night of the murder. Johnson had borrowed two dollars the previous evening and, appearing "a little bit shaken, like he was excited about something," had returned to the garage to discuss the loan, Churchill began.

46   The Master Detective

Martin got in touch with Sh
they quickly made up a party t
Chief of Police, Deputy Alaric
arrived in Albuquerque soon a
"Where's our man?" the Sher
station.
"Upstairs being asked a few
Barney Spears.
Upstairs they found a man h
Albuquerque police officers.
He was Tom Johnson, 31-year
had been sent to the penitent
years before, after pleading gui
He had been freed in July w
to a little less than four years.
in the Andrews Garage as a ca
The man had a prison reco
Born in Birmingham, Alabam
                        sixteer
                        the la
                        ton, (
                        under
                    On
                    Tom
                    gan S
                    years
                    On
                    mittec
                    breaki
                    bery
                    two y
                    In
                    Albuq
                    charge
                    handy

(Above) Oscar Churchill, the garage
attendant, who was brutally slugged
and left for dead by the phantom
suspected of killing Angelina. He is
shown with his wife, who nursed
him back to health

had been committed by the same man and

FIGURE 22. Oscar Churchill, the garage attendant,
and Frank Powers, fingerprint expert.

Reproduced from *Master Detective*, "The Clue of the Lipstick"
(March 1935), in the collections of the Library of Congress.

Crist immediately objected to this characterization, and Otero ordered the jury to disregard it. But the impression had been made, and no ruling could erase it.

Churchill went on from there, telling how Johnson had left the garage for several minutes, returned, and then, unprovoked, bludgeoned him with a hammer.[21] And as Churchill testified to the beating, "his head, the only visible part of his body, trembled" uncontrollably, the *New Mexican* took pains to tell its readers. "At times there was a quaver in his voice," and if "the scars on Churchill's head were healed, he evidently still suffers," the reporter observed together with the jury.[22]

Encouraged by the now hushed atmosphere in the courtroom, Kenney decided to ask Churchill about Johnson's theft of money from the garage, though he knew that it had little to do with the crime for which the defendant was being tried. It was, of course, likely that Crist would object, but there was always the chance that his question might slip past the defense. Besides, there was little to lose if it didn't.

Crist had wanted to first hear the witness's answer before moving to have his statement struck from the record, and so he remained silent for a moment.[23]

Churchill surprised both parties with his response, stating that he had, in fact, not seen Johnson robbing the money, but had only heard the cash register drawer being opened.

As expected, Otero agreed with Crist's objection when he raised it after learning Churchill's answer. The theft from the garage did, indeed, lack relevancy to the charge at hand, the judge noted. The jury was to disregard the entire matter.

But as Crist rose to begin his own examination of the witness, the judge implored him to be as brief as possible. Crist, however, was determined to discredit Churchill's testimony and asked again if he had personally seen Johnson open the register. It was a question aimed at helping the jury understand his prior objection to this testimony.

Churchill at first maintained his earlier response, but after a good deal of further probing by Crist finally acknowledged that he could not actually recall receiving any of the blows he had sustained, nor be absolutely certain that he had, indeed, heard Johnson at the cash register that night.[24]

It was nearly noon when Crist excused Churchill. Everyone was now ready to break for lunch. But Kenney needed to call two additional witnesses before he could put his fingerprint expert on the stand when they returned. J. M. McSparen, a commercial photographer and the owner of Minck's photo shop in Santa Fe, was asked to look at a series of negatives and contact prints that he identified as those he himself had prepared from the glass fragments already in evidence.

Crist had no objection to this material being entered, so long as the place on the one negative pointed to by McSparen as containing a finger-print was so marked, "so that we will be able to refer to it definitely in the future."

Kenney realized that Crist was again attempting to discredit his witness and quickly conceded that McSparen was not a fingerprint expert. That part of the testimony had been "merely voluntary on his part and immaterial," he insisted. "The proper person to point out finger prints is not this witness. I do not want to be bound by the testimony of a witness who is not an expert."

Crist accepted the prosecution's concession, so long as the statement in question was struck from the record.

"Very well," Otero responded, and instructed the jury not to consider the "portion of his testimony wherein he referred to a finger print appearing or alleged to be on this piece of glass."

Satisfied by the judge's ruling, Crist had only one remaining question to ask of McSparen. "Is this an exact reproduction as to size of the piece of glass from which it was taken?"

"No," McSparen acknowledged, "it wasn't measured for that purpose."[25]

Kenney's next and final witness of the morning, R. E. Brunk, was in charge of the fingerprint lab at the New Mexico State Penitentiary in Santa Fe and had come to know Johnson during their time together at the prison. Kenney showed Brunk a glassine print and asked him to identify it. "These are Johnson's fingerprints," he responded, claiming that their impression had been made at the prison in 1927. Kenney handed him a card with another set of prints. They, too, were Johnson's, Brunk testified, recorded by him on November 20, just five days after the defendant's recent arrest. Having made the impressions himself, Brunk noted, he was certain of their origin.

Crist immediately objected to the introduction of both items as evidence, but was just as quickly overruled by Otero. Yet under further questioning, Brunk revealed that the photograph of the earlier set of prints had, in fact, been made by someone other than himself and that while he was present at the time it was shot, he had not been in the darkroom when it was being developed. Nevertheless, he felt certain that the photographic copy being shown to the court was identical to the original 1927 impressions.

Crist once again objected. Only the photographer himself could reliably make such an assertion, he insisted. Kenney countered by offering to call the photographer to the stand, but Crist had a still more serious basis to his challenge. "I object for the reason that the files of the penitentiary are not such official records as are entitled to consideration in the court without further proof," he protested to Otero. Kenney, sensing the danger of this challenge to the crucial testimony he hoped later to present, immediately withdrew his witness's last assertion.[26]

But Crist would not let go. "Do you hold yourself as a finger print expert by training and experience?" he asked Brunk.

"I have only had finger print experience since I have been in the penitentiary," he responded.

"And no other place or time?" Crist inquired further.

"No, sir," he admitted.

"You are an inmate of the penitentiary under conviction for a felony?" Crist asked the witness as a way of compromising his credibility.

"I am," Brunk acknowledged.

"And you know nothing about the taking of the finger prints of 1927?" Crist added

"No, sir; I wasn't there," Brunk responded, his air of confidence suddenly shattered.[27]

It had taken some time, but Crist had managed to ultimately draw out the answer he sought to bring before the jury. There was nothing more to ask of this witness, and so he was excused.

With Crist's final question now answered, everyone broke for lunch and prepared for what promised to be another long afternoon. When Otero called the room back to order at 1:30 P.M., Frank Powers was summoned to the stand. As the *New Mexican* later commented, his testimony "was the first definite evidence to link [Johnson] with the crime. Earlier evidence had dealt largely with suspicious circumstances."[28]

Believing it important for Powers to establish his credentials before beginning his testimony, Kenney asked him to give the jury a sense of his professional background.

Powers responded by telling the court that after eleven years of work in the area of fingerprint identification, he now held the positions of superintendent of the Bureau of Criminal Identification of the El Paso, Texas, Police Department, and of vice president of the International Association for Identification. Over the years, he had examined more than one million fingerprints, he assured the jury. Shown the vase fragments, the fingerprint card, and the photographic copies of each, Powers acknowledged that he had examined each of these prior to the trial. There were, he explained, nine points of comparison used by him to conclude that the prints on the vase had come from Johnson's right thumb and left middle finger.

By now, Powers had moved closer to the jury, and they, in response, had leaned forward to greet him. When asked to produce the photographic enlargements he had made from the various negatives given to him by the prosecution, Powers looked up at the jury, inviting them with his eyes to come even closer if they wanted a better look at the evidence being described.

Upset by what was happening, Crist objected, noting that Powers was "assuming that these are the finger prints of the defendant." Overruled, he again objected moments later when photographs of a second set of prints were brought forward for discussion. To say the prints in this second instance were, in fact, Johnson's was pure hearsay, he argued.

This time, Otero agreed. He could no longer avoid the obvious problem of a witness testifying about prints he had not himself taken from the defendant. But when Crist attempted to revisit his previous objection, Otero refused to change his ruling. Instead he asked Powers to move on with his report of the lab's findings.

As an experienced handler of jurors, Powers passed the enlargements among them and asked that they follow his extensive and detailed analysis point by point. Thrilled by his show of confidence in their innate ability to follow his work, they accompanied him step by step.

A few minutes passed before Crist stopped Powers and objected to his characterization of this analysis as "very clear to the layman."

Aware that no single juror would be willing to admit that he alone was confused by any one of these points, Powers rose in his own defense and insisted that "it is for the laymen on the jury to say whether they are clear or not."

But Otero once again agreed with Crist and ordered the jury to disregard this latest claim.

Angered by the court's decision, and without being asked by either attorney, Powers offered his studied conclusion that the print under analysis undeniably demonstrated Johnson's presence at the crime scene.

An audible sigh of relief filled the courtroom. Crist fumed and counterattacked. If the print now being described as Johnson's was, in fact, identical to "the print found at the scene of the murder," where exactly, and according to his own knowledge, was "that print found?" he demanded of Powers, before insisting that the witness's statement be ruled inadmissible.

Otero, however, denied the defense its wish, setting off yet another round of argument between the two attorneys.

When it finally subsided, Kenney revisited each fingerprint, one by one, all of which Powers identified as Johnson's.

"Where does it put that man?" Kenney then asked.

"At the scene of the crime," Powers answered without equivocation.

Crist raised no further objections. Instead he chose to wait until he could cross-examine the witness more fully.[29] After a brief recess, Crist began his rebuttal. It was already 3:17 P.M. The "battle between an attorney asking carefully phrased questions, and an expert in the fingerprint business," as the *Albuquerque Journal* characterized their confrontation, would last an hour.[30] "The adept wording of the veteran lawyer's questions and his demands for a 'yes or no' answer had Powers squirming at times," the *New Mexican* conceded in its report the following day, "but the expert came through in better shape than most of the witnesses who have had to run through Crist's enfilading cross-examining."

Going to the heart of the matter, Crist asked Powers about the incomplete thumbprint supplied by the prison lab. "Was there no possibility of error?" he demanded to know.

Powers insisted that errors never occurred in his profession. "Not in this business, no sir." Though smears and blurred portions and gilded decorations on the vase fragments had left him with less than precise images to work with, as well as unidentified partial prints on a number of the pieces, it had all made little difference to his analysis. "The reason this isn't complete is due to carelessness in rolling the impression," Powers explained.

But if "there is carelessness in handling this finger print business sometimes," then no analysis could ever be considered definitive, Crist argued in response. And if so, what, then, were they to make of the absence of Johnson's prints from the many other fragments that had been found throughout the house? he asked Powers.

It was merely a function of the way that Johnson had held the piece, Powers replied, though exactly how he had done so remained speculative at best, he admitted.

And so it went as both men continued on in this way for some time, going back and forth over this same ground, until finally Kenney rose from his chair and, seemingly exhausted, announced, "That is all; the state rests."[31] He had presented his case.

As the news spread beyond the courtroom, "there came a stamping of feet and the sound of loud voices from the stairways outside," the *New Mexican* reported. "Johnson turned quickly toward the doors and remained looking in that direction. Sheriff Jesus M. Baca hurried outside to find out what it was all about, but returned in a few seconds smiling. There was no trouble," he was pleased to report.[32]

In His Own Behalf

WITH little of the afternoon remaining, Crist stood, faced the judge, and, in a surprise move, told the jury, "I will not make an opening statement but will let [you] gather the defendant's case from the witness stand."[1] It would now be Johnson's task to convince the jury of his innocence. But as he walked to the witness stand, with his head slightly bowed and his cuffed hands clasped in front of him, as if in prayer, all hope appeared to have left him.[2]

At Crist's urging, Johnson began by briefly telling the story of his early life and of the times he had spent in prison since leaving home as an adolescent. Sentenced to seven years in 1927 for a series of burglaries in Albuquerque, he had been released from prison three years early for good behavior and had found a job at Andrew's Garage the very next day. Washing, polishing, and vacuum cleaning cars, repairing their tires, and performing janitorial duties around the building, he had avoided any contact with the police "up to the time of this trouble." Beginning at six o'clock each morning, he would spend twelve or thirteen hours a day at the garage and would then return at least every other night to help Oscar Churchill "get cars from hotels and bring them down . . . to repair tires and [do] general service work." Even when not working, he would often visit with Churchill for a while, as he had that last Saturday night before Angelina's murder.[3]

Having brought Johnson to this point in his story, Crist asked him to tell the jury about his activities on the day of the crime.

"Sunday morning I woke up about five-thirty and I muttered with myself about whether to go to mass or go to Albuquerque," he continued. "Then I made up my mind that I could go to Albuquerque in the morning if I would be lucky enough to get a ride and I could get there in time to do what I wanted to do and get back in time that evening so I could make benediction."

What was it that drew him to Albuquerque? Crist prompted his client.

"Well it is an old lady in Albuquerque that I lived with when I was living in Albuquerque before I came to Santa Fe," Johnson responded. "I was told by about three or four different parties lately that she was sick, very sick, and she told these people that told me if they seen me in Santa Fe to tell me the first chance I got to come to see her."

And the last time he had received this message? Crist inquired further.

Late Saturday night or early Sunday morning, Johnson answered, his eyes now fixed on the jury. "It was a colored fellow coming through going to Raton" who had stopped him on the street that day. "I was going from Tony's pool hall to my home and he hailed me and asked me if I was the fellow named Tom Johnson. I told him yes and he asked me did I know Miss Glen a lady who ran a rooming house in Albuquerque. I told him yes and he asked me why didn't I go down to see her that she was very sick and she told him if he seen me in Santa Fe to tell me to come right away if I could."

Asked by Crist if he knew the man's name, Johnson replied that he simply never asked. Instead the man merely gave him directions out of Santa Fe and went on his way. Early that Sunday morning, as the Guadalupe church bell rang for six o'clock mass, Johnson left Santa Fe on foot, walking south two miles past the Indian School.

"And then what happened?" Crist asked, only to have Johnson's answer delayed by Otero, who suddenly called for a ten-minute recess.[4] It seemed oddly misplaced with the hour so late, as if calculated to break

Johnson's concentration. Even the *New Mexican* later commented that "Johnson was hardly well launched on his story when the court recessed."⁵

When court resumed at 4:55 P.M., Crist repeated his question. "You said you were about two miles the other side of the Indian School. . . . What happened then?"

"I waived a man down and asked him would he give me a ride to Albuquerque," Johnson told the jury. Given the number of trunks in the car, he appeared to be a salesman. After fixing two flat tires along the way, Johnson arrived in Albuquerque at about 2:00 P.M. Dropped off in front of the Knights of Columbus hall, he then walked the rest of the way to Mrs. Glen's house over at 316 1/2 Third Street. "I knocked on the front door and didn't get no answer," he continued. "I went around to the back and I helloed up stairs and called her name and I didn't get no answer. I waited about fifteen minutes to see whether anybody would come to the house or not and nobody didn't come."

And so he began to walk back toward the road that led to Santa Fe, hoping to find a ride home.

> I just kept walking out Fourth Street and after I got out of the city limits everybody passed I asked them for a ride but people ain't very well you might say, they don't give everybody a ride that asks them, and it was pretty hard for me to get a ride. So I walked well about seven miles out of Albuquerque and I got a ride on a truck and I rides so about twenty-five miles and this fellow that I was riding with one of his tires on the front wheel blowed out, and I and he worked a good while, I don't know how long it was but it was a pretty long while making a boot for it, and when we got through fixing the boot we put the tire back on.

The sun was already low in the sky when they set out again, though he could not say what time it was. And as they drove on, slowly making their way over the hills that day, the two men talked of Albuquerque and Santa Fe and of where Johnson was working. But neither man asked the other his name. Nor had Johnson inquired about the contents of the fully loaded truck.

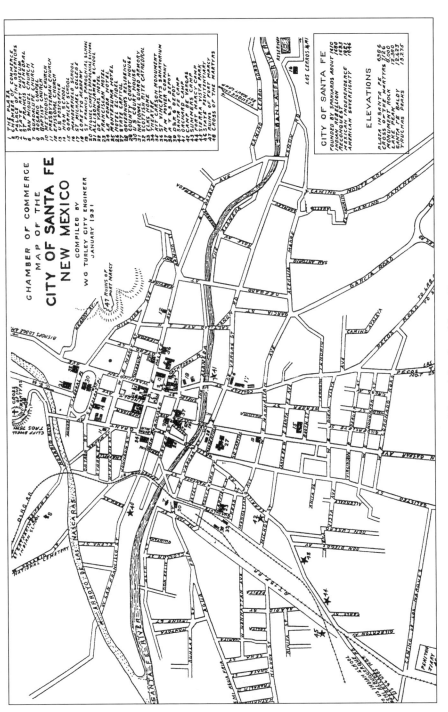

FIGURE 23. Map of the city of Santa Fe, 1931.

When they arrived in Santa Fe, Johnson asked for the time and was told that it was "about nine o'clock." Dropped off by the Phillips 66 gas station at the corner of Cerrillos and Hancock, he continued on foot back to his room, "the second door from the corner" off Water Street on Sandoval. "I stayed in the room about five minutes and then I left my room, went right straight up Sandoval Street to San Francisco Street, and I walked out San Francisco Street to Quintana's." Going west on San Francisco, he then crossed the railroad tracks and continued on for three long blocks. Halfway there and still a few blocks from his destination, he saw Quintana standing in the window of a neighbor's house. "And I didn't stop there to ask him for what I wanted. I went on up to his house, and I knew he wasn't at home because I seen him at this other house. So I sat on the steps and waited until he came home about half an hour later." It was during this time that a young woman came out of the house and drove away with two other men, he told the jury.

Crist wanted to know something more about the car, but before Johnson could respond, Otero once again interrupted. Though only twenty minutes had passed since calling the court back to order, he had decided to bring a halt to the day's proceedings. There would be time enough the following day to bring the matter to its conclusion.

When court resumed the next morning, a sense of finality filled the room.[6] All were now certain that the trial was in its last day. At 8:50 A.M. Johnson returned to the stand to answer the question that had remained unanswered throughout the long night. "Tell us about the car," Crist prompted his client.

"Well, I was sitting on the porch steps and a Ford car roadster drove up and stopped right in front of Quintana's house," Johnson recalled in some detail. "I went over to the car and asked these fellows did they want to see Quintana. They said no they was waiting on a lady and just about that time the woman came out because they had blowed the horn to attract her attention, and after this the car left the house."

Moments later, Johnson heard Quintana's voice approaching from down the block. "I know his voice," Johnson assured those listening to his story. "So I got up off the steps and went to meet him before he got to the house, and I asked him for the favor that I went there for, which I asked him to loan me four dollars and he said yes, come to the house, and

FIGURE 24. Water and Don Gaspar Streets, Santa Fe,
New Mexico, where Tom Johnson lived, ca. 1928.
Courtesy Museum of New Mexico, neg. no. 91795.

I and him went to the house but I didn't go in the house, I stayed on the porch. It seemed to be about ten or fifteen minutes and then he came back out again with the money."

Quintana wanted to know what he planned to do with the money, to which Johnson replied that he had borrowed two dollars from the cash register in Andrew's Garage and now wanted to repay the loan. The other two dollars would enable him to "buy different things with because I didn't have no money."

Promising to repay the loan the following Saturday night, he then headed off to see Churchill. But on his way to the garage, Johnson passed Tony Rael's pool hall and, instead of walking on, stopped and entered. There were about twenty people inside, he recalled, all of them gambling at poker, blackjack, or craps.

When I went in they had a pretty good game shooting craps. Tony Rael was the game banker, and I stopped at the table and I took on

a bet, and as we played there the dice done come around to me, so
we played there quite a while and won some while I was there, and
instead of me going to pay this Churchill the two dollars I stayed
there and tried to win some more and I lost all of the money down
to two dollars back again, and then I quit the crap game and went
to play black jack over at the other table, and how long it was I
played black jack I couldn't say, but I know there was more than me
and Tony in there at the time, and I and Tony never played but one
game of pool since I know him, and that is before they transformed
that place into a gambling joint.

By his own estimate, Johnson had spent upward of two and a half
hours at Tony's until he had lost all of the money he had borrowed, and
then he left. "I went out of Tony's place down to my house and got me a
bite to eat," he continued.[7] Johnson's room was only a few feet down the
street from Tony's pool hall and a few feet away from Andrew's Garage
as well, and so, after he had finished eating, he walked over to explain to
Churchill why he was unable to repay his debt.

When he entered the office, Churchill was lying on a settee, reading
a magazine. Johnson pulled over a chair and asked him what the
proprietor, Al Muller, had said about the loan he had made to him
without the authority to do so.

He said he raised hell, says he bawled him out and told him not to
loan me no more money out of the cash register unless he say so,
and he asked me why in hell didn't I come back and tell him I didn't
have the money or do something that he could straighten it out
himself. I told him I left early that morning and went to
Albuquerque, and he told me that I was a damned liar, I didn't go
no place, and then I explained to him that I went to see grandma
down in Albuquerque, and he said he didn't believe it. I didn't have
no way of proving it, so I didn't say no more about it. He asked me
why didn't I get the money from somewhere so he could get out of
the strain of being bawled out about me. I told him that I went to
borrow some money that evening from this Quintana to pay him,
but I went in this crap game and lost it trying to win some more

money because I had lost about twenty dollars that Saturday night. He said he didn't care where I got them just so long as I had the money to put it in the cash register when he checked out the next morning, that was Monday morning.

Over the next several minutes, the confrontation between the two men grew more heated until what had begun as a verbal dispute became physical. As Johnson explained to the courtroom,

One word brought on another and he cursed me and I cursed him. They was an iron laying on a shelf by a bunch of chains, automobile chains, some sacks of weed chains that they put on car wheels. He made a reach at this piece of iron, and the hammer was standing on its end right by the door. I stepped back and picked up this hammer and at the same time I threw my arm up. Instead of my arm hitting the piece of iron, my arm hit his arm and I knocked it up. At the same time with my right hand I brought the hammer up and knocked him in the head, and I hit him about two or three times as I know of, because when he fell I got scared, and then I went, left out of this place where he was and went out in the garage studying what to do.

Regaining his composure, but still panicked by thoughts of what would happen to him as a black man in a white world, he decided to try to revive Churchill rather than simply run away. "I thought if I left him there and I stayed in town it wouldn't have been no kind of story I could tell nobody to make him believe I didn't jump on him willfully for nothing, because they would believe his story in preference to mine," Johnson continued, looking straight at the jury. "So I went back in there, took a piece of rag from under the cash register, went out to the hydrant and wet this rag and washed his face and put the rag on his throat."

But in the end, nothing seemed to help. And so, with little choice left to him, he fled southward, fearing for his life.

Instead of coming to he just went out like he was going to die or something, and that scared me more, so I thought I better leave

town. I took him and put him back of the boss' desk and piled a
whole lot of rags, rags what we wipe cars with, from under the
counter on the floor first and then I laid him on that and spread a
quilt over him, and as far as tying his hands and like that I don't
know nothing about that. I didn't have no intention of killing
Churchill, and as it happened me being heavy hitting, I hit him a
whole lot harder than I intended to. After I put him back of this
counter I thought I better take some preparation to leave town.

Aware that his client's testimony could be used to demonstrate a
capacity for murder, Crist asked Johnson to speak in greater detail about
his final minutes with Churchill.

Johnson noted that Churchill was unconscious at this point and
bleeding profusely from his head wounds. Afraid that he was dying,
Johnson knelt beside him, placed his head on his knee, and attempted to
revive him by washing the blood from his face. "But I couldn't," Johnson
recalled. It was then that he dragged Churchill to the place behind the
counter where he was later found. In lifting Churchill around his upper
body, Johnson told the court, he had bloodied the front of his coveralls,
as he had earlier the areas around his knees where he had placed
Churchill's head.

Had he succeeded in reviving Churchill, Johnson went on, he would
have called Muller to explain what had transpired between them. But
now he could only think of what would happen to him if he were caught.
"I couldn't have told no kind of story to make nobody believe it; that is
what I thought." And so he began to plan his escape.

I went out in the garage and I studied what way could I get out of
Santa Fe the quickest way. I didn't know nobody that had a car they
would rent it to me, so I took the first car in front there and drove
it out in front to the gas pump and I put in ten gallons of gas, and
then I went back in the office. I opened the cash register. I started to
just take five dollars and I thought I better just get right on out of
the State if I could until I found out how the public felt about it and
I took all of the money.

Before fleeing Santa Fe, he had stopped at his room, grabbed a few pieces of clothing and some toilet articles, and then drove down Water Street to Agua Fria, onto Hancock, and back out on Cerrillos Road going south. It was his first trip in that direction in the dark. He lost his way for a while, but after passing through the towns of Cerrillos and Madrid, he finally arrived in Albuquerque. "It was at night and I never had been on that road before in my life. I just took the road that looked more like the highway than the other," he tried to explain.[8]

Once in Albuquerque, Johnson stopped outside a restaurant on East Central to buy food for the road ahead. But as he emerged from the stolen Buick, a police officer approached him.

> The officer came up to me and he asked me my name, and I told him my name was Tom Johnson. He asked me wasn't I from Santa Fe. I told him yes, and he said you killed a woman up there. I told him I never killed no woman, I didn't know nothing about that, and then he asked me what was that blood doing on my pants, and I noticed the blood was on my knee, looked like that down there, and then before I could say anything else, he ran his hand in my pocket and he asked me where did I get that money, and he said you are the nigger that killed that boy up there too. I told him I didn't know whether I killed him or not but I and him got in a fight and I took the money and this car, and he put a pair of hand cuffs on me and I and him in his car went to the state headquarters in Albuquerque.

Johnson now found himself in the very position that had caused him to flee toward the border with Mexico. As he explained to the jury,

> When they got me in there they sat me in the corner and questioned me. . . . Then this desk sergeant he started to searching me, and he took all of the money out of my pocket and he took the knife I had in my hip pocket and says this is the knife that you killed that woman with and pushed it that close to my nose. I told him no sir, I didn't kill no woman, I didn't know anything about that. So they took all of the things that I had on me out of all my pockets and piled them on the desk there, and then they unloosed the hand cuffs

and fastened them behind my back and left me in another room and put me in the corner and the man sat in a chair right in front of me guarding me, and all of the time he was telling me about me killing some woman in Santa Fe. At the same time he said that I raped a woman.

"Well," Johnson continued, hoping that he might now demonstrate his innocence, "I told him if he thought such as that why didn't he call a doctor to examine me if it was done that very night. Then he told this desk sergeant to call a doctor, and the doctor came and examined me and I think I heard him—I think I understood him to say that I didn't show any signs of raping nobody."

Frustrated by the doctor's findings, Johnson's captors ultimately resorted to other means in an attempt to secure a confession from him.

So pretty soon Mr. Charlton and this officer that was guarding me and some other man, I didn't notice to see who they were, took me upstairs and says to make him talk. . . . And they questioned me over and over and over again about my whereabouts that night and I told them the same thing I am telling the court, and while they was questioning me, I don't know what time it was, the sheriff and officers from Santa Fe came in the room, and Mr. Martin he had received this stuff from down there at the desk sergeant's desk and bring it up to the room up there where we was, and then the first thing he said to me that I killed the woman in Santa Fe, and then he put that knife before me and says this is what you killed that woman with. I told him no, sir, I didn't kill no woman.

With the tacit consent of the others, Martin then raised the level of intimidation, feeling confident that his prisoner would finally break. "He started to take off my clothes and my hands was hand cuffed like they are now," Johnson demonstrated, lifting his arms to show the jury. "So they take the hand cuffs off and Mr. Martin take all the clothes I had on off down to my socks and then the shoes and he piled them up and started to finding blood spots on the underwear and shirt, so he said." Once his clothing had been removed, his hands were again cuffed behind his back.

On his feet, shackled, and now fully disrobed, the questioning began all over again.

> I was backed up against the wall and Mr. Martin came up to me and says nigger you are going to talk. I told him I didn't know nothing to talk about only what I did to Churchill. He says you know you killed that woman, and he said Churchill had made a statement before he died and he know all about that, said they was interested in knowing about this woman being killed. I told him I didn't know nothing about it, and then in the same time he asked me did I know George Kyle, Mr. Martin did. I told him yes, sir, I know him, he appear to be the same kind of man he was, and then they started asking me questions about this woman and my whereabouts and I told them just what I am telling the court where I was, and he took his hand like that and bumped my head back against the wall and then he struck me in the stomach twice with a night stick. . . . He says nigger you might as well come on and tell us the truth because we know you done it and we got the goods on you. I told him go ahead and have the goods, I didn't do it and I ain't going to say I did. The onlyest thing I could say anything about was the trouble between me and Churchill. He said he didn't want to hear nothing about that, said he wanted to know about this woman being killed, and I couldn't tell him nothing because I didn't know nothing about it.

Only then did Martin stop "bothering me," Johnson recounted. Instead he proceeded to examine the clothing he had removed from his prisoner and to count the money found in its pockets. And as Johnson stood there, eyes fixed on his interrogator, a sense of relief began to wash over him after these many hours, as if the ordeal was finally over. But this feeling would last only a few moments. Filling the void Martin had left, the others quickly moved in and began, once again, to accuse him of the crimes committed against Angelina. "I told them all I didn't know nothing about that woman being murdered," but they didn't believe him. And so the questioning continued on into the morning, with each of the officers taking his turn. Martin would occasionally break the unending flow of questions by pointing to one of the bloodstains on Johnson's clothing, but as far as Johnson could recall, he was never asked about any of them.[9]

There was more than a hint of exhaustion in Johnson's eyes now as he looked pleadingly at his attorney, hoping that his time on the stand was nearing its end. But Crist knew that there were still a number of important points that needed to be clarified further before he could pass his client along to the prosecution for cross-examination. "Is that the knife they took out of your clothes there in Albuquerque that night?" he asked Johnson, showing him the knife that had previously been entered as evidence.

It was, he acknowledged, purchased "to make model airplanes with" and to use "around the garage sometimes" to repair tires. He normally carried it in a pocket on the lower leg of his overalls but had transferred it to a hip pocket when he climbed into the Buick at the garage so that it wouldn't stick him in the leg as he sat down behind the wheel. When told in Albuquerque that he had killed Angelina with this knife, "I told them no, I didn't kill no woman with that knife; that knife ain't never cut a person," he insisted.

And what of the red spot on the knife? Crist asked.

"It is red paint on that knife," Johnson explained. "I paint around the garage a lot. I paint gas pumps out in front." It might even have been from the red paint he had used for the bed in his room, he added.[10]

Hoping that the jury now had a clearer sense of the red dot's origin, Crist turned next to the issue of the clothing that Johnson was given to wear for the ride back from Albuquerque. It was, perhaps, his last chance to win a bit of sympathy for the accused.

The interrogation had gone on for several hours, Johnson explained, while he stood there naked until, finally, a few police officers went back to the Buick and retrieved a suit, a shirt, and a pair of shoes for him to put on. It was all that he would ever again see of the things he had grabbed from his room that night. Among the missing items was his underwear. He had asked repeatedly for a pair of his shorts, but they simply refused to bring him any, Johnson recalled pointedly.

Amidst these images of the prisoner and his captors, Crist asked, "Is this the pair of coveralls that they took off of you that night?" And as Johnson sat there silently, looking at the several pieces of clothing set out before him, Crist proceeded to inventory each of the articles said to have been in his pockets.

They were all his, Johnson told the jury, explaining which of the shirts he had worn over the other so that they might have a clearer picture of how he had been dressed that night.

"Explain to the jury how the blood got on these overalls," Crist prompted his client, hoping that repetition might lend credibility to his assertions.

"That blood on them overalls down on the legs and all up the side of the overalls, if any on the sleeve it is the same way, all that there came from when I was handling Churchill," Johnson responded. "I had his head right up in my hand and part of his body was on my leg and that is where I got blood on me down there and in front here."

And the blood that had been found on the top, palms, and between the fingers of both of his hands? Crist continued.

"I put my hand in back of Churchill's head and his hair was hanging down in his face and blood running down all over his head like; that is when I, while my hand was handling his head, that is how blood came on my hands," he tried to tell the jury as graphically and as convincingly as he could. "The reason the palms of my hand like that was the blood wasn't so thick there, I handled the steering wheel of the car like that."

Had he washed his hands, face, or any part of his body "at any time from the time you came back from Albuquerque until you arrived at Albuquerque the morning of Monday?" Crist inquired further.

"No, sir," Johnson responded. "I didn't take time to wash nothing. When I left Santa Fe I just kept going." Only once during his hastily organized flight did he stop, "just slowed up the car and urinated and kept going."[11]

Crist was clearly pleased with his client's explanations, but felt that one last issue remained for him to address, the claim made by Kyle that he had seen Johnson near the Jaramillo home on the night of the murder.

They had first met while both were inmates in the state prison, Johnson told the jury. Kyle "ran a curio shop there and I made waste baskets and airplanes and different little articles and I sold them to him for a pretty reasonable price."

"Did you have any difficulty with him in your business transactions?"

Crist asked Johnson, knowing that the answer would explain to the jury why Kyle had fabricated the story of an encounter between the two men on the night of the murder. It would be a long and detailed response, but Crist knew how important it was for his client's defense, and so he gave him the time to tell it all, hoping not to lose the jury's attention before he had finished. "Just tell the jury about that difficulty," he instructed Johnson.

> Well, I sold those little airplanes there in the store to him and he didn't want to pay no better price, he wanted every kind I made, big ones and small ones, all for the same price, and I wouldn't sell them to him like that. I put them in the store in my own name and a lot of visitors buy them and got pretty fair prices for them, and some how or other he made some trouble for me and stopped me from making them. I didn't make any airplanes or anything until Mr. Swope and Mr. Summers came back on this last administration and then I made a little money that way, and at the same time Mr. Kyle was taking the stuff he bought from me and all of the rest of the fellows out there and sending it up in town and getting two prices for what he paid for it and I refused to sell him anything, and I could see he was mad, he didn't say or no body tell me, but the way things happened. I knowed if I didn't sell them to him it wasn't no use to make them, so when I got out of the penitentiary I went over to his house, because I didn't know nobody here in Santa Fe, and asked him would he give me a chance to try to make something until I could get a job. He said no he didn't have no regular job and couldn't give me a job or place to stay there in that part of town. So I see he was still sore at the way things happened out at the penitentiary. That was the same day I got out. I went over to the Andrews garage and asked for a job and they said that they didn't have no open place then. They rented the wash rack and service like that out to another fellow. I worked there, just flunking around and they give me a dollar a day just to stick around there, and I worked myself up a pretty good job. So I had left some designs, Indian designs and things over to Mr. Kyle's house. One day I went to take a car back to a gentleman over at the—over to the Federal building, and on my way back from the Federal Building, I stopped at Mr. Kyle's house

and asked him to let me have my designs. That was after I paid him the money that he loaned me. He didn't loan it to me, but just give me so much money on material to build things and sell, and then I went after my designs, and when he came out he started at once after the designs. He said you wouldn't work for me, you rather work for them people that don't mean you no good. I asked him what did he mean by saying that. I told him I had a job and when I first came out I came to him and asked for a job and he didn't have nothing for me, and the man that he was talking about, that was the man that give me the chance to work and make a living. He said that is all right you will find out Alfred Muller don't mean no nigger no good. You wouldn't work for me, and he got mad and started bawling me out, cursed, told me not to talk back to him and things like that. I told him I didn't care nothing about but the onlyest people that meant me some good, I didn't care what nobody else said to make up for it; so he said well that is all right, get on out of my place. I told him I wouldn't have come there if I didn't have my designs there, and I left the place and never did see him no more. But before this happening of me going over there to get my designs, it can be proved that he came down to the garage and tried to make trouble for me, telling me if he didn't get his money he was going to get the police and things like that, and Mr. Muller had a little bank in the safe that I saved my tips in. Instead of wanting to have trouble with him, because I knowed he wasn't a man that would treat a fellow right, I didn't hesitate, I went and opened my—got the cash register key from Mr. Muller and opened my little bank and counted out four dollars and went right straight up to his store and paid him and I haven't seen Mr. Kyle since then.

To give Johnson a final chance to convince the jurors of Kyle's treachery, Crist decided to walk his client back over the same ground one last time.

No, he had not seen Kyle since that last encounter when they talked about his designs. "When I went to pay the money I paid it to his wife at the store," Johnson emphasized. Nor did he "even say anything about him to her."

Had the conversations between himself and Kyle been at all cordial? Crist went on.

"Well, it wasn't friendly at all," Johnson responded without hesitation. "No kind of way, because when a man talk about putting another person in jail because he think you don't have the money to pay off his debts that ain't very friendly, I don't think." And though he tried to be "as plain and decent as I could" in explaining to Kyle why he couldn't work for him, the kindness had not been reciprocated.[12]

There was little else that Crist felt his client could now add to his testimony. But before turning him over to the prosecution, he tried again to humanize his image as best he could. "Have you any relatives in this section of the country?" he inquired.

"No, sir; not a soul," Johnson replied sadly.

"Have you any intimate friends in this section of the country?" Crist continued, broadening the picture he wished to paint for the jury.

"Well, no, sir; I did have but I don't think I got them now," Johnson answered.

"Have you any money or means of any kind?" his attorney added.

"No, sir," Johnson again responded, not a penny.[13]

"Now, is there anything else Johnson you would like to tell the jury about this matter?" Crist added, wanting to overlook nothing and to give Johnson a chance to make a final plea to those sitting in judgment of him. "If there is," he continued, "tell it."

"Well, Mr. Crist and Gentlemen of the Jury," Johnson began, knowing that his life depended upon these final remarks,

All I can say I don't know anything about this murder of Angelina Jaramillo. I never seen her before in my life. I don't even know she lived there on that Johnson Street wherever they said she lived. And this story that Mr. Barnes told about me being over there about two months ago during the Fiesta, something like that, I was over there, but not the way he told that story about it, the way he seen me etc., not even the spot where he told the court that he seen me. When I met Mr. Barnes I was on Johnson Street at the side of Mr. Robinson's house, and he came around the corner of Griffin Street coming from the North. He just turned around the corner, me being right there at Griffin Street right at the side of Mr. Robinson's house. . . . Griffin Street was in front of me. When this car rolled past me he says Hey boy, what are you doing. I told him that I was going down to Bill Alexander's house. He says come here and I went over there to him and he questioned me about where I worked and examined the overalls I had on. They wasn't that striped overall, they was a white suit of overalls I had on and they were Andrew's Garage Overalls, and he asked me what was I doing going to a person's house this time of night. I asked him what time it was and after he told me it was away round one o'clock I told him I didn't know it was that late. I told him I was at my house working a little while and didn't have no clock there, building toy airplanes and I thought then I would go over to Bill Alexander's house, and the very words I told him that I would go over there. I didn't say what I was going after, anything like that. He told the court that I couldn't tell the fellow's name or didn't know where I was going, and Gentlemen of the Jury, if any officer meet a man out on the street and he couldn't give account of his self or where is he going, he is subject to be locked up as a suspicious character, anybody knows that. As an officer he wasn't telling the truth in making that statement.

Crist quickly stopped his client and cautioned him not to characterize statements made by someone else.

"I am just telling it like it is; I have to tell it like it is," Johnson wanted all who were listening to understand.

"That is all right," Crist gently responded, bidding his client to move forward without any further accusations against the police officer.

"All right, I take that back," Johnson apologized, fearing that he might have hurt himself by making such an assertion. "I wouldn't say that." Instead he continued to relate only what he had observed, allowing the facts to do the work for him.

At the same time he claimed that he went up—I don't know the name of the street, but he went east, just opposite from the direction he went. I went on around the corner and after he drove off he went straight down Johnson Street to the next block and then he turned at this next block up—I don't know the name of the street but it is the next street east after Johnson . . . and just as I got at the corner him and another man walked around there with a flash light and pistol in their hands, each one of them, and I walked right on past them, and I seen them standing there watching me. I didn't stop no place when they left me, I just kept walking and I didn't stop no place until I turned back to go back home after I found them watching me with them flash lights and pistols. As I walked back past them, they asked me, says you ain't going no where, I thought you was going to a friend's house. I told them I was until I found out they was watching me and walking around behind me, and I turned around and went home. And I went home and after I got there about fifteen minutes, I was in bed and three officers came there and knocked on the door and told me to put on my clothes, and after I put on my clothes, this fellow that seemed to want to recognize me, said I had done something like that, he talked with them, one of them was Mr. Holmes and another fellow that walked that beat by my house, and they said—they must have come to some conclusion that I wasn't the one they were looking for. They asked me where did I work and what was my name and then they told me to pull off my clothes and go on to bed, and that was all about that.[14]

Though Johnson had ably countered the important elements in the prosecution's case against him, Crist felt certain that he would have to assist him during the difficult cross-examination that lay ahead. Nodding to the judge that he had finished his questioning, Crist took his seat and waited.

Johnson had spoken for an hour and a half, but at 10:12 A.M., Otero instructed the jurors to retire to their room for ten minutes.[15] Everyone seemed grateful for the chance to catch his breath.

A Lawful Verdict

THE *New Mexican* would publish two editions on that last day of the trial. Delaying the first until all of the testimony had been completed, the reporter rushed his copy to the editors shortly after 2:00 P.M. "On the stand at the opening of the morning session today, Johnson flatly contradicted the testimony of [the] state's witnesses," he wrote of Johnson's early morning responses to Crist's final questions.

Far less neutral, however, was the newspaper's characterization of Johnson's treatment of the cross-examination that immediately followed. "Ready with an explanation of everything—everything but the fingerprints on the shattered glass vase," Johnson was said to have "glibly" told a story that "was at wide variance with the testimony of a half-dozen or more of the state's witnesses. Once on cross-examination he almost slipped," the reporter noted. "District Attorney J. J. Kenney was quizzing him about the road to Albuquerque." But "Johnson quickly recovered himself," he added with disappointment, "and from that point all the way into the Duke City his memory was a perfect blank."[1]

Ultimately, it would be left not to the newspaper's readers, but to the jury to decide whether Johnson or the prosecution had spoken the truth.

It was clear from the beginning of Kenney's cross-examination that he intended to portray Johnson as a liar whose every word was rightfully suspect. But as the day's testimony ended, Kenney would acknowledge that he had been "unable to tangle Johnson in any part of the story."[2]

"Were you ever known as Thomas Fisher?" Kenney began his efforts.

"No, sir," Johnson answered truthfully.

"When you were at Dayton, Ohio, three years, did you have a criminal record under the name of Thomas Fisher?" he asked again.

And again Johnson answered no.

Kenney responded by asking the question a third time. Receiving a third negative response, he showed Johnson a copy of his record from the New Mexico State Penitentiary and asked him to tell the jury what it told of his criminal past.

Crist immediately objected. "The card, it speaks for itself," he protested, aware that Kenney wanted Johnson to repeat this history point by point in order to have him destroy his own credibility.

"Overruled," the judge responded.

"Exception," Crist noted.

Kenney, however, withdrew his request for a reading of the card, perhaps fearing that he might be offering Crist yet another avenue of appeal. Instead he tried a fourth time to have Johnson admit that he had once been known as Thomas Fisher.

He had been arrested and jailed in Dayton, Johnson replied, but he had used his given name of Bishop, and not Fisher.[3]

Embarrassed for not having caught his own error, Kenney moved on from this line of questioning and inquired about "the colored man" who told Johnson that "grandma" was ill.

Johnson repeated what he had earlier related to the court, that he did not know or ask the stranger his name.

But Kenney refused to accept his response. "And yet he stepped up to you on the street and knew who you were?" he asked disbelievingly.

Not exactly, Johnson rebutted. "He didn't appear to be that he knowed me because he asked me did I know a person in Albuquerque by the name of M. T. Glen."

"He just stepped out of the clear sky," Kenney responded, "and told you grandma was sick?"

"No, sir," Johnson answered. "He didn't step out of the clear sky, he drove up on the curb in a car and called me to him."[4]

Perhaps Johnson hadn't been to grandma's at all, Kenney implied with his next set of questions. Johnson had testified to knocking on her door, but, "Why didn't you use the bell?" he asked.

"I didn't ring the bell because they was no bell there when I was there before and I always knocked on the door; otherwise when I went there I just open the door and went past." And so, as before, he had "tried the door and knocked," but there had been no answer.

"You know there is a bell there, don't you?" Kenney pressed further.

"No, sir, not until you said so,"[5] Johnson replied without a sign of wavering.

Nor could Kenney shake Johnson's testimony concerning the person who had given him a ride to Albuquerque, just a white man with a Colorado license plate who appeared to be a salesman "according to the looks of the luggage he had."

"And you don't know who you came back with either?" Kenney went on in an incredulous tone.

"No, sir; I didn't ask his name and he didn't ask mine," Johnson responded, repeating his earlier testimony.

Could he provide a physical description? the DA asked.

"He was a tall white man," Johnson offered, "drove an International truck, appeared to be a mercantile or commercial truck according to the goods he had on the truck."

More significant for the prosecution, however, was Johnson's alleged time of return to Santa Fe, about which Kenney now pressed even harder.

"According to this man that I was on the truck with," it was about 9:00 P.M., Johnson insisted.

But Kenney remained unsatisfied. Key witnesses had testified to seeing him in Santa Fe much earlier that evening. If Kenney could crack the foundation of his story, the rest would crumble. "Was it long after dark?" he asked, his tone more agitated than before.

"Yes, sir; it was dark before we got in the city limits, long before we got in the city limits," Johnson held firmly.

But if so, where had he been when he noticed it had gotten dark? Kenney wanted to know.

Being unfamiliar with the area made it impossible to pinpoint the spot, Johnson responded.

Could he describe it, then? Kenney wondered.

He couldn't "because it was dark and I don't know where I was," he answered. He had, of course, noticed a number of things along the road as he passed them on his way to Albuquerque that morning, "but places you cannot see at night you cannot tell exactly."

Growing more exasperated with each response, Kenney tried to shake Johnson's testimony by mentioning specific sites, hoping he would misspeak.

But again, he would not be caught. "I don't know that either," Johnson remarked concerning the last location on the prosecution's list. "I wouldn't say I did because I don't remember that place."

"But you wouldn't say you didn't?" Kenney insisted.

"I don't know how to answer that," Johnson retorted.[6]

Frustrated by Johnson's persistence, Kenney then tried to pin him down to certain precise times for his movements once he was dropped off at Cerrillos Road.

But after several attempts, Johnson shot back, "I already said I don't know, and I wouldn't figure the time, because I don't know."

Undeterred, Kenney decided to walk Johnson back through his own testimony. Had it not already grown dark long before he reached Santa Fe? he asked. And if so, would he not have reached Quintana's steps "mighty close to ten o'clock?"

"I presume it was," Johnson was willing to concede.

Then why had Quintana testified to a time nearly three hours earlier? Kenney inquired incredulously, as if he had finally broken through his adversary's defense.

Because "he didn't tell anybody he wasn't at home when I got there," Johnson responded without hesitation, hoping that the jury would accept his explanation for this discrepancy.

And so it went, with Kenney setting specific times to each of Johnson's movements about town and Johnson refusing to agree to any of them. Only when they reached his struggle with Churchill was Johnson willing to set a time. "They have a big clock in the corner," he noted, "and I noticed it was twelve o'clock and a little bit past." "I am sure it wasn't over two minutes past twelve," he insisted when Kenney questioned his recall. "I saw that when I sat down and looked at the clock."

"Isn't it the truth," Kenney dramatically interjected, leaping forward for emphasis, "that you went straight to the garage from the home of Angelina Jaramillo?"

"No, sir," Johnson responded just as dramatically. "I never was in that neighborhood that night."[7]

But Johnson's denial could not uproot the seed Kenney had planted. Allowing it to germinate, Kenney moved on with his questioning, readying his return. "You saw Churchill laying here and testifying that there wasn't any argument between you," he pointedly remarked.

"I couldn't help what he said," Johnson replied. "I said we argued."

"Which of you is telling the truth?" Kenney asked after detailing the discrepancy in their testimonies.

"Mr. Kenney, I will tell you these things right in front," Johnson rebutted. "Anybody coming in that door to trade or do anything a person could see him not laying on the settee like he said he was."

But Kenney continued to press Johnson on this point, trying again and again to portray him as a liar, asking him if he would "swear Churchill is not telling the truth."

"That is just what I did," Johnson reminded everyone present, despite Kenney's insinuation to the contrary.[8]

Moving next to the blood found on his clothing, Kenney wanted Johnson to explain how drops had gotten on the inside of the coveralls.

"Put my hands on the inside" reaching for "my shirt there with cigarettes on the pocket," he replied.

"These are drops of blood here, aren't they?" Kenney then asked, pointing to the stains on the shirt.

"Not to my knowing, sir; that is what you say," Johnson responded.

"No, I am not saying that, I am asking you," Kenney angrily shot back, asking if the other spots on the shirt were blood as well.

And once again, Johnson answered, "I don't know whether drops, that is what you say."

Kenney knew that without having analyzed the spots in the lab, there was no proof that they were, in fact, blood. Yet he continued to ask questions as if it had been demonstrated conclusively that the spots had come from Angelina's wounds.

Each time, of course, Johnson disputed the assertion. He would, however, concede that there was blood on the shirttails, as he had in the area of his shirt pocket, but there was an explanation other than the one Kenney wanted the jury to accept. "I stopped out there on the road to urinate," he reminded the prosecutor. "That is when I got blood on there."[9]

But since he had gone back to his room before leaving Santa Fe, surely he had washed after his struggle with Churchill, Kenney asserted.

"No," Johnson insisted repeatedly. He had spent only two or three minutes in his room before leaving Santa Fe and hadn't time to wash before he fled.[10]

"Now you deny absolutely having been anywhere near the Jaramillo house that night?" he asked Johnson, returning finally to the central issue in the trial.

"Yes, sir; I absolutely do," Johnson responded, slowly emphasizing each word.

"You know where the Jaramillo house is?" Kenney probed further.

"No, sir; I don't know, no more than what I hear," he answered.

"You knew Angelina Jaramillo in her life time," Kenney continued, as if he were stating a known fact.

"No, sir; I didn't," he replied. "If I knew her I didn't know her by name; just seeing her on the street, I didn't know who she was."

"You know Bob Smith?" the prosecution pressed on, still attempting to drag the desired admission from the defendant, if only indirectly.

"Yes, sir; I know Bob Smith but that is not Angelina Jaramillo," Johnson answered, quickly drawing an important distinction for the jury to consider.

"You have seen him many times at your garage?" Kenney added.

"That is all, just seeing him," Johnson replied.

"You have seen him there with Angelina?" Kenney tried again.

"No, sir. Never noticed him there with a woman since I have been working there,"[11] Johnson once again insisted, unwilling to be moved an inch away from his earlier testimony.

Kenney found him equally unmovable when he turned next to the night in question. "I don't know anything about that night of the murder," Johnson insisted in response to the prosecution's repeated assertions to the contrary.

How, then, could he explain his fingerprints being on the vase, "if these should happen to be your finger prints?" Kenney asked.

"Well, according to what that man said they must be them, but I don't see how they got there, because I wasn't in that neighborhood," Johnson responded, a quizzical expression suddenly appearing on his face as he stared at the jury. There was clearly something wrong with the whole matter of the fingerprints, was there not? he asked Kenney as he turned the tables on the prosecution. "You know there is just as many ways to prosecute a man by his finger prints as there can have some falseness about it," he remarked further.

"I don't know that," Kenney responded impatiently.

"You would know it because you are the prosecuting attorney," Johnson snapped in return.

"Think I would prosecute a man I believed to be innocent?" Kenney asked, attempting to court the jury's support.

"I don't know," Johnson responded, lingering again over each word for emphasis.[12]

Crist covered much the same ground as Kenney during the redirect questioning that followed this final exchange. There were several issues raised by the prosecution that simply had to be gone over again. He especially wanted Johnson to show the jury how he had been dressed at the time of the murder. It was important for those who were to judge his client to have a vivid image of how the blood had gotten onto his hands and clothing. But only after Johnson struggled for several minutes to put on the two shirts he had worn that night did the judge finally instruct the sheriff to unshackle his hands.

"I have left the hand cuffs on, as you understand, because I considered it to be for the public interest and safety, as well as the safety of the defendant himself," Baca disappointedly told Otero as he removed the cuffs.

Johnson then knelt down as he had that night. Showing how Churchill's "head was laying right in my hand," he explained that his blood ran "all over my hands . . . between my fingers and wrist and every place that was in the way." After he moved around and put his hands in his pockets, the blood had ended up in a number of places and had remained there, Johnson explained.[13]

However, the spot on the knife, contrary to the prosecution, was not blood, he asserted before Crist could ask.

"What does that stain on there look like to you, basing your answer on your experience and use of red paint?" Crist asked as a follow-up.

"That look like red enamel which it is," Johnson maintained.

But when Crist began to ask that the knife and one of Johnson's shirts be passed to the jurors for comparison, Kenney suddenly interrupted with a startling concession: "I might say at this time the state makes no contention this mark on the knife is blood; I was inclined to think it was but now I doubt very much whether it is blood." Forced to reverse his earlier claim, he tried to further minimize his embarrassment by adding, "It is not material anyhow."[14]

But of course it was, and had most certainly colored the jury's perception of the prosecution's entire case against Johnson. Crist only hoped that the jury understood the problem with this particular piece of evidence and would begin to look on the clothing, the fingerprints, and all of the eyewitness testimony as similarly suspect. Each was riddled with obvious problems, as was the women's burnt stocking recovered by the police from Johnson's stove. Were the remnants from the fire "similar or not to the stockings which you say Mr. Muller gave to you?" Crist now asked Johnson in an attempt to counter the claim that they were similar to those found in Angelina's bedroom drawers.

Both were silk stockings, he responded, explaining that they were used to make a cap to keep the grease from his hair as he oiled the cars in Andrew's Garage. The bottom part of the stockings, however, was not used, and after it was cut away, he sometimes tossed the material into the stove—as he sometimes did with the dirty stocking caps he wore home from work.[15]

Finally, one last question remained, Crist told Johnson and the jury. "Did you tell the officers at Albuquerque the same story you told your attorney when you first talked with him and the same story that you have told here in court?"

"The identical thing," Johnson declared without hesitation.[16] With his testimony now completed, he stepped down from the witness stand. The shackles were then put back on his wrists, and he was returned to his seat at the defendant's table.

With just a few minutes remaining before the noon recess was to begin, Crist recalled Ben Martinez to the stand. "At the request of the court," Martinez had made a detailed drawing of the interior of the Jaramillo house, which Crist was now anxious to use for his own summation.[17] But before offering it to the court as evidence, he failed to ask why it was that Angelina's uncle had been so intimately involved in a police investigation involving a member of his own family. Nor did Crist seek the identity of the unnamed person who Martinez said had assisted him in measuring the rooms and, more disturbingly, in listing their contents.

When court resumed at 1:30 P.M., Ethel Wilson, Mrs. Glen's granddaughter, was asked by the defense if there was any truth to Johnson's assertion that his trip to Albuquerque had been prompted by her grandmother's wish to see him.

There was, Wilson responded, as there was to his statement that no one was at home when he arrived there that Sunday afternoon.[18]

Brought forward as the defense's final witness, Al Muller then corroborated Johnson's assertion that he had gotten the charred stockings from the garage.[19]

In rebuttal, Tom Stewart was recalled by the prosecution and claimed that Johnson had "made a pass" at him while still in Albuquerque, though he did admit under cross-examination that he had not felt at all threatened by the "stark naked" man.[20]

Jesus Baca was similarly recalled and assured the court that Johnson had told him that he washed his knife before leaving Santa Fe.[21]

Oliver Holmes then confirmed Baca's statement.[22]

Crist countered with some additional questioning of Ed Swope regarding the dinner Johnson had cooked on the night of the murder, and when Swope finished his response, the defense rested. It was exactly 2:00 P.M. on the fourth day of the trial.

Judge Otero reconvened the court after a ten-minute recess and gave the jury its instructions. Beginning with a reading of the indictment and a detailed description of the crime Johnson was alleged to have committed,

Otero went on to explain that "the acts constituting the crime may be proved by circumstances" and that in this particular case, "it is upon circumstantial evidence . . . that the prosecution relies to convict the defendant." "The proof need not be the direct evidence of persons who saw the offense committed," he further stressed. It was proper to convict a defendant if the "circumstances connected with or surrounding the commission of the crime" pointed, beyond a reasonable doubt, to his guilt—so long as these circumstances, and any other demonstrable facts, were "incompatible upon any reasonable hypothesis" to the contrary.[23]

Crist had, of course, been right in his pretrial effort to strengthen the diluted definition of "circumstantial evidence" that Otero was now using. Had he prevailed, the jury would have been told that "every hypothesis or theory" had to be "excluded" for a guilty verdict to be found—that the circumstances presented by the prosecution had to be "such as to apply exclusively to the defendant and be irreconcilable with any other theory than his guilt . . . beyond a reasonable doubt."[24]

But Otero allowed his own far broader definition to stand and, instead, reminded the jury not to permit their prejudices or sympathies to play a role in making a determination, as the court itself had not. "By nothing which the Court has said in these instructions, nor by rulings upon the trial, has it been the intention of the court to express, nor does it express, any opinion upon any of the facts in issue in this case," he asserted.[25]

Of course, neither the jury nor the court could succeed in following this dictum. Johnson, Negro ex-convict, stood before them as he was, and in comparison to his alleged victim. As Dolores Otero DeBurg scolded the *Albuquerque Journal* on the last day of the trial, "The fact still remains that the Jaramillos are the Jaramillos, therefore, worthy of the dignity, respect and honor due them, because they are the Jaramillos." Was it not true "that Miss Jaramillo's father, had he lived to attain the fruition of his career, might today be occupying the governor's mansion or gracing a seat in the senate of the United States?" Did the reporters not know of the "social distinction which the family maintained?" How egregious, then, to use such a term as "girl" when referring to the daughter of this notable family and thereby place her "by inference in the same social strata as the negro who allegedly committed the crime against her." To do so, Otero

DeBurg angrily protested, was to utterly disregard "the small courtesies and deferences due to a member of one of New Mexico's representative families."[26]

Judge Otero had already forewarned the jury "not to consider as evidence the statements of counsel"[27] when Crist walked slowly over to the jury and began his two-hour summation. "There was an overwhelming public sentiment against this man," he argued with great passion. Yet they must not allow themselves to be swayed by it, for "when popular clamor enters the jury box, we might as well go back to the six-shooter and the Bowie knife to get justice."[28]

"Until this trial showed there was some question about his guilt, he would have been torn limb from limb if the mob could have gotten hold of him," Crist reminded those who sat in judgment of the accused. But Johnson had been fortunate enough not to be lynched or shot outright and now stood before them seeking a just acquittal based on a fair assessment of the evidence. The defendant's life was clearly in their hands. A wrongful conviction would surely result in his execution, Crist stressed, and "no wrong can be righted" once that had occurred.

Still, however elegant and impassioned he made his plea, however long he reasoned with the jury, Crist knew how little chance there was of overcoming the force of this "public clamor." "Full of surprises all the way through the trial, J. H. Crist, veteran defense counsel, ran true to colors in his arguments before the jury in the Johnson case late today," the *New Mexican* would later begin its characteristic reporting of the trial's final hours. "Grasping the cylindrical part of the glass vase found in the Jaramillo home, as Babe Ruth holds a bat, Crist swung it before the jury," attempting, as before, to discredit the state's position.

How could the state's witness claim to have found a usable thumbprint when it was clear to all that the "thumb stuck out as a knot on a log"? Crist asked the jury. "It was a physical impossibility to get more than a quarter of the top joint of the thumb on the glass," he argued as he grasped the vase. "How much of my thumb can I get on that piece of glass? Take hold of it yourself," he demanded. "See how much of your thumb you can get on it."

Ultimately, Crist asserted, neither he nor the jurors could "check up on the testimony of this expert." Wishing to appear understanding rather than confrontational, he said of Powers that it was "human to err." Yet they were being asked "to convict this defendant on the uncorroborated testimony of [this] one man," he reminded the jury, when, quite simply, "you and I don't know." There was sufficient doubt for an acquittal, he emphasized, and asked in conclusion that they be motivated by Abraham Lincoln's example of compassion: "If I err let it be on the side of mercy."[29]

Speaking of the fingerprint testimony in his own summation, Kenney assured the jury that "no contradiction is possible, not if all the experts in the world were here. . . . The finger print evidence stands before you uncontradicted by the defense and beyond contraction. The state has established this evidence to a mathematical certainty. . . . There is no possibility of error or mistake."

Praise, nonetheless, was due to opposing counsel, Kenney was willing to concede. Crist had "constructed a brilliant defense on absolutely nothing," and for this accomplishment alone he was deserving of recognition. So, too, were "the people of Santa Fe . . . entitled to the highest praise for their marvelous self-control in this case," as most certainly were the many investigators who had helped to solve it, Kenney cleverly added.

But for the defendant there could be nothing but the basest contempt. Echoing the judge's characterization of Johnson's defense as being little more than "an alibi,"[30] Kenney cut further into it by declaring, "How rotten an alibi it must be when it has to depend upon the statement of a defendant, a three-time convict whose credibility amounts to zero." What was his account of that night worth when it contradicted all of the other witnesses? he asked. "Told by the police in Albuquerque that he was wanted for murder, he told his story then and he tells his story now because he was faced with the absolute necessity of protecting himself." There should be no doubt of Johnson's guilt simply because "Mr. Crist tells you that this man told the jury the same story he told the police in Albuquerque," Kenney advised.

"Who knows how long this man was in that house," he added in an attempt to raise anew the fears that had first gripped the community just three weeks earlier. And then, with the attention of the courtroom once again riveted on the accused, Kenney lifted his face upward and shouted, "The blood of Angelina Jaramillo cries to heaven for vengeance," before turning back toward the jury and pleading with them to do what was right: "This mother, broken in spirit, and this man, Oscar Churchill, fiendishly beaten, are to be avenged."[31]

It was 6:00 P.M. when Kenney finished, but Otero was confident that little time would be needed by the jury to reach a verdict. And so he sent the jury out to deliberate. Ten minutes later, one of the bailiffs returned to the courtroom and announced that a decision had been reached. Judge Otero reconvened the court and reminded those present against any outburst after hearing the verdict. But word soon came back that the jury was reconsidering its decision. Otero once again recessed the court. Disappointed, "the crowd slumped in its seats and resumed its waiting," the New Mexican would later report.[32]

For the next two hours, Johnson sat shackled and utterly alone at the defendant's table, wondering how it had all come to this, here in this desert town, thousands of miles and so many years away from where his life had begun. None of his relatives now knew where he was. Years earlier, he had chosen to spare them the heartache and embarrassment that his imprisonment for a far lesser crime would have caused them.

Crist suddenly appeared, lit a cigarette for his client, and quietly told him that a hung jury now seemed possible. The spectators themselves feared as much. Johnson hesitated a moment and then managed a slight smile as Crist got up and left the courtroom again, believing there was still time enough for a quick dinner.[33]

But he had miscalculated. At 8:45 P.M., the jury returned and the court was called back to order. Crist, who was still in a nearby restaurant, had to be summoned before the verdict could be read.[34] "I want to repeat at this time to the audience that we don't want any demonstration whatsoever," Otero began, and then, turning to the jury foreman, asked to be handed the verdict. "We, the jury," Otero read aloud, "find the defendant, Thomas Johnson, guilty of murder in the first degree in manner and form as charged in the information." "So say you all, gentlemen?" he asked.

"Yes, sir," they answered as one voice.[35]

"Johnson sat unmoved as Judge Otero read the verdict," the New Mexican reported the next day. There would be no display of sympathy by the press, no ground yielded to this murderer, no attempt to understand his lack of outward response as anything other than proof of his cold-

FIGURE 25. The jury that convicted Tom Johnson
gathered outside the courthouse.

Reproduced from *Master Detective*, "The Clue of the Lipstick"
(March 1935), in the collections of the Library of Congress.

blooded nature, though a similar blanket of silence had suddenly fallen
over the courtroom as well that evening. A sacred ritual was about to be
enacted, and reverence of a kind was due the sacrificial lamb. The gods
would have their revenge, and the community would be restored. Justice
was about to root out the evil that had been visited upon them all. So
quiet had it become that "several whoops, muffled by the closed doors,"
could be heard coming from the stairway below.[36]

Crist broke the spell by asking that the jury be polled. "As your
names are called, gentlemen, stand up," the judge ordered. And as he ran
down the list of twelve, each stood in turn to affirm the verdict as written
and read. But when he read out the last name before him, a puzzled

expression came over the juror's face. "That isn't his name," the court interpreter told Otero as he handed him the correct name to call. The man stood and affirmed his decision, and then, together with his fellow jurors, was excused.[37]

There was only one matter now remaining, but Otero chose to first thank those involved in the proceedings before dealing with it. The police, bailiffs, and spectators were each acknowledged by him with appreciation. So, too, were the jurors. "I believe your verdict is correct," he told them. "The court concurs."

Crist, who had labored without payment on behalf of his client, was the next to receive Otero's praise. "I fulfilled my duty to the best of my ability," he responded. But it was Kenney for whom Otero had reserved his final words of thanks. Speaking at some length about the "absolutely fair" manner in which the prosecution had conducted its case, he told those assembled in the court that "the people of this district are to be congratulated upon having a district attorney like Mr. Kenney."

Taking his cue from Otero, Kenney stood and addressed them as well. "My gratification is based upon the wonderful spirit of law observance which has been shown by the public generally," he began. "I do not believe any other community anywhere could have behaved more admirably under the strain of the situation."[38]

As Kenney sat back down, Otero turned to Johnson and ordered him to stand. Unsure of what he was to do at this point and apparently dazed by the reality of an outcome he had feared from the moment he was first accused of Angelina's murder, Johnson stepped onto the witness stand. Told to come to the front of the judge's bench, he was asked by Otero, "Have you anything to say before sentence is passed upon you?"

"No, sir," he answered in a barely audible voice.

"Have you any reason to state why sentence should not be passed?" Otero added.

"No," Johnson again responded, his handcuffed arms folded in front of him, as if trying to shield himself from what he knew would come next.

"Thomas Johnson, the crime of which you have been convicted is perhaps the cruelest ever committed in the State of New Mexico," the judge began. "No useful purpose can be served by repeating the details which have been presented to the jury. I wish to add this, however: Let the doom that awaits you serve as a solemn warning to any person who on any future date may even contemplate a like crime."[39]

With this said, Otero then issued his decree, reading a well-prepared statement as if the verdict had long been anticipated:

> It is the Judgment and Sentence of the Court that the said defendant be taken into custody by the sheriff of Santa Fe County, New Mexico, and be by him forthwith delivered to the Warden, otherwise known and designated as the Superintendent, of the New Mexico State Penitentiary; that on Friday, the twelfth day of February, a.d. 1932, at some time between the hours of 12:01 am and 11:59 p.m. of said day, the said Warden is hereby ordered and directed to place said defendant in the Electric Chair situated within the walls of said penitentiary and that the said defendant be then and there executed in the manner provided by law by electrocution, that is, by the passing of a current of electricity through the body of the defendant of sufficient intensity to cause his death, and by the continuance and application of such current through his body until he is dead."[40]

It was as if Otero, having first offered words of praise for Crist's efforts, had sought to mock his final plea and then to disparage the defendant's race. Even the *New Mexican* felt moved to comment on the date chosen. "There was a touch of irony in the sentence passed on Johnson by Judge M. A. Otero, Jr., in the crowded smoke-filled district court room last night—unintentional, of course. The date set for the electrocution . . . is the birthday of Lincoln, the Great Emancipator, whom J. H. Crist, defense counsel, quoted in his final remarks to the jury."[41]

Shortly after 9:00 P.M., Judge Otero lowered his gavel and the court's business was concluded. It was but three weeks since Angelina's lifeless body had been discovered, but in that time, Johnson had been arrested, charged, tried, and convicted. With sentencing now completed, he was hurried into an adjoining room, and there he waited with Sheriff Baca and his armed deputies until all of the spectators had left the courtroom. Then, as Otero had ordered, he was delivered to the state penitentiary to await his execution.

"There was a crowd of 100 or more waiting outside when the sheriff came downstairs with the prisoner, waiting to get a glimpse of the negro," the *New Mexican* reported. "But there was no demonstration." None was needed. The process had gone as smoothly as Angelina's grandfather had promised his people it would.

"On the way out to the penitentiary Johnson maintained silence," the newspaper again noted.[42] But what more could he have said?

Innocence Abandoned

"IN a cell at the state penitentiary today, Tom Johnson began the first of the few more than 60 days that are to pass before he goes to the electric chair," the *New Mexican* was pleased to report to a community whose well-being now seemed more assured. The Negro rapist and murderer had been placed under the tightest security. As a "safe-keeping" prisoner, he was being held in solitary confinement and would remain there until the period allotted for an appeal had elapsed, at which time he was to be transferred to the "death house," the last stop before his final walk.[1]

Not that there was much chance of Johnson filing such an appeal, the report continued. The cost of a typed copy of the trial transcript, without which such an effort would certainly prove futile, was itself far more than a penniless convict could hope to manage. There was, of course, the chance that some might feel a sudden touch of sympathy for the condemned man and seek to help him. But the *New Mexican* cautioned against such a decision, advising its readers to recall instead that "the negro [had] committed eight felonies and one misdemeanor in the space of three hours" and that even if the jury had found him innocent of the murder charge, a "conviction under any one of the felonies . . . would [still] have resulted in imprisonment for life of the negro under the New Mexico habitual criminal law."[2]

The next day, the *New Mexican* issued a short editorial statement to honor the work done by the "Counsel for Defense." "In the legal annals of the state the performance of Jacob H. Crist will go down as a classic," Dana began his commentary. "Mr. Crist put on one of the finest public-defender exhibitions in judicial history, despite the fact that appearing for an abhorred criminal charged with a frightful crime is a distasteful and unpopular role. The manner in which the veteran lawyer discharged his duty in the midst of an atmosphere of bitter community hostility and indignation was most creditable and has added laurels to a picturesque and brilliant career."[3]

Similar sentiments were expressed by the Santa Fe Bar Association in a personal letter to Crist, a copy of which the association had sent to the newspaper for publication as well. A certain level of professional effort was expected of court-appointed attorneys, regardless of the "atrocious character" of the crime being charged. But Crist's services had been "exceptional," the association's president noted with pride. "Your efforts on behalf of the defendant were untiring, and showed outstanding skill as a lawyer"—"a high compliment to our profession," of which Crist was surely "an honored member." More importantly, though, "Your conduct in this case and the able service rendered by you forecloses any charge that might have been made that the defendant was not properly defended, or that he did not have a fair trial."[4]

But Crist knew that the same could not be said for the court. A number of errors made by the bench might be exploited on appeal. Yet for the moment, his hands were tied. Unless sufficient funds could be found, there was no chance of continuing the fight for his client's life. Even if Crist had wanted to undertake the appeal pro bono, his own financial reverses made it impossible for him to do so.

Judge Otero had by this time sent an official notice of the judgment and sentencing to Governor Arthur Seligman,[5] as well as a "Death Warrant" to Warden Swope at the state penitentiary. It would be his responsibility "to execute the provisions of said order and judgment in the manner and on the date therein provided."[6]

And there were other directives issued by the court that day, including those concerning the payment of fees to several of the prosecution's professional witnesses. Frank Powers, the prosecution's fingerprint expert, was to receive the highest of these, $125 per diem, five times that of Detective Martin, plus mileage.[7] Only Loren Elliott, who testified at the request of the defense concerning the physical examination he gave Johnson, would have to bill the state and then wait a period of seven months to be compensated.[8]

Two days after the death warrant was received at the prison, the *New Mexican* ran a story about the heroic "labor of two young men who are known by numbers at the state penitentiary," without whose "care and skill of a high order" the fingerprint evidence "generally believed to have cinched Johnson's conviction" would certainly have been destroyed. Working nonstop for more than twenty-four hours, "from Tuesday night until well into Wednesday night," they had removed the dust from the prints, "speck by speck," so that they could be photographed.

No mention, of course, was made of the possibility of error, or worse. Instead the newspaper, in its implied contrast between the Negro killer and the white inmates who had helped to convict him, chose to give back to the "pleasant-looking young convict" and the "front office employee" the identities that had been taken from them at the time of their own incarceration. Where the *New Mexican*'s editors had long labored to strip Johnson of his humanity and to make of him a dark and fearful symbol, they now publicly elevated the two named convicts.[9]

Johnson as a matter of course found himself further demonized the next day when the *New Mexican* reported that Sheriff Baca was now developing a new theory concerning the convicted killer's trip to Albuquerque on the day of the murder. Nearly a month after searching Johnson's room, Baca suddenly announced that jewelry had been found among his possessions and that several items had proved to be part of a collection stolen from a home in Santa Fe. The other half of the collection was still missing, he said, as was all of the jewelry from another home. Nevertheless, both thefts were now being laid at Johnson's feet. It was Baca's claim that Johnson, rather than attempting to visit with Mrs. Glen, had, in fact, gone to Albuquerque to sell the stolen items. The "Negro's story" was once again shown to be a lie, the newspaper asserted. There could be no further doubt of his guilt.[10]

From the very moment of his arrest, Johnson had expected both the verdict and the sentence that followed. Yet however certain he had felt about the trial's outcome, nothing could have prepared him for the shock of hearing the words *guilty* and *death* pronounced against him. What little spirit had remained after four long days in court had been drained away in an instant. It would take another week before he could begin to conceive of continuing the fight to save his own life.

On December 15, Crist reported to the *New Mexican* that Johnson was at last ready to appeal his conviction.[11] A motion would be filed as soon as the necessary funds could be raised. In the meantime, Crist was studying the possibility of filing a separate motion for a completely new trial, a far shorter process than the lengthier appeal, for which he would need Otero's permission to proceed.[12]

The *New Mexican* reported to its newly concerned readers that while time was running out on both possibilities, neither deadline had yet been reached. And so, as an extra measure of precaution, it had been determined that custody over Johnson would be transferred from the sheriff to the warden, thereby moving the process a step closer to its completion.[13]

Ironically, this change in Johnson's status came on the very day that the national office of the NAACP elected not to involve itself in his case. Following the lead of its Albuquerque chapter in choosing to believe that Johnson was guilty simply because "the court found him so," they, too, had abandoned Johnson to his fate.[14] Established in August 1913 by five men and one woman, the Albuquerque chapter of the NAACP had, over the years, actively pursued opportunities for improving the treatment of its small community (numbering 441 in 1930).[15] Now fearing the damage their support for a convicted rapist and murderer might cause them, they had chosen not to involve themselves in Johnson's struggle.

But a small ad hoc group of Albuquerque blacks, outraged by the local chapter's decision, had quickly organized themselves in an effort to raise funds for his appeal and had independently approached Walter White in New York. It was Ethel Wilson, the granddaughter of Mrs. Glen ("Grandma") and a witness for the defense, who, as pro tem of the Defense Club, telegraphed him about the case and told him of Crist's belief that Johnson had a "fair chance to escape [the] chair" if he could appeal the verdict to the state supreme court. The majority of Albuquerque's black community had long supported the NAACP's national office, she reminded White. She hoped it would now be reciprocated. Never before had a request come from New Mexico for political and financial assistance, and though a public meeting on Johnson's behalf was scheduled for the following day, only help from New York could save him.[16]

When the association's final decision not to assist Johnson was reached in New York, it fell to White's assistant, Roy Wilkins, to send the disappointing news to Wilson. Perhaps wanting to first learn of the support enjoyed by the Defense Club for its efforts, he had waited until the day after the public meeting to notify the group of the national office's response. Yet rather than contact Wilson directly, Wilkins sent a telegram to a member of the association's local chapter. "Case is not one coming within [the] scope of [the] association," he told them. "We understand branch also takes this attitude. Please advise signers we cannot aid."[17]

A week later, the *New Mexican* reported that "the negro" was being held in "close confinement," though still not at the Death House, a small, "high-ceilinged, glaringly white" building consisting of just two rooms, one for those men whose last appeals were exhausted and the other for the chair that awaited them. Until those last days, the condemned were routinely kept in cells adjoining those of other prisoners with lesser sentences and allowed to exercise in the prison yard for up to forty-five minutes each day. But Johnson was being denied this "privilege" of a "breathing spell." Instead he was under strict confinement, day and night, as a "disciplinary measure." His offense, prison officials reported, was a "sullen" attitude. He was guilty, they said, of "brooding over his fate" and of speaking only when addressed. And even then he would volunteer nothing and respond in only the briefest way possible.[18]

Crist, unfortunately, was out of town at the time and unable to monitor his client's situation.[19] But someone whose car Johnson had often washed at the garage did show him a bit of kindness a few days later and sent him a carton of cigarettes for Christmas.[20]

Whether anyone could have successfully interceded on Johnson's behalf is, of course, uncertain, given the prevailing atmosphere. Conditions for blacks throughout the northern region of New Mexico had only gotten worse since his arrest. A letter, perhaps fearfully sent in an effort to curry favor with the authorities, appeared in the *New*

Mexican soon after the trial. Signed "A Negro" and addressed to Baca, it praised his efforts in the days immediately following Johnson's arrest. "Please accept my congratulations," the writer urged, "for I feel that we as a whole should congratulate a man of your stability."[21]

On December 30, a black man was arrested "for allegedly attempting to entice a young white girl into his automobile." Accused of approaching the girl as she walked to the store for her mother on Christmas morning, he denied the charge. Brought before the police court several hours after his arrest, he was found guilty of disorderly conduct. "Negro Fined $60 for Advances to White Girl," the *Albuquerque Journal* announced in bold type on its front page the next day.[22]

By the end of the following week, the tiny black community of Taos, a total of eight men and women, had been ordered to leave town within twenty-four hours. A "vigilance committee," formed after several young Spanish women were seen frequenting a black-owned speakeasy, had given the group until 9:00 P.M. to be gone or they would be forcibly removed, the *New Mexican* reported. Though its shortest front-page story, running only three brief paragraphs, its title, "Order Eight Negroes Out Of Town," was printed in the second-largest typeface used that day.[23]

The follow-up piece, buried midway through the newspaper ten days later, gave more graphic details of the incident. A letter had been sent to Will Moss, owner of the Hot Tamale restaurant, and signed anonymously by "Citizens of Taos," that demanded, in large lettering, that "Niggers Get Out and Get Quick." "This is to inform you and your associates and all people of your race, that your presence in Taos or Taos County is no longer desired," it began. "To make it more plain, we warn all colored people to leave Taos within 24 hours." Escorted to the town line by the sheriff, his deputy, "and citizens overseeing the migration," the restaurant's owners, together with a group of musicians who had for some time been presenting concerts on the town plaza, were all gone by the following day. "Once again, Taos has been kept clean of Negroes," the local Spanish language newspaper, *Revista Popular de Nuevo Mexico,* would report several days later.

In truth, the issue was not simply one of morals or even of cultural survival, but of finance as well. The economic rigors of the Depression were now being played out in the racial arena. The recent trial in Santa

Fe had merely emboldened its sister community to the north. What the *New Mexican*'s editor had earlier proposed for Santa Fe, the good people of Taos had now managed to accomplish—and with the Anglo community's apparent blessing as well. "The Negroes who were here held a place that won a very evil name, and it was a disgrace to the town, and if they are permitted to come here again, we well know what the result will be," the editor of the *Taos Valley News* noted shortly after the handful of blacks were expelled. "Taos has a future to look forward to, and the present is not all we are to consider. We want no negro residents here, as it is well realized that if they purchase property, and make homes in Taos, that all living on adjoining lots will be placed in a position most grave, and their property will be of absolutely no value." Clearly, "the action taken by our citizens was with intent for our future good."[24]

On that same day in early January, when Will Moss received his frightening letter from the citizens of Taos, the *New Mexican* reported that a decision to import an electrician for Johnson's execution had been reached by Warden Swope. Though in place for more than two years now, the electric chair had still not been tested. Others sentenced to die during this period were still pursuing their appeals. Johnson's scheduled execution, now a month and a half away, promised to provide a much needed opportunity for training. An expert in the proper functioning of this new device would be needed. But since Johnson might yet file an appeal, Swope had decided to wait before making the necessary arrangements. There was no point in paying twice for the services of an out-of-state executioner, he told the press.[25] The use of taxpayer money implied a sacred trust that could not be violated.

By law, Johnson should have had six months to file his motion, but Judge Otero had shortened the period by scheduling his execution one-third of the way through the allotted time. The de facto violation of Johnson's rights seemed not to catch anyone's attention, neither Crist's nor that of Johnson's supporters as they continued their feverish search for funds. The filing fee itself was minimal, but nearly three hundred dollars was needed for a copy of the trial transcript, without which Crist could not prepare his brief, nor plead the case before the state's supreme court.

On January 22, with only three weeks left before the switch was to be thrown, Leila Smith sent a direct appeal to the governor. "I am writing you in regards to the case of Thomas Johnson, 'negro.' I am a white woman," she wished him to know, "and all I have heard of the case was through the newspapers." But what she had read had left her with sufficient doubt about his guilt. A second investigation of the case was clearly needed.

There were, however, only three weeks remaining before Johnson's scheduled execution, Smith reminded Seligman. "A party of colored people" were working to gather the funds needed for an appeal, but with "so few colored people in this section of the country," great numbers of whom were suffering terribly under the current "unemployment situation, it is hard to raise the money in such a short time."

Sensing that a grave injustice might soon be committed, she implored him to grant a stay of execution, promising that if he did, "I will gladly help them to raise the necessary funds."[26] The governor, however, chose not to respond to her directly, but instead passed her request back to his secretary, who informed Smith that "it will be necessary for you to take this matter up with the Negro's attorney."[27]

But a second request, sent to Seligman on February 3, would require a more personal response from him, particularly given its disturbing, if incomplete, disclosure. Thirty years earlier, E. D. Williams had been appointed New Mexico's commissioner to the Negro Department of the South Carolina Interstate and West India Exposition by territorial governor Miguel Otero, the father of Johnson's trial judge. Since then, Williams's position as an influential attorney within the state's black community had grown considerably. He would be more difficult to brush aside than Leila Smith proved to be. "On the part of many people of the state of New Mexico, I request clemency in behalf of Tom Johnson, a colored man, who is sentenced to electrocution on the 12th of this month," Williams urgently wrote Seligman. "The fact that Johnson is an ex-convict, coupled with his inability to hire ample counsel to defend him, rendered the situation somewhat against him."

Still more troubling, however, was the recently disclosed possibility of another's guilt, Williams told Seligman. Until this evidence was brought to his attention, he himself had remained unwilling to accept the possibility of Johnson's innocence. But he was no longer that certain. "If he is allowed to live," Williams argued, "it may be he will, in the process of time, prove his innocence." To avoid the irreversibility of a wrongful execution, he was now requesting that Johnson's sentence be commuted to life in prison. In response, Seligman personally assured Williams that he would give the matter his "most careful consideration."[28]

Two days earlier, Crist had visited Johnson at the state penitentiary, setting off a round of speculation that an appeal was in the offing. In fact, it still remained a financial impossibility. But fear was already running high, and the *New Mexican,* in its continuing policy of attack at every turn, chose to stoke its fires by reporting that "penitentiary authorities are inclined to believe that an 11th-hour appeal will save Johnson from the chair . . . and add months at least to his life."[29]

On Saturday, February 6, Crist unexpectedly received a phone call from the Defense Club informing him that the three hundred dollars needed for the transcript had finally been collected.[30] For nearly two months now, it had seemed all but certain that an appeal could not be pursued. But over the last several weeks, the club's members, along with a growing number of other supporters, had become ever more convinced of Johnson's innocence. As they told Crist that night, they "would help him toward the chair instead of away from it" if they thought him guilty.[31]

On Tuesday, February 9, a "Motion for Allowance of Appeal" was filed by Crist in district court.[32] It was a procedural formality that Otero was utterly powerless to block. Granted on receipt,[33] Johnson automatically received a minimum ninety-day stay of execution.

That afternoon, Warden Swope was served by the court with a certified notice of Johnson's intent to appeal his conviction. The execution, already being planned, was now postponed indefinitely. Kenney was, of course, disturbed by this latest development, but put the best possible face on the news when he met the press shortly afterward. "This particular prisoner has, in law, exactly the same right to appeal his conviction as anybody else," he explained. And because of this appeal, he continued, "There is no other comment I could have to make about the subject, at least at this time," other than "there is not the faintest doubt of his guilt."[34]

Crist proved similarly closemouthed that day. His plan was to substantiate reversible errors in two or three of the decisions made by the judge in the course of the trial. If he succeeded, a new trial would have to be scheduled for his client. But as he told the *New Mexican,* he would not as yet indicate what those errors were. "We'll talk about them when the time comes," he promised instead. Nor would he discuss in any detail the new information that had come to light since the trial, information that appeared to have significant bearing on Johnson's innocence. For the moment this, too, would have to remain unspoken.[35]

Given the newspaper's handling of the case, it seemed a wise decision. By afternoon, his own interview, together with the prosecutor's, would both be reported under the single heading "Negro's Guilt Certain, District Attorney Says."[36]

An Abiding Conviction

"IT IS TO THE DISGRACE OF THE AMERICAN NEGRO, and particularly of his religious and philanthropic organizations, that they continually and systematically neglect Negroes who have been arrested, or who are accused of crime, or who have been convicted and incarcerated," W. E. B. DuBois protested that April in the NAACP's journal, *The Crisis.* "One can easily realize the reason for this," he continued, for "ever since Emancipation and even before, accused and taunted with being criminals, the emancipated and rising Negro has tried desperately to disassociate himself from his own criminal class." But in this struggle for acceptance, DuBois argued passionately, "he has been all too eager to class criminals as outcasts, and to condemn every Negro who has the misfortune to be arrested or accused." In May of 1934, DuBois would choose to resign from the association rather than support the integrationist desires of the small black bourgeoisie over the needs of the many accused and abandoned.[1]

Though helped by the handful of individuals who had organized the Defense Club and had raised the little he needed to begin his appeal, the absence of this larger organization's support would soon threaten to compromise all efforts to save Johnson. Filed with the district court[2] on March 2, the Notice of Appeal was accompanied by a request from Crist for all documents in the case. This was to include the complete transcript of the trial as prepared by the court stenographer.[3] But Judge Otero would wait until April 29, more than two months after the request had been made, before authorizing the delivery of this material.[4] After an additional delay of a week, the documents finally arrived at Crist's office, together with a bill for $263.40.[5]

On that same day, May 6, the State of New Mexico was served with a "Citation on Appeal" ordering it to appear in state supreme court thirty days after the appellant's brief was received. It would be the task of Attorney General E. K. Neumann "to answer said appeal and to show cause, if any there be, why the judgment of the said District court should not be corrected and speedy justice administered to the parties in this behalf."

Yet however much the onus now appeared to rest with the state, in truth, it sat squarely on the shoulders of the condemned and his attorney. As the *Albuquerque Journal* prominently noted in its front-page report, Crist had but "thirty days to file his brief . . . in the appeal of Tom Johnson, negro."[6] But on June 4, Crist submitted a second motion with the court requesting a two-week extension. As he told the court, "pressing professional work and business absences from his office had detained [him] from giving the necessary study and work to the preparation of a competent brief in a case of such grave importance." With the consent of the attorney general, the extension was quickly granted.[7] "Crist Gets More Time On Appeal In Case of Negro Tom Johnson," the *New Mexican* reported two days later as part of its effort to keep its readers fully informed.[8]

The appellant's brief, filed on June 20, spoke of five reversible errors in a case whose evidence was "wholly circumstantial."[9] The first of these concerned Dr. Livingston's reference to the criminal assault committed against Angelina. As he had previously argued during the trial, Crist again asserted that this was a completely separate crime, for which his client had not been charged, and that mention of it had clearly been prejudicial. To have subsequently ruled such testimony admissible, over the objection of the defense,[10] was particularly egregious given the fact that "the Defendant is a colored man," he stressed. "With a highly inflamed public sentiment against him, speedily put on trial while that sentiment was at fever heat, charged with the most serious of all crimes—the murder of a young girl in the midst of the Capital City—surely if ever there was a case that called for the utmost caution on the part of the trial court, to see that the rule against other crimes was strictly enforced and a departure clearly justified, the case at bar was such [a] one."[11]

To have then introduced a washer during redirect examination that was allegedly found "under the bed of the deceased" and to identify it as something used in automobile repair was again both procedurally improper and "highly prejudicial," Crist argued further. "In a case depending entirely on circumstantial evidence, it quite naturally would have influence on the minds of the jury." Such, in fact, was the inevitable influence of all "suspicious circumstances" in any "purely circumstantial case . . . and in a case of human life, the law of evidence should be strictly applied," he reminded the court.[12]

Unfortunately, this lack of care had prevailed throughout the trial. "A study of the transcript," he emphasized, "will show the careful student that there are a number of peculiar and inexplicable things in the circumstances and exhibits, and the mind of the Jury must have been befogged." Such a mind was certainly "fertile ground for prejudicial lodgment and fruitful germination of a suspicious circumstance."

Of these, surely Cleofas's failure to say whether her daughter's assailant was white or black, despite her close proximity to him in a well-lit room, "must have been puzzling to the Jury."[13] Nor "is it conceivable that he would have dragged her through 3 rooms [while] continuing to beat her with a vase that must have been broken into bits by the first blow," he insisted. Furthermore, if Johnson's motive had been to cover up his crime, why hadn't he merely stabbed Cleofas to death? Surely the court understood that by not considering these obvious questions, the prosecution had clearly sought to "induce speculation by the Jury."[14]

So, too, did the use of the lipstick "confuse the Jury in a case confusing on the whole," Crist added. The defense had objected to its admission after the district attorney had failed to prove that it was, in fact, the same lipstick purchased by Angelina and used by her on the afternoon just prior to her murder. "No one saw her put it in the dresser in her mother's room where Martin found it," he reminded the court, "and unless it was clearly shown that the tube of lipstick which [the] deceased used the afternoon of the homicide was the same tube Martin found in her mother's room after the homicide, it was inadmissible."[15]

Equally objectionable was the hearsay basis on which photographs of fingerprints alleged to be Johnson's had been accepted by the court. Though the prosecution's expert witness had made neither the prints nor their photographs, he nonetheless had used them to identify prints found on the vase fragments. Otero had initially agreed with Crist's objection, that no link had been established between the accused and these photographed fingerprints, and had ruled that "if they don't connect it up it will be stricken." But when a direct connection could not be established, he simply reversed himself. "These inconsistent rulings were undoubtedly confusing to the Jury," which surely must "have found itself in a maze" by now, Crist further asserted.

Compounding this problem of a "study and comparison" using a "hearsay standard based on hearsay photographs" was the prosecution's failure to corroborate the witness's opinion. Instead "THAT VERDICT WAS BASED ON THE ABSOLUTELY UNCORROBORATED TESTIMONY OF ONE MAN," Crist typed in capital letters, and had to be reckoned with by the high court, as did the fact that far too many hands—Martin's, Swope's, Brunk's, and others'—had "meddled with the finger prints on the broken glass." Such "testimony and exhibits do not appeal strongly to credibility," which they must, he insisted, if the state is "asking the forfeiture of a life."[16]

In ending the brief, Crist argued, finally, that aside from these numerous evidentiary problems, the very instructions given by the trial judge on how this circumstantial evidence was to be used in reaching a verdict "did not fully cover the law as laid down by this court on that subject." Instead of instructing the jury that it could convict on such evidence only after "excluding every other reasonable hypothesis," Otero had used the poorly constructed, grammatically incorrect, and highly confusing expression, "incompatible upon any reasonable hypothesis." Citing case after case in which the word *exclude* was held as essential when instructing a jury regarding circumstantial evidence, Crist asked that reversible error be found in the judge's refusal to use this language when asked to do so by the defense, and particularly where "life is at stake."[17]

On July 19, Crist was served with the state's response.[18] In it, Neumann and his assistant, Frank H. Patton, asserted that "there was no error by the trial court" in any of the five points being relied on by the appellant for a reversal of his conviction. Using a differing set of precedents than Crist, they began by arguing that the "causal relation" between the rape and the murder of Angelina was sufficient to warrant its introduction. Rather than being highly prejudicial and, therefore, reversible error, "We think the state was entitled to show all the facts surrounding the crime at the time of its commission."[19]

Nor had the trial judge erred in allowing testimony regarding the location of the washer, "Instead of being confusing, this testimony enlightened the jury," Neumann and Patton told the state's supreme court justices. Though "merely a circumstance," the jury nonetheless had "a right to consider it for what it was worth"—as they did "the remainder of the 'inexplicable things'" Crist had cited. Each of these difficulties, including even the matter of the lipstick, which, admittedly, Marie Gonzales "did not actually see Angelina place . . . in her bureau drawer, must have been reconciled in view of the verdict," they assured the court.[20]

Similarly without merit was the defense's notion that the photographic fingerprint evidence was based merely on hearsay and, therefore, lacked credibility. Neither could Crist claim that it had been "meddled" with. Such evidence, the state asserted, was admissible, and its applicability to a verdict, "a question for the jury [that] cannot now be disturbed."[21]

Furthermore, the court was within its rights to refuse to use the specific language requested by the defense in giving the jury its instructions, provided that the instruction given was "correct in substance and is so expressed that the jury can comprehend the meaning of the language employed." And both conditions had been effectively met,[22] the state's attorneys maintained. In fact, there was "nothing in the entire case to show prejudice or that the defendant did not have a fair trial," they assured the court.[23]

A week after receiving the state's response, Crist filed his reply and requested that a date be assigned for oral arguments to be heard. "Even if it be admitted for the sake of argument" that a causal relationship did exist between the rape and the murder, Crist began his counterarguments, "the evidence of the rape could in no wise aid the jury in determining the guilt or innocence of the defendant of the crime charged," which is the single act of murder. "The rules of evidence forbid the introduction of that which is immaterial and irrelevant," he repeated, "especially when its introduction is in violation of a well established rule and unquestionably tends to prejudice the defendant before the jury." To permit exceptions to this rule was to emasculate it "until the body of the general rule is dissolved into thin air and we have nothing left of it but a fragmentary mass."[24]

And so he went, point by point through the state's response, noting the violations of accepted practice and established law committed by the district court and emphasizing once again that "in a case involving human life, the rules of evidence and as to the conduct of trials shall be strictly construed." There could be no space left for error in such matters, he stressed, nor could that which was "measurably prejudicial to the defendant"[25] be allowed over the objections of the defense. "For all that is known to the contrary," Crist argued, any one of these pieces of evidence or testimony "may have been the deciding factor, or at least a weighty item which, together with other evidence, produced in the mind of the jury the necessary 'abiding conviction' of guilt."[26] This was particularly troublesome given the court's failure to offer "component instruction" that was unequivocally clear, even to the "unlettered juryman."[27]

For the next six months, while waiting for the state supreme court to act on the matter before it, Johnson sat alone in his cell, seemingly forgotten by the world outside. Finally, on January 22, 1933, Grace Mott Johnson, a white sculptor of some repute, broke the silence that had descended upon the case and sent a telegram to Walter White. Born in New York in 1882, Mott Johnson had studied at the Art Students League and in Paris and was now represented by works in the Whitney Museum of American Art and at the Brookgreen sculpture garden in South Carolina, as well as in numerous private collections. Having visited Taos and Santa Fe sporadically since 1917, she had decided at the age of fifty to migrate westward from New York and had settled in Santa Fe the previous June.[28]

Though familiar with the difficulty blacks faced in the courts, she, as yet, remained "perfectly convinced" of the condemned man's guilt, she told White. A "comprehensive interview" with Detective Martin had left her believing that the convicted murderer was, indeed, "a very dangerous criminal."[29] Still, there was something about the matter that merited attention by the NAACP, she believed. Had the association investigated the case? she asked White. Did he know that the state supreme court's hearing on the latest filing was now scheduled for the twenty-fifth?[30] She planned to attend this next hearing and to meet with Crist later that evening. Should "any [new] material evidence" be presented, she would send it along, "if indeed you need or want any." But beyond this, she foresaw no further personal involvement in the matter, "unless something new should develop."[31]

Two days later, while reading a copy of the trial transcript obtained from Otero, and after meeting with Crist, Mott Johnson contacted Walter White for a second time. "Wish to reverse statement that I am convinced of Johnson's guilt," she advised him by telegram. "No verification of detective's statements to me yet found." Instead, something new had developed that had now transformed her curiosity into concern. There would be a second lengthy letter following this cable, she promised White, though she was still "awaiting your reply to my first."[32]

Roy Wilkins, and not White, responded the following day. Although there had been some communication with "certain individuals" in Albuquerque opposed to the local NAACP's decision not to assist Johnson in his appeal, the association remained without details of the crime or the trial or of the appeal now under way, he informed her. Yet even with the little that was known, Wilkins was certain that it was not the type of case "which comes within the Association's work." Nor did he believe it possible, "at this late date," for the association to be of any extra help, particularly since Johnson appeared to have competent legal help and "ready access to all the instruments of the law in order to effect his release, if possible."

More importantly for the NAACP, "no elements have operated because of race prejudice to deprive him of his constitutional rights," Wilkins felt confident to add. And since "the deprivation of these rights because of color is the particular basis upon which this Association enters into cases," it did not feel itself "justified in making a move in his behalf." Wilkins was, however, willing to pass on to the association's Legal Committee any new information or thoughts that might develop from her reading of the transcript.[33]

Within the week, Mott Johnson was again cabling New York. She had made contact with the Defense Club through one of its Santa Fe members (a woman who worked in the governor's mansion) and had taken on the responsibility of acting as a go-between for the group. "Johnson Defense wish you can advise at once of or send good detective to secure evidence not cleared in trial now for either event Supreme Court sustaining or reversing decision," she telegraphed Roy Wilkins on the first of February. A more detailed "statement of matters and opinion" was to follow, as before.[34]

"Now I did read the Transcript of Record thoroughly—almost without food or sleep—together with the Attorney General's and Mr. Crist's briefs in the space of 48 hours," Mott Johnson wrote Wilkins the next day, "and would not take a thousand dollars for the experience." Out of her reading had come a firm belief "that at the trial Johnson was not proved either guilty or not guilty by the evidence presented (all of it circumstantial) which by no means excluded the guilt of another party or other parties instead of the accused beyond a reasonable doubt."

This had not always been her opinion in the matter, she reminded Wilkins that day. Detective Martin, on whose testimony and exhibits so much of the state's case rested, had seemed convincing when they first met. But with time and further reflection, his statements to her, "*many* of them altogether additional to anything appearing in the record . . . gave me good reason to think there must have been strong prejudice or animus on Mr. Martin's part."

It was for this reason, "as a matter of jurisprudence," that she preferred to see the defense win the right to a new trial. If granted, the defense could then introduce the "new facts" that had suddenly been made available to it, facts that Mott Johnson believed would help separate out what was true in the case from what was not. The NAACP's financial help would, however, be needed before a detective could be hired to further develop these leads—if, indeed, this was the reason for Crist's delay in introducing what was already known, she added with apparent cynicism. After dealing with both sides, she had grown suspicious of the whole lot. Each "it appears to me . . . have much to hide and parties to shield in the case and that their reasons are of a personal and political nature."[35]

In an article being prepared for publication in the following month's issue of *The Crisis,* the NAACP noted once again that "for the most part, the Negro is arrested by an ignorant, prejudiced and venal white policeman and his mere arrest usually means conviction. He gets little to no legal defense, and even if innocent, is apt to receive the 'limit of the law.'" Indeed, "the chances of his getting the worst of it at the hands of the law are ten times as great as those of the white man."[36] This, as Mott Johnson was soon to learn, would be Tom Johnson's fate as well.

Shortly after the article appeared, the Supreme Court of New Mexico issued its decision in the matter of the *State v. Johnson.* First summarizing the "damaging and highly incriminating evidence" presented by the prosecution against "Thomas C. Johnson, a negro," Justice Daniel Sadler, speaking for the court, noted the "apparent improbabilities embraced in the story as related by [the defendant, who] was unable to corroborate it in any material particular." It was, therefore, the opinion of the court that the state had, in fact, "impeached it in many respects" and that the verdict of murder in the first degree returned by the jury was "substantial." On this there could be no doubt.[37]

Dispensing with the appellant's five points and with the oral arguments Crist had presented in support of them, the court concluded on March 28, 1933, that "a careful study of the entire record fails to disclose error in the conduct of the trial. Defendant, represented both below and in this court by the able counsel of long experience, appointed by the trial court, was convicted of a heinous crime and given the sentence prescribed by law. The judgment and sentence so pronounced must stand affirmed and IT IS SO ORDERED."[38]

Final Days

"IT IS A SHAME that the Tax Payers of New Mexico have to feed Tom Johnson for 2 or 3 years," Thomas Hanna, an Albuquerque realtor, wrote Governor Seligman a week later. "He should have been hung the night he committed the Cold Blooded Murder that he did. There never was a worse crime committed in New Mexico. It makes people think there is no justice in our courts. To keep men alive like him is a great Injustice to our Tax Payers." Outraged, but feeling stifled by propriety, Hanna added that "a person cannot write on paper the kind of a man Tom Johnson is."[1]

Responding "with kind regards," Seligman reminded Hanna that since the matter might still return to the courts, it had "not as yet come before the Governor's office."[2]

The *New Mexican,* in its lead story on the afternoon of the court's decision a week earlier, had already warned that while "Tom Johnson's conviction [had been] sustained," there was still a chance, however minimal, that he might yet file a motion asking for a rehearing of the appeal. Though the "Supreme Bench [was] to Issue [an] Order Fixing [the] Date [the] Negro [was] to Pay [with the] Death Penalty," as the newspaper's headline indicated, no one could be certain—nor feel absolutely safe—until this next twenty days of waiting had passed. Nor should anyone begin to feel even the slightest bit of sympathy for the condemned man, they were once again graphically reminded. Such heinous crimes as Johnson had committed—the rape and murder of a young woman, with a knife driven "into her brain"—deserved no less.[3]

Johnson had not as yet decided whether he would file for the rehearing when, on April 10, the *New Mexican* reported that following a series of successful appeals, the first of several new verdicts in the Scottsboro case had been reached. It came as no surprise to all involved that while one of the two white women alleged to have been raped by the young black men now awaiting execution had, in fact, recanted her earlier testimony, the defendant had nonetheless been found guilty a second time. Moreover, the chief defense counsel, Samuel Liebowitz, was himself being accused by the prosecution of buying witnesses "with Jew money." In response, Liebowitz angrily protested that the verdict was nothing less than "an act of bigots spitting upon the tomb of the immortal Abraham Lincoln."[4]

Over the next several months, journalists north and south would concur. *The Nation, The New Republic, The New York Times,* and Philadelphia's *Ledger* would each attack the prosecution and its jury, as would Richmond's *News Leader* and Raleigh's *News and Observer.* Wrote the *News* of Chattanooga, "The Scottsboro case was a battle of prejudices. Indeed it has become such a mixture of propaganda and prejudice that we can not conceive of a civilized community taking lives on the strength of this miserable affair."[5] Nor could Edwin Borchard, the Yale University law professor, who that year wrote in his book *Convicting the Innocent,* "How many wrongfully convicted persons have actually been executed, it is impossible to say. But that these cases offer a convincing argument for the abolition of the death penalty . . . can hardly be gainsaid."[6]

But no such outcry was heard when Johnson's conviction hit the news wires, nor when his appeal was denied—nor when Crist filed the motion for a rehearing. Even *The Crisis,* which that April had carried the story of a Philadelphia man's success at overturning a murder conviction, remained silent, though the NAACP was now more fully informed about Johnson's case than it claimed to have been previously.[7]

After again being granted a two-week filing extension, the "Motion for Rehearing" was presented to the state supreme court on April 27. As before, Crist had been "constantly engaged" in a great number of cases pending before the district court (one of which, the *New Mexican* reported, involved a "Negro Charged With Burglary"[8]) and had been unable to give sufficient time to Johnson's case until then.

It was now Crist's contention that the supreme court, in reaching its decision, had itself made eight identifiable errors. There was no supporting testimony for the alleged cause of Cleofas's head wound, he noted, nor for the existence of a cloth gag whose use was said to have resulted in the lipstick particles being caught under Johnson's fingernails.[9]

Similarly lacking in corroboration was the testimony given by Tony Rael. "The reputation of many of the pool rooms in these latter days" as little more than "gambling and bootlegging parlors" should have thrown a shadow over Rael's claim that Johnson had stopped in earlier than he himself had testified, Crist asserted. As for Kyle's placing of Johnson near the scene of the crime, it was simply the word of a convicted murderer who had previously exchanged "'harsh words' with the defendant, and, as is generally known, has since committed suicide in good health—a suicide of unreported and unrumored cause."[10]

Crist was, however, willing to concede that not all of his previous objections were "aptly" presented, particularly those concerning the location of the washer, the identification of the lipstick found in the dresser, and the claim of "genuineness" regarding the photographed fingerprints. But if poorly stated, the "ground of objection" was nonetheless apparent in each instance and should have been acted upon, he reasserted. To have failed to do so on the basis that the jury must draw its own conclusions from this evidence was to have placed the fate of a defendant in the hands of "unlettered men . . . without ability to check up or analyze"—a most dangerous precedent, he concluded.[11]

The attorney general responded with a short document, dismissing the first five points presented by the defense as beyond the purview of the court. In fact, the "sufficiency of the evidence" used by the jury to reach its verdict was not open to their consideration, at least not according to accepted rules, Neumann argued further. That the court nevertheless chose to examine both the appellant's arguments and the objects in question, and still found no evidentiary insufficiency, was, in effect, a new verdict of guilt. This being the case, what then remained to be considered?

he asked rhetorically. "From all that now appears, we think the motion should be denied."[12]

The justices, however, had not waited until after hearing from the attorney general to begin their deliberations or to reach a preliminary conclusion. By May 1, one day prior to receiving the state's response, Daniel Sadler was already circulating his "Comment On [the] Motion for Rehearing" among his colleagues on the bench. "I have read and analyzed defendant's motion for rehearing. Most of it involves a contention that in our statement of the facts we have misconstrued the testimony of this or that witness. All of this argument, however, would go to the substantiality of the evidence to sustain the verdict. Upon this question I understand none of the Justices entertain any doubt, nor do I."[13]

On May 15, "the judgment and sentence aforesaid" became final. Warden Swope was now *"directed and commanded"* to carry out the state's will on July 21, three and a half weeks short of the maximum allowable time between the issuing of such a warrant and the execution itself.[14]

The *New Mexican* was relieved to finally be able to announce the following day that, "Tom Johnson, negro convicted of the murder of Angelina Jaramillo, will go to the electric chair." Yet still there were two remaining avenues of escape—a governor's pardon or a federal court decision to overturn the verdict on constitutional grounds. Even by 1930s standards, the use of an all-white jury could have been considered a denial of Johnson's right to a fair trial.

But Crist was unfamiliar with the growing number of appeals that had been won on this basis. Nor was the NAACP there to advise him on the matter. And so, Johnson was left with only a governor's pardon to be hoped for—and Seligman had yet to comment on the case. As he told the press, he was still waiting for a petition from Crist on behalf of the "negro" before doing so.[15]

Isolated in his cell, though after a year allowed to exercise out in the yard but only after all other prisoners had been brought inside,[16] Johnson remained unaware of his fate for several days. Swope, never before called on to execute a man, now sought the attorney general's advice as to when in the process he was to read the execution warrant to his prisoner. When told five days later of the court's decision to hold his execution on July 21, Johnson received the news without comment.[17]

FIGURE 26. New Mexico Territorial Penitentiary, Santa Fe, ca. 1890.
Courtesy Museum of New Mexico, neg. no. 15206.

His supporters, however, could not remain silent. On June 14, the governor's "Old Standby Friend J. W. Lindsay" wrote Seligman that "all of your Friends here [in Yado, N. Mex.] have Sign Petition and have sent it up to you all asking you all to Please Don't let Tom Johnson Hang." Lindsay was one of Seligman's oldest black political backers. In his postscript, he asked the governor to "Remember" that he and another man named Brunk "are with you for any thing you wants us to do for you."

As with other blacks before him, Seligman's secretary answered Lindsay's letter, promising only that the petition would have the governor's "consideration."[18]

Over the next several weeks, others feverishly continued their efforts in an attempt to demonstrate Johnson's innocence. With only days remaining before the scheduled execution, Mott Johnson, in a desperate act, cabled Walter White after five and a half months of silence between them. "Please wire Governor Seligman immediately," she pleaded on July 14, asking that the NAACP request a reprieve for Johnson because of new evidence "strongly indicative of his innocence."[19]

But once again, it was Roy Wilkins who responded to her plea. Explaining that White was out of town on business, he reminded her of the local chapter's recommendation "that this was not properly a case for the activities of the N.A.A.C.P." Still, if it would help to secure a stay of execution, the association was now willing to send the governor a telegram. It had now become their belief that Johnson should have "every chance for his life."[20]

Sent to the association at 3:09 A.M., Wilkins had found Mott Johnson's telegram waiting for him when he arrived at his office that morning at nine o'clock. At 6:14 P.M., he forwarded the wire to the governor over White's signature. It had taken the entire day to reach this decision to intercede, but only after he had carefully reworded Mott Johnson's cable so that the task of proving Johnson's innocence would continue to fall outside the association itself: "National Association for Advancement of Colored People respectfully requests Your Excellency grant a reprieve and stay of execution for Thomas Johnson, sentenced to die July 21st, because we are informed new evidence is now being received which strongly indicates Johnson's innocence."

Seligman waited until the next day to respond. With a single sentence, he assured White that his request "will have consideration."[21]

Though Mott Johnson had "given [herself] to the investigation of the case since the beginning of the year," she had not been completely convinced of Johnson's innocence until the previous Sunday, she wrote Wilkins in her follow-up letter of July 16. Nor was she alone in this conclusion. "The majority of the people" were now similarly convinced, including the late archbishop, who earlier had urged Crist to continue this "last ditch" fight. Crist had himself long believed that another man was responsible and, in May, had received a letter confirming his suspicions. Since then hundreds of others had signed a "Petition for Commutation of Sentence," among them, "a blood relative of the murdered girl."[22]

What at first had been quietly whispered about within Angelina's family had soon spread among a small circle of people close to the case and, in time, throughout the city. An "English Canadian whose

FIGURE 27. Chevy dealership, Water and Shelby Streets, Santa Fe, ca. 1928.
Courtesy Museum of New Mexico, neg. no. 91148.

propensities are well known here—an uncle by marriage of the murdered girl," was said to have committed the crime, Mott Johnson told Wilkins. That he was "not brought to witness at the trial" served only to support this claim, she added.[23] That he disappeared shortly after the trial had only added weight to these suspicions.

According to several accounts, Smith had grown ever closer to Angelina throughout the fall of 1931. He had been working at a Chevrolet dealership down the street from Loretto Academy when she reenrolled there for her senior year. It seems likely that their relationship as uncle and niece began to change soon after school began. During the first weeks of the term, she would occasionally stop in to see him while on her way home. Just how frequently these visits occurred at first is unclear.

We do know from her outburst on the afternoon of her birthday party that by early October, Angelina was no longer willing to contain her emotions. Others were bringing boyfriends, but she was prevented from having one. As an eighteen-year-old, kept from the young men of her own community by a set of traditional strictures imposed by her mother, Angelina appears to have found Smith's attention in the weeks that followed too flattering to reject. His Anglo background must surely have heightened his appeal the more that she grew to reject her own cultural world.

It is not at all surprising that Angelina spoke of feeling "queer" in the days before her murder. The many confusing emotions she was now experiencing must certainly have left her adrift between these two worlds and without anyone to confide in. How could she have explained herself to family or friends? How could she tell them of her daily visits with Smith over the last number of weeks?

What actually happened that terrible night will never be known. It is clear, however, that there was no forced entry into the Jaramillo home and that against her mother's wishes, Angelina had worn her best nightclothes that evening. When confronted by Cleofas, she had merely smiled and walked back to her room to await Smith's visit.

Sometime before midnight, once the others in the house had fallen asleep, she quietly let him in. Was she, then, the victim of a sexual encounter that had gone farther than she had initially intended, and that when she tried to stop him, Smith lost control and became violent? Was alcohol a factor, given his history? Or was she, perhaps, already pregnant (the "queer" feeling?) and the victim of a hastily attempted abortion—or of a panicked lover when she refused to consider it?

As an elderly woman, Smith's daughter would state only that talk of her father's guilt had begun immediately after the crime was discovered. Still denying her father's involvement in the death of her cousin, she angrily protested the repetition of this charge, puzzled as to why it was still being whispered around town from time to time. Her cousin, however, was far more willing to acknowledge that it had long been known within the family that her uncle had, indeed, raped and murdered his niece.[24]

It seems now to have been simply a matter of protecting the family from this damaging truth. Position and influence would have meant that they could depend on all of the local authorities—police, sheriff, district attorney, judge, and U.S. senator—to cooperate in the framing of a "negro" whose presence most already agreed was unwanted. The "moral case" against Johnson, as Cutting had written his mother shortly before the trial began, was itself sufficient to warrant his execution.

Without adequate funds, those working to free Johnson continued to find themselves unable to hire the "unprejudiced detective" who was needed to further develop the evidence that was already pointing to Smith's guilt. In these final weeks, Mott Johnson and the others had been left trying "in haste" to save him and had grown "very much exhausted by our last moment efforts to obtain evidence for the warrant for the arrest of the suspected party," as she reported to Wilkins that July 16.[25]

With less than five full days remaining before Johnson's execution and with objections beginning to arrive from notables as far away as New York[26] and as near as Taos (Mabel Dodge Luhan among them[27]), Seligman continued to promise that "the matter will have my very careful consideration."[28]

But there was, of course, more to be considered than the mere issue at hand. As always, a host of political factors were at play. Anglo fraternities and sororities at the state university in Albuquerque had for decades routinely discriminated against "Spanish-speaking" students seeking membership. In an attempt to root out this problem, a survey questionnaire titled "Attitude Toward Natively Spanish-Speaking People of the Southwest" had been sent to three thousand English-speaking high school students earlier that spring.[29] Yet powerful leaders within the Spanish community, men whose positions were dependent on accommodation and coexistence and who, in turn, were looked to by Anglo politicians for their support, were strenuously opposed to the survey and to its underlying assumption of continuing disharmony between the two groups. As Gilberto Espinosa, a well-placed attorney in Albuquerque, had written Seligman on April 27, "I sincerely trust you will not permit this work to go on and that you will take positive and proper action toward putting an end to such foolishness. . . . It is high time that we in New Mexico realize that we are but one people and stop attempting to perpetuate class differences. . . . So long as ignorance exists," he concluded, "racial misunderstanding and prejudice will continue."[30]

On May 8, in the midst of the court's deliberations concerning Johnson's motion for a rehearing of his appeal and only a week prior to the issuing of the execution warrant, a public forum had been held in Old Town, the heart of Albuquerque's Spanish quarter. Under extraordinary pressure, the authors of the survey were forced to agree that it was perhaps misconceived,[31] after which the Resolution Committee, organized by the university's president and board of regents and chaired by Espinosa, forwarded its report to the governor. In it the questionnaire was declared to be without purpose other than "to raise [the] race question that tends to discriminate and disenfranchise the Spanish speaking people." As a consequence, the committee demanded that those responsible for the survey be punished as "an example to future employees" who might forget that "the welfare of the public" was paramount.[32]

The resolution proved to be a reminder for Governor Seligman that the political connections and social position enjoyed by Angelina's powerful Hispanic family had to be factored into any decision he would reach. Their needs could not be violated if he wished to find victory at the next election.

To deal forthrightly with the new evidence available in Johnson's case would have meant certain political death. It would have taken far greater courage than Seligman was willing to express to truly reconsider the case, particularly after a special session of the New Mexico state legislature met with Warden Swope on Monday morning, July 17. A political appointee of Seligman, Swope had quickly risen through the ranks to become chairman of the state Democratic Party. Already scheduled to oversee Johnson's execution that coming Friday, it had become his responsibility as well to select someone to fill the unexpected vacancy caused by the death of one of New Mexico's U.S. senators. Seligman had at first appeared to be on his way to Washington, but support for his selection was now suddenly eroding.[33]

Late that afternoon, Seligman convened a hearing at Crist's request. By now, Warden Swope had already sent for J. E. Owens, a skilled executioner at the Oklahoma state penitentiary with thirty-seven electrocutions to his credit. Owens was to begin preparations for his work as soon as he reached Santa Fe.[34] If carried out, Johnson's electrocution would become New Mexico's first. By statute, the electric chair had replaced the hangman's noose in 1929. Still untried, it was decided by Swope that the prisoner-built device would have an expert conduct its maiden run. For Seligman to stop the execution at this point would clearly have angered his party's chairman.

FIGURE 28. New Mexico Governor Arthur Seligman.
Courtesy Museum of New Mexico, neg. no. 50548.

Behind closed doors, and with only the governor and his attorney general present, Crist began his plea for Johnson's life, stressing that he had come forward not as an attorney, but "as a citizen and a man" charged with speaking for the hundreds who had lent their signatures to the many petitions he now held in his hand. There was substantial new evidence pointing to another's guilt, Crist explained, but additional time was needed before these "leads" could be developed into something that a court would not dismiss as pure hearsay. His request, then, was for a sixty-day stay of execution.[35]

FIGURE 29. New Mexico Territorial Penitentiary, south entrance, ca. 1912.

Photo by Jesse L. Nusbaum, courtesy Museum of New Mexico, neg. no. 61406.

Seligman refused to comment on what he had heard, but promised instead to take the matter under advisement.[36] By Tuesday afternoon, no decision had yet been reached,[37] nor did Seligman take action of any kind the following day. At 1:00 P.M. on Thursday, with no word yet received from the governor, Swope ordered Johnson moved to the Death House, along with Santiago Guardano, a three-time convicted murderer who was scheduled to die right after Johnson.[38]

"Two Scheduled to Die in Pen Tonight: Johnson, Guardano To Chair," the *New Mexican* promised Santa Fe's citizens that afternoon. The exact time had not yet been made public, but it was said that the execution would take place before dawn. The dozen selected witnesses had already been advised to be at the prison by midnight, and "many requests for admittance to the execution chamber have been received by state authorities," the newspaper reported. "In some cases political wires have been pulled by persons who wish to be witnesses," and "quite a few applications have come from women," it added with surprise. There was, of course, still time for the governor to intervene, but it now appeared more doubtful than ever that he would.[39]

Preparing for the end, Guardano had already said good-bye to his family. But no one had come to visit Johnson. Instead, much of his last day was spent together with Guardano in prayer as Father Leonard, the Franciscan monk who had earlier presided over Angelina's funeral, administered their last rites. The *New Mexican,* of course, compared the behavior of the two men and, to the end, filled its portrait of Johnson with negative imagery. "During the day, Johnson, the negro, seemed more nervous than Guardano, although Johnson repeatedly has been described by those who knew him in prison as 'a mean and bad negro.'" And while Johnson, apparently unable to make peace with his God, "could not eat a hearty supper . . . Guardano dined heartily on fried chicken and vegetables," seemingly ready to meet his end, the newspaper reported.[40]

"Shortly before midnight the motor cars, large and small, shiny and drab, began to turn out Cerrillos Road" on their way to the prison gates. Despite the late hour and the chilling rain, the crowd soon swelled to over a hundred excited spectators, men and women alike. "A number of people showed positive delight in the expected pleasure of seeing revenge," the *New Mexican* later commented, while "others seemed to shudder at the spectacle," though they, too, had chosen to participate.

Among the dozen required witnesses was Angelina's uncle, Ben Martinez, an early arrival at the prison gate. A likely accomplice in the cover-up of his former brother-in-law's crime, he appears to have needed the added assurance of watching as the sacrificial lamb was put to death. Howard Kerr, a black Santa Fe barber, was there to represent Johnson. The remaining ten were selected from the city's professional class, all of them doctors, lawyers, or businessmen. Additional seating had been offered to a few area law officers, but more than fifty others from throughout the state had requested admission. Curiously, only Albuquerque would remain unrepresented.

There would, of course, be several journalists present, as would be the state's attorney general. Father Leonard was to pray with Johnson as he walked his last steps and sat waiting in the chair to die, and two physicians, sworn to save lives and to do no harm, had accepted an invitation to play a role in the killings as well. It would be their responsibility to pronounce Johnson dead once the electric current had been sent coursing through his body.

As each of the seventy male witnesses arrived in the warden's office (several dozen women had sought entrance, but were denied), he was searched for weapons and told that smoking was prohibited for fear that someone might become ill in the hot, crowded room. Once assembled and given their instructions, they descended a set of rear door steps and made their way across the prison yard and toward the Death House. A black cat suddenly dashed in front of them and then disappeared into the darkened night. Unsettled, they continued on, and as they entered the room where Johnson would soon be put to death, they filed silently into their waiting seats.

Dressed in his "discharged prisoner's uniform"—a dark suit, striped shirt, and dark shoes—and with his head shaved, Johnson was now led from his cell to the death chamber. Flanked by armed prison guards, he entered the room and waved to the spectators, taking special note of Sheriff Baca's presence. Making no statement when asked if he wished to, he sat himself down and gave a final wave—as if he were "in a hurry" to get it over with, one witness later commented. Whatever his final thoughts, he chose to keep them to himself. Leaving no written message, he remained silent to the end. As the *New Mexican*'s headline conscientiously reported to its readers the next day, "Negro Says Nothing."

Strapped into the chair, a saline solution was applied to his scalp to improve the electric current's conduction, and a hood was then placed over his head. An electrode, similarly bathed in the salted water, was attached to the hood, and a second placed on his leg just below the knee. Father Leonard stood fifteen feet to the left of the chair, asking God to receive the soul of the man who was soon to appear before Him, while Johnson, a crucifix in his right hand, sat silently praying. Owens took up his position five feet to the rear of the chair and waited for the signal from Swope, who stood ten feet in front of Johnson. The equipment itself had undergone three days of testing as a precaution against a "botch" of the operation. Assurance was needed that none of the participants or spectators would be hurt.

FIGURE 30. New Mexico electric chair, New Mexico State Penitentiary,
Santa Fe, ca. 1950.

Photo by Tyler Dingee, courtesy Museum of New Mexico, neg. no. 73466.

At 12:30 A.M., Swope nodded and the current was turned on. Neither
morphine nor a sedative had been offered to Johnson, only the 2,400 volts
that shot through his brain and spread quickly throughout his body over
the next forty seconds. The crowd outside the prison's gates, seeing the
lights dim, sent up a cheer, while a mouse, seemingly frightened by what
it saw, darted across the death chamber floor in search of a safer haven.
As smoke rose from Johnson's stiffened leg, Swope signaled Owens to
lower the power to 220 volts and then to raise it again to 700, a procedure they repeated several times more. After eight minutes, Johnson was
declared dead.

Swope later said that he was certain that Johnson "felt no pain." The
body, after all, had not been "horribly burnt," as some had feared. Only
a "blister halo" on his shaved scalp and a small dark mark on his leg were
later found. "Carried out in a business like manner, there was no show

about the affair either," he was pleased to report that next morning. "We were prepared for any trouble, but no person in the death cell had any firearms and there were no blackjacks." Spectators had been forewarned not to speak or to react should the condemned man make a statement, whatever its content. "There was no hitch at all," Swope proudly concluded. "The executions were a perfect success from a scientific standpoint."

But while all had gone as planned, not all of the witnesses emerged untouched by the experience. As one reporter observed, "The electrocutions were a tremendous nerve strain to most of the spectators who came out of the death chamber pale and excited. Even Warden Swope, who had prepared for days for the event, showed signs of the responsibility of the ordeal."

Yet by morning, he was able to hold forth on the virtues of various methods of execution and on the benefit to all of the death penalty over life imprisonment.[41] Johnson's body had by now been sent to the Rising-Roberts Funeral Home, where embalming had begun before sunrise, though there was as yet no one to claim his remains. Unless someone came forward within the next three days, he was to be buried in the prison cemetery as dictated by established procedure.

Outside the mortuary, a large crowd had gathered in the early morning air and was now demanding to see the body. Hours later, dressed in a striped suit, white shirt, black tie with yellow dots, and high black shoes, all donated by Rising-Roberts, Johnson was laid out in a gray casket, and for the next four days, a period longer than originally intended, many hundreds of men, women, and children filed through the building to see "the negro who was electrocuted."[42]

In death, as in life, public sentiment continued to run passionately against him. Throughout the city, the dominant feeling was that Johnson had received precisely what he deserved.[43] The rumor of Smith's guilt no longer seemed of interest to most. "With few exceptions," Mott Johnson wrote in a three-page press release sent to the NAACP, the National Urban League, and the International Negro Youth Movement, "every Nordic interviewed of whatever station or education considered it a 'nigger crime' and based his or her opinions largely on this assumption."[44]

The *New Mexican* made no editorial comment about Johnson's

demise, but instead reserved its space for praising Swope's "efficient, orderly and workmanlike" manner in carrying out the state's first electrocution. Yet there was displeasure in the fact that so many had gathered outside the prison, Dana noted with disappointment. "It is amazing how widespread is the morbid and grisly desire to see life leave a human body, or to be able to boast that one has witnessed it." Having worked so hard and for so long to promote the image of Johnson as negro rapist and murderer, he was now suddenly disturbed to see the final act begin "to take on the character of a show."[45]

On the afternoon of July 24, Johnson's body was taken to the penitentiary cemetery for burial, leaving the unending crowd no longer able to view the killer they had learned to hate and to fear. As Father Leonard prayed over the casket, it was lowered into the ground. No permanent marker was placed over the grave, and in time, its exact location would be forgotten.[46]

Disquieting Shadows

IT was, as Mott Johnson wrote Roy Wilkins several days after the burial, "a very complicated case with many mysteries, some at least of which we had hopes of solving, had a reprieve been granted." Unable at first to accept the loss, she promised herself some last act of restitution, telling Wilkins, "I still hope to have a somewhat enlightening further statement of this case to send you in the future."[1] But she never would. In time, she, too, would grow anxious to leave it in the past.

Few, in fact, would again ever speak of it, except as rumored folklore or as a bit of local color in this fabled land. It was perhaps best to move on. Within days of the execution, the *New Mexican* reported that "a new colored church" was soon to open in Santa Fe, on Johnson Street. There had been another some years earlier, but with so small a congregation, it had closed. Now it would be resurrected by this same tiny community, on a street perhaps chosen as a sign of protest and continuity.[2]

There seemed to be, in fact, a strange and unsettling irony to much of what followed the murders of Angelina Jaramillo and Thomas Johnson, almost as if the Fates were sitting in judgment over this double tragedy, even unto the next generation. Or so it now appears from afar. Robert Smith had remained in Santa Fe throughout the trial. To have left before it had ended would have cast even greater suspicion on him. But with Johnson safely convicted, Smith, together with the truth of what had actually happened, was sent away by the family whose honor and reputation he had threatened to destroy. Returning to Montreal, he sold life insurance for a while, but by the time of Johnson's execution, he was again unemployed. Leaving the shelter of his parents' home a year later, he remained somewhat adrift until his early death in 1941, though documentation about his later life is sketchy at best.[3]

Mae, too, would ultimately leave Santa Fe as life there grew more difficult for her in time. After her tearoom foundered, she worked for a while as a waitress in the Mayflower Café and then settled in El Paso, Texas, where she remarried.[4] But in 1936, her ten-year-old son Carlos became ill and died. With her family once again gathered at the Rosario Cemetery, she laid him to rest beside his cousin Angelina.[5]

By now, Bronson Cutting, too, was dead, killed when his plane crashed near Atlanta, Missouri, while en route back to Washington. "One of the nation's great men is gone," a federal judge was said to have commented when he heard the news. "Senator Cutting was the friend of the friendless and a pillar of strength for the weak," Santa Fe's mayor noted with a "sense of personal loss," adding that Cutting's "benevolence and charity knew no bounds." Lauded by his newspaper's editor as a great "champion of the poor" and of the native Spanish people, it was "his wisdom and counsel, sorely needed in the nation and the state," that would be greatly missed by all. "Senator Cutting's place cannot be filled soon—possibly never," Dana felt certain. "Later we will realize more keenly than we do now, the loss we have sustained."[6]

"In the untimely and tragic death of your son we, too, have lost a deeply loved friend,"[7] Walter White wrote Cutting's mother, adding his voice of praise to the many others she would hear in the days immediately following the distinguished senator's crash. "In dealing with a subject around which encircles so much prejudice and misunderstanding, as is the case with the race problem, one frequently encounters, especially in public life, individuals . . . as prejudiced as those who indulge in lynching and other evil practices." But not her son, he told Mrs. Cutting. A week later, the NAACP itself would pass a resolution emphasizing that, "Throughout his career, [Cutting] manifested an unsurpassed interest in the well-being of Negro Americans and could always be counted upon to lend his influence to the wisest and most effective means of combating injustice based on race or color."[8]

Six months earlier, Cutting had revised his will to reflect his appreciation for those who had helped to provide him with the opportunity to support this principle. A long list of mostly Spanish names appears. Each person on it was to be given a $1,000 gift of thanks. Miguel Antonio Otero, the judge's father, was a member of this list, as was Angelina's uncle, Ben Martinez, whom Cutting had assigned the task of investigating alleged Democratic voter fraud during his reelection the previous year.[9] But to his editor, Dana Johnson, Cutting left the far greater sum of $25,000, while Jesus Baca, his closest associate, was willed the largest single amount given to any person outside Cutting's own family—$150,000 plus ownership of the *New Mexican*. Several institutional legatees were named by Cutting as well, but only Venceslao Jaramillo's Spanish American Normal School in El Rito received an equally high sum, and one that was many times more than what the others would inherit.[10]

And then, a year and a half later, Dana Johnson himself died of a heart attack at the age of only fifty-eight. "Probably few readers read his page in the light of the objective he had in mind," the *New Mexican*'s new editorialist wrote the following day, December 11, 1936. "We, of course, had the benefit of the knowledge of it. He subscribed, and wholeheartedly and from personal conviction, to Senator Cutting's theories of American government, liberal, progressive, and humane."[11] "What he gave to Santa Fe and New Mexico will always be a part of its finest development," memorialized another.[12]

Eight years later, and only a few weeks after purchasing Cutting's former home, Jesus Baca died unexpectedly at the age of forty-five. He had sold the *New Mexican* not long after acquiring it and, over time, had successfully invested the money in real estate throughout the region. Having built up a large fund over these years, he was finally able to purchase his friend's estate, an acquisition having the deepest personal meaning for him. But death soon robbed him of the happiness he had waited so long to enjoy.

As with the others, the *New Mexican* spoke warmly of Baca and his accomplishments. In an extensive obituary appearing on August 28,

1944, the citizens of Santa Fe were reminded of how he had become, under Senator Cutting's close tutelage, a "popular" official who "handled many important cases" after winning election as sheriff. The loss by the community of one of its most loyal sons, "known for his cheerful disposition and his energizing smile," would be mourned for some time to come.[13]

In the end, only three of the individuals most closely connected to Johnson's death would die in the fullness of their years. Crist had continued to practice law to his last day and, on April 25, 1935, at the age of seventy-eight, had argued a case in federal court. But after a short walk the next morning, he began to feel uncharacteristically tired and complained of a slight pain in his chest. Nevertheless, he returned to his office across from the Martinez family's residence on Grant Street and prepared for a hearing that was scheduled for early afternoon in Judge Otero's court. He lay down for a short rest and never got up. The coroner's inquest, hurriedly convened that day, ruled the cause of death to be a cerebral hemorrhage.

A lengthy obituary filled the *New Mexican*'s front page a few hours later and spilled over inside, as if his death had long been anticipated. "All Santa Fe and New Mexico will be shocked today to hear of the sudden death of Mr. Crist," the paper told its readers. "Learned in the law," he had remained busy "until the end," still practicing his profession as "one of the oldest lawyers in the Southwest." And with good reason. The economic downturn that had previously affected his defense of Johnson had not yet abated for him. During his walk that last morning, Crist had commented to a friend that "collections have been poor." Settling his estate would prove to be a messy affair, and when the proceeds were finally distributed six years later, all of his assets went to cover unpaid debts. In fact, he had left no will, aware that nothing but the home he shared with his wife in Pojoaque would remain.[14]

Judge Otero fared far better financially and lived long enough to be thought of as a distinguished jurist, dying in 1977 at the age of eighty-five, his reputation undeservedly intact.[15] But it was Cleofas Jaramillo who truly acquired a saintly patina with the passing of each year. For weeks after her daughter's murder, Cleofas suffered an "anguished heart," made worse by a host of "sad faces" who came to offer their sympathy, as she would later note in her memoir. "I tried to be cheerful. Tears must be shed in the heart, in secret, and like St. Monica, we must meet the world with a smile."

And so gradually she emerged from her grief and returned to the larger world, first to pack Angelina's things or to give them away ("the piano, the Edison phonograph and her ukulele . . . for music brings more tears when the heart is sorrowing") and then to lease their home, "for I could not stay in it for more than a few hours at a time."[16] In time, Cleofas would move back to their house, only to sell it soon afterward to Hazel Hyde, who, adding it to the adjacent property she had purchased in the summer of 1931, would begin to put together the complex now standing at the corner of Griffin and Mackenzie. A large party attended by a great many of the town's notables, Otero and Kenney and Baca among them, would celebrate the completion of this first phase of her project. Ironically, Hyde's husband, George Blodgett, for whom she had made the initial purchase and built its adjoining studio, had abandoned it and her only a few days before Angelina's murder.[17]

But none of this was of interest to Cleofas. Her thoughts were by now almost exclusively directed toward the work of the Sociedad Folklórica she had succeeded in establishing as the culmination of efforts her daughter had long ago encouraged her to begin. Launching the organization in June 1935 as an attempt to preserve Spanish culture and language against the Anglo incursion that threatened to destroy it, she had come to devote nearly all of her time to recording the stories, recipes, and ways of her people.[18]

Only once in the four books that grew out of this work did she discuss Angelina's murder, remaining steadfast in her condemnation of Johnson and in her repudiation of all talk of another's guilt, though by 1947, Helen McCrossen, a prominent citizen of Santa Fe, would write New Mexico's governor, Thomas Makay, that "according to popular belief among the Spanish people here, that Negro [Tom Johnson] was innocent."[19] Perhaps it was this erosion of support for the verdict against Johnson that led Cleofas to finally admit that the killer was not wearing the clothing Johnson had on when captured, though she had identified these garments at the trial as belonging to her daughter's murderer. Could her late correction to this key element in her testimony have been her way

FIGURE 31. Cleofas Jaramillo, in the years after her
daughter's death, as a proponent of Spanish tradition.

Courtesy Museum of New Mexico, neg. no. 9919.

of expressing doubt without being openly disloyal to those who had nurtured her?

In late October 1956, with her health failing, Cleofas was brought to Texas by her sister and placed in the El Paso Nursing Home, where she died on November 30.[20] When the will she had written at the close of World War II was probated, Mae and her three grown children were named as the principal legatees. There was a small piece of property remaining in El Rito, some worn-out furniture, and an old typewriter. The appraised value totaled $305. In addition, the proceeds of an insurance policy, "on the life of a deceased daughter," remained for others to claim.[21] When an agent for New York Life had tried to pay Cleofas shortly after Angelina's murder, she had refused to accept the check. "I left the money with the company," Cleofas wrote in her memoir. "I could not force myself to touch what I had sacrificed to save for my daughter."[22]

Twenty years after Cleofas's death, Anita Thomas, an archivist at the New Mexico State Archives, placed a brief note in a small, obscure, and unread file of material concerning Johnson's execution: "The murder of Angelina Jaramillo—*uncle-in-law Bob Smith* believed to be guilty. She had a crush on Bob and would come down past the garage to visit before going home." The family physician, Ward Livingston, called it a "Nigger killing," Thomas added. Smith, it was said, "left New Mexico" after the murder.[23] With her historian's ear to the wind, she had heard the persistent rumors that Cleofas had sought to silence and had set them down for others to find.

But when the *New Mexican* published an article the following year describing the complex of apartments at the corner of Griffin and Mackenzie Streets, no mention of this suspicion was made. Two decades earlier, the newspaper, in a memorial tribute to Cleofas, had spoken of "the tragic death of her daughter at the hands of an unknown marauder" and of the "cruel gossip" that persisted afterward.[24] But now, only a short sentence was offered concerning the entire affair, as if an old promise was again being kept.[25]

My own last visit to what remains of the Jaramillo home had left me still haunted by its story, and so when I left, I took the long walk out to where Johnson was put to death. The prison is now long gone, its place occupied by the strip malls that have sadly invaded the southern edge of the city. Across the road and behind a gas station and a Dunkin' Donuts shop, Johnson's body lies abandoned in a barren graveyard.

With proper homage paid, I then made my way to the opposite end of town, where I hoped to visit Angelina's grave. I found her beside her family in their large tree-covered plot, graced by the adobe chapel whose bells had once tolled her death. But her spirit seemed no more at peace to me than did his. And as I stood there and thought further about these two victims, now joined forever by a shared tragedy, I could not help but dream of how much might be gained if we could but redress the wrongs committed in our own names—and of how much more was still to be lost to us if we failed.

Santa Fe, August 2000

Notes

In Pursuit

1. Dan Burrows, "The Clue of the Lipstick," *The Master Detective* (March 1935): 46.
2. Ibid., 47.
3. Ibid.
4. Ibid., 47–48.
5. Ibid., 43.
6. Ibid., 42.
7. Ibid., 45.
8. Ibid., 42.
9. Ibid., 45.
10. Ibid., 45–46; "Negro Is Brought to Prison" and "Confesses Murder of Churchill," *Santa Fe New Mexican,* 16 November 1931, 1, 3. (Hereafter referred to as *SFNM.*)
11. Burrows, "Clue," 46.
12. "Negro Is Brought," 2.
13. Robert Torrez, "Voices from the Past," *Santa Fe Pride* (February 1995): 2; and Judith Johnson, "A Mighty Fortress Is Our Pen," in *Essays in Twentieth Century New Mexico History* (Albuquerque: University of New Mexico Press, 1994), 120–26.
14. "Negro Is Brought," 2; and Burrows, "Clue," 48.
15. "Negro Is Brought," 1–2; and Cleofas Jaramillo, *Romance of a Little Village Girl* (San Antonio: Naylor, 1955), 161.

16. "Call Special Term to Hear Murder Case," *SFNM*, 17 November 1931, 2.
17. "Girl Attacked, Killed; Negro Is Held," *SFNM*, 16 November 1931, 1.
18. "Slain Girl Student at Loretto, Member of Old Spanish Family," *SFNM*, 16 November 1931, 1, 6.
19. Ibid.
20. Ibid.
21. George Brown Tindall, *South Carolina Negroes, 1877–1900* (Columbia, S.C.: University of South Carolina, 1952), 300–302.
22. Ibid., 184; and Donald L. Grant, *The Way It Was in the South: The Black Experience in Georgia* (New York: Carol Publishing Group, 1993), 289.
23. "Thomas Johnson," Kansas Penitentiary, Prison Ledger U, 72, Kansas State Historical Society, Topeka, Kans.
24. H. A. Goette, *Goette's Savannah City Directory for 1902* (Savannah: Savannah Morning News, 1902), 215; *1910 U.S. Census*, "Chatham County, Savannah, Georgia," National Archives, Washington, D.C.; John Dittmer, *Black Georgia in the Progressive Era, 1900–1920* (Urbana: University of Illinois, 1977), 28; and Grant, *The Way It Was in the South*, 220.
25. *Census;* and H. A. Goette, *Goette's Savannah City Directory for 1910* (Savannah: Savannah Morning News, 1910), 601.
26. Dittmer, *Black Georgia in the Progressive Era*, 8–9, 17–22.
27. Kansas Penitentiary Prison Ledger.
28. Ibid.
29. Ibid.
30. H. A. Goette, *Goette's Savannah City Directory for 1921* (Savannah: Savannah Morning News, 1921), 559.
31. Grant, *The Way It Was in the South*, 291.
32. "Bishop, Thomas," Register of Statistics of Arrests, v. 34, 1921, Wright State University, Paul Lawrence Dunbar Library, Archives and Special Collections, Dayton, Ohio.
33. Kansas Penitentiary Prison Ledger.
34. Register of Statistics of Arrests, Ohio.
35. "Johnson, Thomas," Michigan State Penitentiary Register, Michigan Department of State, Michigan Historical Center, State Archives, Lansing, Mich.
36. "Johnson, Thomas," New Mexico State Penitentiary Register, New Mexico State Archives, Santa Fe, N.Mex.; "Negro Confesses Seven Robberies," *Albuquerque Journal*, 25 July 1927, 1; "Negro Jailed in Burglary and Firebug Outrage," *Albuquerque Journal*, 20 July 1927, 1; and "Negro Is Held For Burglary of Eight Homes," *Albuquerque Journal*, 26 July 1927, 1.
37. "Jury Makes Report on Murder, Evidence Points to Johnson," *SFNM*, 17 November 1931, 1–2; and "Coroner's Jury Blames Negro," *Albuquerque Journal*, 17 November 1931, 2.
38. "Jury Makes Report," 2.
39. Ibid.; and "Negro Is Brought," 2.
40. "Coroner's Jury," 2.

41. "Jury Makes Report," 2.
42. Ibid.
43. "Coroner's Jury," 2.
44. Ibid.; and "Negro Was Seen," *SFNM*, 18 November 1931, 1.
45. "Call Special Team," *SFNM*, 17 November 1931, 1–2.
*46. Ibid.; and "Negro Was Seen," 1.

An Enchanted Land

1. Jaramillo, *Romance*, 151–52; and "People," *SFNM*, 18 May 1931, 6.
2. Jaramillo, *Romance*, 152–53.
3. Ibid., 153.
4. Ibid.
5. Cleofas Jaramillo, *Shadows of the Past* (Santa Fe, N.Mex.: Seton Village, 1941), 10.
6. Jaramillo, *Romance*, 14.
7. Ibid., 115.
8. Ibid., 57–58.
9. Ibid., 65–67.
10. Marriage Records, Our Lady of Guadalupe, Taos, 27 July 1898, Archives of the Archdiocese of Santa Fe, Santa Fe, N.Mex.
11. Jaramillo, *Romance*, 74, 79–81; and Reyes Martinez, "The Martinez Family of Arroyo Hondo" (1936, WPA Files, History Library, Museum of New Mexico, Santa Fe, N.Mex.), 5. For brief biographical accounts of Cleofas Jaramillo, see Tey Diana Rebolledo, "Cleofas Martínez Jaramillo," in *Notable Hispanic American Women*, edited by Diane Telgen (Detroit: Gale Research,), 219–20; and Ramón Sánchez, "Cleofas M. Jaramillo," in *Dictionary of Literary Biography*, vol. 122 (Detroit: Gale Research, 1992), 154–58.
12. Jaramillo, *Romance*, 122.
13. Ibid., 114–15.
14. Ibid., vii.
15. Ibid., 87–88.
16. Ibid., 65.
17. Ibid., 64.
18. Ibid., 116.
19. Ibid.
20. Ibid., 121, 123, 125–28.
21. Ibid., 128, 130, 131.
22. Ibid., 137.
23. Ibid., 70, 124.
24. Ibid., 61.
25. Jaramillo, *Shadows*, 51.
26. Jaramillo, *Romance*, 81.
27. Ibid., 14.

28. Jaramillo, *Shadows*, 97.
29. Jaramillo, *Romance*, 140, 112; and Lynne Marie Getz, *Schools of Their Own: The Education of Hispanos in New Mexico, 1850–1940* (Albuquerque: University of New Mexico, 1997), 22.
30. Jaramillo, *Romance*, 140–41.
31. Ibid., 143.
32. Ibid., 141, 145.
33. Jaramillo, *Romance*, 145–46.
34. Ibid., 145.
35. Ibid., 147.
36. Ibid.; and Maria Higuera, "Academy Grad Recalls School," *Albuquerque Journal*, 2 May 1984, 1, 4.
37. Jaramillo, *Romance*, 148.
38. Marriage license of Robert Alexander Smith and Salome Martinez, 5 July 1919, Department of Records, Santa Fe County, Santa Fe, N. Mex. and baptismal record of Robert Alexander Smith, 7 June 1896, St. Antoine Church, National Archives, Montreal, Quebec, Canada.
39. "Santa Fe Keeps Remarkable Record of Three Weddings a Week," *SFNM*, 5 July 1919, 5.
40. Divorce complaint, filed 20 August 1929, Records of the District Court of Santa Fe County; and Deed to 359 Garcia, Department of Records, Santa Fe County, Santa Fe, N. Mex.
41. *Santa Fe City Directory*, 1930/1931.
42. Jaramillo, *Romance*, 140.
43. *Santa Fe City Directory*, 1930/1931.
44. Ibid.
45. *Santa Fe City Directory*, 1932/1933.
46. Jaramillo, *Romance*, 148.
47. Ibid., 147–48.
48. Ibid., 149.
49. Ibid., 151.
50. Ibid., 150–51.
51. Ibid., 153–54.
52. Ibid., 151–52.
53. Ibid., 162.
54. Ibid., 145.
55. Ibid., 156.
56. Ibid., 157.
57. Ibid., 157–58; and Burrows, "Clue," 44.
58. Jaramillo, *Romance*, 158; "Coroner's Jury," 1.
59. Jaramillo, *Romance*, 158.
60. Ibid., 158–59; and "Mother Taken to See Body of Dead Girl," *SFNM*, 18 November 1931, 1.
61. Ibid.

In the City of Holy Faith

1. "Negro Was Looking for 'Angelina': Man in Pen Identified by Woman," *SFNM*, 18 November 1931, 1.
2. Ibid.
3. Ibid.
4. "Handprints of Negro Sent to El Paso Expert," *Albuquerque Journal*, 19 November 1931, 1.
5. Ibid.
6. "Murder Case Hearing at Pen Friday," *SFNM*, 19 November 1931, 1.
7. Ibid.
8. Ibid.
9. "Murder, Politics and the Administration of Justice in Frontier New Mexico: The Hanging of Perfecto Padilla," *La Crónica de Nuevo Mexico* 32 (December 1991): n.p.
10. "Noted Criminal Lawyer Dies Today," *SFNM*, 26 April 1935, 1, 3.
11. "Quietly Married at Presbyterian Manse," clipping, n.d., Prince Papers, New Mexico State Archives, Santa Fe, N.Mex.
12. Jacob H. Crist Probate Record, Santa Fe County Clerk's Office, Santa Fe, N.Mex.
13. "Churchill Comes to; Identifies His Assailant," *SFNM*, 20 November 1931, 1.
14. Burrows, "Clue," 49.
15. "Lipstick Is Found under Fingernails," *SFNM*, November 20, 1931, 1–2.
16. Ibid., 2; and "Finger Marks of Negro in Girl's Room," *SFNM*, 21 November 1931, 1, 3.
17. "Handprints in Jaramillo Home Identified as Tom Johnson's," *Albuquerque Journal*, 21 November 1931, 1.
18. "Lipstick Is Found," 2.
19. "Finger Marks," 1–2.
20. Ibid., 1.
21. "Lipstick Is Found," 2.
22. Ibid.; "Handprints in Jaramillo Home," 1; and "Negro Confesses Seven Robberies," 1.
23. "Lipstick Is Found," 2.
24. "Finger Marks," 1.
25. "Churchill and Mrs. Jaramillo Are Improving," *SFNM*, 21 November 1931, 1.
26. Jaramillo, *Romance*, 159.
27. "State of New Mexico, Plaintiff, vs. Thomas Johnson, Defendant, Criminal Information, Criminal No. 4708," 21 November 1931, Clerk of Court, Santa Fe District Court, Santa Fe, N.Mex., 1–2; and "Finger Marks," 1.
28. "Warrant," 23 November 1931, Santa Fe District Court, Santa Fe, N. Mex. 1–2.
29. "Crist Says May Ask for Venue Change," *SFNM*, 28 November 1931, 1.

The Negro Crime

1. "Nothing to Show Negro Was Possible Killer Says Muller," *SFNM*, 21 November 1931, 6.
2. "Confesses Murder of Churchill."
3. E. Dana Johnson, "A Lesson," *SFNM*, 16 November 1931, 4.
4. E. Dana Johnson, "Obituary as Written by Mr. Johnson," in Alice Corbin Henderson, "E. Dana Johnson," *New Mexico Historical Review* (January 1938): 125.
5. Henderson, "E. Dana Johnson," 122.
6. Ibid., 126.
7. Ibid., 127.
8. Ibid., 121–22.
9. Ibid., 123.
10. Ibid., 121–22.
11. "E. Dana Johnson," *SFNM*, 11 December 1937, 4.
12. Henderson, "E. Dana Johnson," 122.
13. Ibid.
14. Johnson, "A Lesson."
15. Ibid.
16. Anita Scott Coleman, "Arizona and New Mexico," *Messenger* 8 (September 1926): 275–76.
17. U.S. Department of Commerce, Bureau of the Census, *Historical Statistics of the United States* (Washington, D.C., 1975), 27.
18. Quintard Taylor, *In Search of the Racial Frontier: African Americans in the American West, 1528–1990* (New York: W. W. Norton, 1998), 104.
19. Ibid., 35. The earliest-known black in what became New Mexico was the fabled Estevan, a Moroccan slave who scouted for the 1539 expedition of Fray Marcos de Niza, but who was killed by the Zuni and left no issue, by all accounts. (Quintard Taylor, "African Americans in the Enchanted State: Black History in New Mexico, 1539–1990," in *History of Hope: The African American Experience in New Mexico,* edited by Quintard Taylor [Albuquerque, N.Mex.: Albuquerque Museum, 1996], 1, 10.)
20. Charles P. Henry, "Blacks and Competing Groups in American Society," *Western Journal of Black Studies* 4 (winter 1980): 230.
21. "Finger Marks," 1–2.
22. Reyes Martinez, "The Martinez Family of Arroyo Hondo," 1; and Chris Wilson, *Myth of Santa Fe: Creating a Modern Regional Tradition* (Albuquerque: University of New Mexico Press, 1997), 29.
23. Jaramillo, *Romance,* 68–69.
24. Ibid., 55.
25. Reyes Martinez, "The First Negro Passes" (1937, WPA Files, Museum of New Mexico History Library, Santa Fe, N.Mex.), 1–3.
26. Ibid., 3.

27. Marta Weigle, ed. *New Mexico in Cameo and Camera: New Deal Documentation of Twentieth-Century Lives* (Albuquerque: University of New Mexico Press, 1985), 15, 113–15, 154.

28. Albert Rosenfeld, "New Mexico's Fading Color Line," *Commentary* 20 (September 1955): 204.

29. Gilbert Thomas Stephenson, *Race Distinctions in American Law* (London: D. Appleton, 1910), 351.

30. Pauli Murray, *States' Laws on Races and Color* (Cincinnati: Women's Division of Christian Services of the Methodist Church, 1950), 290.

31. George Stark, *El Delirio: The Santa Fe World of Elizabeth White* (Santa Fe, N.Mex.: School of American Research Press, 1998), 28–32.

32. "Far West," *The Crisis* 38 (August 1931): 275.

33. Thorsten Sellin, "The Negro and the Problem of Law Observance and Administration in the Light of Social Research," in *The Negro in American Civilization,* ed. Charles S. Johnson (New York: 1939), 451; and Coramae Richey Mann, "The Sexualization of Racism: The Black as Rapist and White Justice," *Western Journal of Black Studies* 3 (fall 1979): 168–70. For an insightful discussion of how "white" was redefined during these years in the American South, see Grace Elizabeth Hale, *Making Whiteness: The Culture of Segregation in the South, 1890–1940* (New York: Pantheon Books, 1998).

34. A. Leon Higginbotham, *Shades of Freedom: Racial Politics and Presumptions of the American Legal Process* (New York: Oxford University Press, 1996), 139–47.

35. Katherine Gay to E. Dana Johnson, 16 November 1931, NAACP Papers, Library of Congress, Washington, D.C.

36. Katherine Gay to Walter White, 17 November 1931, NAACP Papers, Library of Congress, Washington, D.C.

37. For an account of Bronson Cutting's life and career, see Richard Lowitt, *Bronson M. Cutting: Progressive Politician* (Albuquerque: University of New Mexico Press, 1992).

38. "An Old Subscriber" [Bronson Cutting] to E. Dana Johnson, *SFNM,* 17 November 1931, 4.

3 9. "Santa Fe for Law and Order," *Albuquerque Journal,* 18 November 1931, 4.

40. "Let Us Modify It," *SFNM,* 18 November 1931, 4.

41. "Excluding the Negro," *Raton Range,* 26 November 1931, 2.

42. Director of Publicity, NAACP, to Katherine Gay, 18 November 1931, NAACP Papers, Library of Congress, Washington, D.C.

43. Walter White to E. Dana Johnson, 19 November 1931, NAACP Papers, Library of Congress, Washington, D.C.

44. Walter White to Bronson Cutting, 19 November 1931, NAACP Papers, Library of Congress, Washington, D.C.

45. E. T. Puryear to Walter White, 21 November 1931, NAACP Papers, Library of Congress, Washington, D.C.

46. Bronson Cutting to Walter White, 10 December 1931, NAACP Papers, Library of Congress, Washington, D.C.

47. Lowitt, *Bronson M. Cutting,* 320.

48. Bronson Cutting to Olivia Peyton Cutting, 30 November 1931, Bronson Cutting Papers, Library of Congress, Washington, D.C.

Not of One's Peers

1. "Johnson on Trial for Murder Friday," *SFNM*, 1 December 1931, 1–2.

2. "Subpoena," 1 December 1931, *State of New Mexico vs. Thomas Johnson*, First Judicial District Court, Santa Fe County, No. 4708, Criminal, Santa Fe, N.Mex., n.p.

3. "Claims Johnson Trouble Maker at State Prison," *SFNM*, 4 December 1931, 1.

4. Ibid.

5. "Prisoner Shows No Interest," *SFNM*, 4 December 1931, 1–2.

6. *State of New Mexico vs. Thomas Johnson*, Appeal from the District Court of Santa Fe County, Transcript of Record, 6 May 1932, Case No. 3814, Supreme Court of the State of New Mexico, Santa Fe, N.Mex., 22. [Hereafter indicated as TR.]

7. Ibid; and "Prisoner Shows No Interest," 1–2.

8. "Prisoner Shows No Interest," 2.

9. Ibid.

10. Ibid., 1.

11. "Mrs. Jaramillo, Slain Girl's Mother First Witness Called," *Albuquerque Journal*, 5 December 1931, 1.

12. TR, 23.

13. "Prisoner Shows No Interest," 1–2.

14. TR, 23.

15. "Requested Instruction By Defendant," 4 December 1931, *State of New Mexico vs. Thomas Johnson*, First Judicial Court, Santa Fe County, Criminal No. 4708, Santa Fe, N.Mex., n.p.

16. "State Asks Death for Tom Johnson," *SFNM*, 5 December 1931, 1, 3.

17. TR, 25–27.

18. Ibid., 27–29.

19. Ibid., 29.

20. Ibid., 29–30.

21. "Mrs. Jaramillo," 5.

22. TR, 34–38.

23. "Mrs. Jaramillo," 5.

24. TR, 45–47.

25. Ibid., 48–50.

26. "Mrs. Jaramillo," 1.

27. Jaramillo, *Romance*, 135.

28. Ibid., 160–61.

29. TR, 50–52.

30. Ibid., 52.

31. Ibid., 53.

32. Ibid., 53–54.

33. Ibid., 54.

Facts Not in Evidence

1. "Submits Clothing to Jury," *SFNM,* 5 December 1931, 3.
2. "Probe Negro Lynching by Maryland Mob," *SFNM,* 5 December 1931, 1; and "Maryland Mob Lynches Negro," *Albuquerque Journal,* 5 December 1931, 1.
3. "11-Year-Old Girl Tells of Lipstick," *SFNM,* 7 December 1931, 1.
4. "Crist Batters Evidence of Bloodstains," *SFNM,* 5 December 1931, 1.
5. TR, 54–56.
6. Ibid., 56–58.
7. Ibid., 59–60.
8. Ibid., 60–62.
9. "Submits Clothing to Jury," 3.
10. TR, 62–64.
11. Ibid., 64–65.
12. Ibid., 66–68.
13. Ibid.
14. Ibid., 68–69.
15. Ibid., 69–70.
16. "Subpoena" issued to Loren Elliott, 5 December 1931, *State of New Mexico vs. Thomas Johnson,* First Judicial Court, Santa Fe County, Criminal No. 4708, Santa Fe, N.Mex.
17. Ibid.
18. TR, 76–78.
19. Ibid., 79–82.
20. Ibid., 89–95.
21. Ibid., 97–99.

Of Your Own Knowledge

1. TR, 101–5.
2. Ibid., 105.
3. Ibid.
4. Ibid., 106–7.
5. Ibid., 107–10.
6. Ibid., 112.
7. Ibid., 114–15.
8. Ibid., 116–19.
9. Ibid., 119–23.
10. Ibid., 124–26.
11. Ibid., 126, 129.
12. "11-Year-Old Girl," 2.
13. TR, 130.
14. Ibid., 131.

15. Ibid., 135–39.
16. Ibid., 139–41.
17. Ibid., 142.
18. Ibid., 146–48.
19. Ibid., 143–44, 147–49.
20. Ibid., 145–56, 148.
21. Ibid., 148.
22. Ibid., 148–49.
23. "11-Year-Old Girl," 1.
24. TR, 150–51.
25. Ibid., 151–52.
26. Ibid., 152–54.
27. Ibid., 154–55.
28. Ibid., 155–57.
29. "11-Year-Old Girl," 2.
30. TR, 157–59.
31. Ibid., 159–63.
32. Advertisement for the Paris Theater, *SFNM*, 6 December 1931, 6.
33. TR, 163–64; and "11-Year-Old Girl," 2.

Red, Blue, White, and Green

1. "El Paso Fingerprint Expert Says Marks on Vase Made by Prisoner," *SFNM*, 7 December 1931, 2.
2. Ibid.
3. TR, 164–67.
4. Ibid., 167.
5. Ibid., 168–70.
6. Ibid., 170–71.
7. Ibid., 171–72.
8. Ibid., 172–76.
9. Ibid., 177.
10. Ibid., 177, 179.
11. Ibid., 179.
12. Ibid., 180.
13. Ibid., 181.
14. Ibid., 181–82.
15. Ibid., 182–83.
16. Ibid., 188–89.
17. Ibid., 189–90.
18. Ibid., 190–92.
19. Ibid., 193.
20. "El Paso Fingerprint Expert," 2.

21. TR, 193–95.
22. "El Paso Fingerprint Expert," 2.
23. TR, 195–97.
24. Ibid., 197–98; and "El Paso Fingerprint Expert," 2.
25. "El Paso Fingerprint Expert," 2; and TR, 198–201.
26. TR, 202–4.
27. Ibid., 204.
28. "El Paso Fingerprint Expert," 2; and "State Closes Case Against Johnson," *SFNM,* 8 December 1931, 1.
29. "State Closes Case," 5; and TR, 206–18.
30. "Negro Recites Actions on Day of Santa Fe's Girl's Murder," *Albuquerque Journal,* 8 December 1931, 2.
3 1. TR, 218–32.
32. "State Closes Case," 5.

In His Own Behalf

1. TR, 232–33.
2. "Negro Recites Actions," 1.
3. TR, 233–38.
4. Ibid., 238–40.
5. "State Closes Case," 1.
6. TR, 240–46.
7. Ibid., 246–49.
8. Ibid., 249–55.
9. Ibid., 255–60.
10. Ibid., 261–62.
11. Ibid., 263–65.
12. Ibid., 265–69.
13. Ibid., 269.
14. Ibid., 269–72.
15. Ibid., 272.

A Lawful Verdict

1. "Negro Sticks to Story; Explains Everything But Fingerprints on Vase," *SFNM,* 8 December 1931, 2.
2. "Johnson is Grilled On the Stand," *Raton Range,* 8 December 1931, 1.
3. TR, 272–73; and Register of Statistics of Arrest, vol. 34, 1921, Wright State University, Paul Lawrence Dunbar Papers, Archives and Special Collections, Dayton, Ohio, "Thomas Bishop," n.p.
4. TR, 273–75.

5. Ibid., 275.

6. Ibid., 275–77.

7. Ibid., 277–81.

8. Ibid., 281–82.

9. Ibid., 282–84.

10. Ibid., 284–85.

11. Ibid., 285–86.

12. Ibid., 287.

13. Ibid., 291–92.

14. Ibid., 293–95.

15. Ibid., 295–96.

16. Ibid., 296.

17. Ibid., 296–98.

18. Ibid., 301–3.

19. Ibid., 306–7.

20. Ibid., 308–9.

21. Ibid., 310–11.

22. Ibid., 311.

23. Miguel Antonio Otero, Jr., "Instructions to the Jury," TR, 6–10; and *State of New Mexico vs. Thomas Johnson,* Instructions to Jury, Criminal No. 4708, First Judicial District Court, Santa Fe County, Santa Fe, N.Mex.

24. Jacob Crist, "Requested Instruction By Defendant," TR, 13.

25. Otero, "Instructions to the Jury," 12.

26. Dolores Otero DeBurg, "Miss Jaramillo Versus the Jaramillo Girl," *Albuquerque Journal,* 13 December 1931, 6.

27. TR, 12.

28. "Verdict Seals Fate of Negro Who Killed Angelina Jaramillo," *SFNM,* 8 December 1931, 1, 5.

29. Ibid., 1; and "Execution on Birthday of Emancipator," *SFNM,* 9 December 1931, 6.

30. Otero, "Instructions to the Jury," 9–10.

31. "Verdict Seals Fate," 5.

32. Ibid., 1.

33. "Execution on Birthday," 6.

34. Ibid.; "Verdict Seals Fate," 1; and TR, 312.

35. TR, 313.

36. "Execution on Birthday," 6.

37. TR, 14, 313–14; and *State of New Mexico vs. Thomas Johnson,* Verdict, Criminal No. 4708, First Judicial District Court, Santa Fe County, Santa Fe, N.Mex.

38. "Execution on Birthday," 6; and "Negro Murdered Miss Jaramillo in Santa Fe, Is Jury Verdict," *Albuquerque Journal,* 9 December 1931, 1, 5.

39. "Negro Murdered Miss Jaramillo," 1, 5.

40. "Judgment and Sentence," TR, 15.

41. "Execution on Birthday," 6.
42. Ibid.

Innocence Abandoned

1. "Execution on Birthday," 1, 6.
2. Ibid.
3. "Counsel for Defense," *SFNM*, 10 December 1931, 4.
4. "Bar Association Sends Tribute to Crist for Defense of Negro," *SFNM*, 11 December 1931.
5. Miguel Antonio Otero, Jr., to Arthur Seligman, 9 December 1931, and Arthur Seligman to Miguel Antonio Otero, Jr., 10 December 1931, Governor Arthur Seligman Papers, Penal Records, State Records Center and Archives, Santa Fe, N.Mex.
6. "Death Warrant," 9 December 1931, *State of New Mexico vs. Thomas Johnson*, Criminal No. 4708, First Judicial District Court, Santa Fe County, Santa Fe, N.Mex.
7. "Petition" and "Order," 8 December 1931, and "Petition for Allowances of Fees For Expert Witnesses," 9 December 1931, *State of New Mexico vs. Thomas Johnson*, Criminal No. 4708, First Judicial District Court, Santa Fe County, Santa Fe, N.Mex.
8. "Petition for Allowance of Fees," 15 June 1932, *State of New Mexico vs. Thomas Johnson*, Criminal No. 4708, First Judicial District Court, Santa Fe County, Santa Fe, N.Mex.
9. "Pen Inmates Labored Hours to Recover Negro's Prints Used in Case Against Killer," *SFNM*, 11 December 1931.
10. "Believe Johnson Made Duke City Trip to Dispose of Stolen Goods," *SFNM*, 12 December 1931.
11. "Johnson Seeking Funds to Take Appeal to High Court," *SFNM*, 15 December 1931, 1; and "Johnson Appeal Depends on His Aged Grandpa," *Albuquerque Journal*, 16 December 1931, 1.
12. Ibid.
13. "Order," 16 December 1931, *State of New Mexico vs. Thomas Johnson*, Criminal No. 4708, First District Court, Santa Fe County, Santa Fe, N.Mex.
14. Ethel Wilson to Walter White, 14 December 1931, Bronson Cutting Papers, Manuscript Division, Library of Congress, Washington, D.C.
15. Quintard Taylor, "African Americans in the Enchanted State," 7, 9; and Barbara Richardson, *Black Directory of New Mexico* (Rio Rancho, N.Mex.: Panorama Press, 1976), 31.
16. Ethel Wilson to Walter White, 14 December 1931, Bronson Cutting Papers, Manuscript Division, Library of Congress, Washington, D.C.
17. Roy Wilkins to Mrs. W. A. McDonald, 16 December 1931, NAACP Papers, Manuscript Division, Library of Congress, Washington, D.C.
18. "Johnson in Close Confinement; Not Yet Moved to Death House," *SFNM*, 23 December 1931, 2.

19. Ibid.
20. "Will Import Electrician for Execution of Johnson," *SFNM*, 30 December 1931, 2.
21. "Negro Pays Compliment to Sheriff's Office," *SFNM*, 17 December 1931, 2.
22. "Negro Fined $60 for Advances to White Girl," *Albuquerque Journal*, 31 December 1931, 1.
23. "Order Eight Taos Negroes Out of Town," *SFNM*, 8 January 1932, 1.
24. "'Niggers Get Out Quick' Was Warning Up in Taos," *SFNM*, 19 January 1932; and "Salin [*sic*] Los Negroes [*sic*] de Taos," *Revista Popular de Nuevo Mexico*, 3 January 1932, 4.
25. "Will Import Electrician," 2.
26. Leila Smith to Arthur Seligman, 22 January 1932, Governor Arthur Seligman Papers, Penal Records, State Records Center and Archives, Santa Fe, N.Mex.; and Taylor, *In Search of the Racial Frontier*, 227–29.
27. Secretary to the Governor to Leila Smith, 23 January 1932, Governor Arthur Seligman Papers, Penal Records, State Records Center and Archives, Santa Fe, N.Mex.
28. E. D. Williams to Arthur Seligman, 3 February 1932, and Arthur Seligman to E. D. Williams, 4 February 1932, Governor Arthur Seligman Papers, Penal Records, State Records Center and Archives, Santa Fe, N.Mex.
29. "Johnson to Die on February 12," *SFNM*, 1 February 1932, 2.
30. "Johnson Appeal of Execution to Be Decided Today—Crist," *SFNM*, 6 February 1932, 1, 4.
31. "Says Friends Believe Man Is Innocent," *SFNM*, 8 February 1932, 1.
32. "Motion for Allowance of Appeal," TR, 16; and "Negro's Guilt Certain, Dist. Attorney Says," *SFNM*, 9 February 1932.
33. "Order Granting Appeal," TR, 16; and "Negro's Guilt Certain."
34. "Negro's Guilt Certain."
35. Ibid.
36. Ibid.

An Abiding Conviction

1. For a full discussion of this struggle, see David Levering Lewis, *W. E. B. DuBois: The Fight for Equality and the American Century, 1919–1963* (New York: Henry Holt, 2000).
2. "Praecipe," TR, 17–18.
3. "Notice of Appeal," TR, 18–19.
4. "Order Settling Bill of Exceptions," TR, 315.
5. "Clerk's Certificate of Costs" and "Clerk's Final Certificate," TR, 316–17.
6. "Negro's Appeal From Death Sentence Is Perfected," *Albuquerque Journal*, 8 May 1932, 1.
7. "Motion for Extension of Time for Filing Brief," TR, n.p.
8. "Crist Gets More Time On Appeal in Case of Negro Tom Johnson," *SFNM*, 6

June 1932.

9. "Brief of Appellant," *State of New Mexico vs. Thomas Johnson,* no. 3814, 20 June 1932, Supreme Court of New Mexico, Santa Fe, N.Mex., 2–3.

10. Ibid., 5, 7.

11. Ibid., 7.

12. Ibid., 10–11.

13. Ibid., 11–12.

14. Ibid., 12–13.

15. Ibid., 14–15.

16. Ibid., 16–19.

17. Ibid., 20–24.

18. "Acceptance of Service," *State of New Mexico vs. Thomas Johnson,* no. 3814, 19 July 1932, Supreme Court of the State of New Mexico, Santa Fe, N.Mex.

19. "Brief of Appellee," *State of New Mexico vs. Thomas Johnson,* no. 3814, 16 July 1932, Supreme Court of the State of New Mexico, Santa Fe, N.Mex., 2–3.

20. Ibid., 8.

21. Ibid., 8–9.

22. Ibid., 10–12.

23. Ibid., 6–7.

24. "Reply Brief of Appellant," *State of New Mexico vs. Thomas Johnson,* no. 3814, 27 July 1932, Supreme Court of the State of New Mexico, Santa Fe, N.Mex., 1–2.

25. Ibid., 5–6.

26. Ibid., 7.

27. Ibid., 8–10, 18–19.

28. "Johnson, Grace Mott," in *Who's Who in American Art,* vol. I, ed. Alice Coe McGlauflin (Washington, D.C.: American Federation of Arts, 1935), 224; "Johnson, Grace Mott," in *Who's Who in American Art,* ed. Dorothy Gilbert (New York: R. R. Bowker, 1962), 308; and "Grace Mott Johnson," in *Contemporary American Sculpture* (San Francisco: National Sculpture Society, 1929), 174.

29. Grace Mott Johnson to NAACP, 22 January 1933, NAACP Papers, Manuscript Division, Library of Congress, Washington, D.C.

30. Grace Mott Johnson to Walter White, 22 January 1933, NAACP Papers, Manuscript Division, Library of Congress, Washington, D.C.

31. Grace Mott Johnson to NAACP, 22 January 1933, NAACP Papers, Manuscript Division, Library of Congress, Washington, D.C.

32. Grace Mott Johnson to Walter White, 24 January 1933, NAACP Papers, Manuscript Division, Library of Congress, Washington, D.C.

33. Roy Wilkins to Grace Mott Johnson, 25 January 1933, NAACP Papers, Manuscript Division, Library of Congress, Washington, D.C.

34. Grace Mott Johnson to Roy Wilkins, 2 February 1933, NAACP Papers, Manuscript Division, Library of Congress, Washington, D.C.; and Richardson, *Black Directory of New Mexico,* 30.

35. Ibid.

36. "Color Caste in the United States," *The Crisis* 40 (March 1933): 60, 70.

37. "Appeal From the District Court of Santa Fe County, *The State of New Mexico, Appellee, v. Thomas Johnson, Appellant,* no. 3814," 28 March 1933, Supreme Court of the State of New Mexico, Santa Fe, N.Mex., 1, 5–6. Also in *Pacific Reporter,* second series, vol. 21, May–June 1933 (St. Paul: West Publishing, 1933), 813–19.

38. "Appeal From the District Court," 19–20.

Final Days

1. Thomas Hanna to Arthur Seligman, 4 April 1933, Governor Arthur Seligman Papers, Penal Records, State Records and Archives Center, Santa Fe, N.Mex.

2. Arthur Seligman to Thomas Hanna, 7 April 1933, Governor Arthur Seligman Papers, Penal Records, State Records and Archives Center, Santa Fe, N.Mex.

3. "Tom Johnson's Conviction Sustained," *SFNM,* 28 March 1933, 1.

4. "Negro Guilty of Attack on White Woman," *SFNM,* 10 April 1933, 1.

5. "Opinion on Scottsboro," *The Crisis* 40 (June 1933): 135.

6. Edwin M. Borchard, *Convicting the Innocent: Errors of Criminal Justice* (New Haven: Yale University Press, 1932), xix.

7. "Willie Brown," *The Crisis* 40 (April 1933): 94.

8. "Motion for Extension of Time for Filing Motion for Rehearing," *State of New Mexico v. Thomas Johnson,* no. 2814, 14 April 1933, Supreme Court of the State of New Mexico, Santa Fe, N.Mex.; and "Negro Charged With Burglary," *SFNM,* 20 April 1933.

9. "Motion for Rehearing," *The State of New Mexico v. Thomas Johnson,* no. 3814, 27 April 1933, Supreme Court of the State of New Mexico, Santa Fe, N.Mex., points 1–2.

10. Ibid., points 3–5.

11. Ibid., points 6–8.

12. "Brief of Appellee on Motion for Rehearing," *State of New Mexico vs. Thomas Johnson,* no. 3814, 2 May 1933, Supreme Court of the State of New Mexico, Santa Fe, N.Mex., points 1–4.

13. "Comment on Motion for Rehearing," *State of New Mexico vs. Thomas Johnson,* no. 3814, 1 May 1933, Supreme Court of the State of New Mexico, Santa Fe, N.Mex.

14. "Warrant of Execution," no. 3814, 15 May 1933, Supreme Court of the State of New Mexico, Santa Fe, N.Mex.; and "Comment on Motion for Rehearing."

15. "Johnson to Death Chair," *SFNM,* 16 May 1933, 1.

16. "Johnson Not Told Time Is Set," *SFNM,* 18 May 1933, 1.

17. "Negro Notified of Date of Execution," *SFNM,* 20 May 1933, 1.

18. J. W. Lindsay to Arthur Seligman, 14 June 1933, and Secretary to the Governor to J. W. Lindsay, 17 June 1933, Governor Arthur Seligman Papers, Penal Records, State Records and Archives Center, Santa Fe, N.Mex.

19. Grace Mott Johnson to Walter White, 14 June 1933, NAACP Papers, Manuscript Division, Library of Congress, Washington, D.C.

20. Roy Wilkins to Grace Mott Johnson, 14 June 1933, NAACP Papers, Manuscript Division, Library of Congress, Washington, D.C.

21. Walter White to Arthur Seligman, 14 July 1933, and Arthur Seligman to Walter White, 15 July 1933, Governor Arthur Seligman Papers, Penal Records, State Records and Archives Center, Santa Fe, N.Mex.

22. Grace Mott Johnson to Roy Wilkins, 16 July 1933, NAACP Papers, Manuscript Division, Library of Congress, Washington, D.C.

23. Grace Mott Johnson to Roy Wilkins, 16 July 1933, NAACP Papers, Manuscript Division, Library of Congress, Washington, D.C.

24. Author's interviews with Rosa Montoya, cousin of Angelina Jaramillo, and Marian LaNoue, daughter of Robert and Mae Martinez Smith, 28 July 1999.

25. Ibid.

26. William Morris Houghton to Arthur Seligman, n.d., Governor Arthur Seligman Papers, Penal Records, State Records and Archives Center, Santa Fe, N.Mex.

27. Mabel Luhan to Arthur Seligman, 15 July 1933, and Arthur Seligman to Mabel Luhan, 17 July 1933, Governor Arthur Seligman Papers, Penal Records, State Records and Archives Center, Santa Fe, N.Mex.

28. Arthur Seligman to Theodore M. Brinson, 17 July 1933, Governor Arthur Seligman Papers, Penal Records, State Record and Archives Center, Santa Fe, N.Mex.

29. "Close Investigation of Race Quiz," SFNM, 6 May 1933, 1.

30. Gilberto Espinosa to Arthur Seligman, 27 April 1933, Governor Arthur Seligman Papers, New Mexico State Records and Archives Center, Santa Fe, N.Mex.

31. "Close Investigation of Race Quiz," 1.

32. Resolution Committee to Arthur Seligman, 8 May 1933, Governor Arthur Seligman Papers, New Mexico State Records and Archives Center, Santa Fe, N.Mex.

33. Glisson Winkler, "Governor Is Blocked for Senate," SFNM, 17 July 1933, 1.

34. "Enter Plea for Johnson," SFNM, 17 July 1933, 1.

35. "No Decision on Johnson," SFNM, 18 July 1933; and "Johnson, Guardano First in State Sent to Chair," SFNM, 21 July 1933, 3.

36. "Governor Hears Clemency Plea for Johnson; No Decision," Albuquerque Journal, 18 July 1933, 1.

37. Ibid.

38. "No Action on Two Appeals," SFNM, 19 July 1933, 1; and "People Stand At Pen Gate As Two Die," SFNM, 21 July 1933, 1.

39. "Two Scheduled to Die in Pen Tonight: Johnson, Guardano to Chair," SFNM, 20 July 1933, 1.

40. "People Stand," 1.

41. "Two Scheduled to Die," 1, 3; "Johnson and Guardano Pay Penalty in First Electric Executions in New Mexico," Albuquerque Journal, 21 July 1933, 1; "Bury Johnson at N.Mex. Pen," SFNM, 24 July 1933, 1; and "Johnson Y Guardano Sufren la Pena de Muerte en la Silla Electrica," Revista Popular de Nuevo Mexico, 26 July 1933, 1.

42. "People Stand," 3; "Two Scheduled to Die," 3; and "Bury Johnson," 1.

43. "People Stand," 3.

44. Grace Mott Johnson to N.A.A.C.P. et al., 21 July 1933, NAACP Papers, Manuscript Division, Library of Congress, Washington, D.C.

45. "The Chair," *SFNM*, 21 July 1933, 4.

46. "Bury Johnson," 1.

Disquieting Shadows

1. Grace Mott Johnson to Roy Wilkins, 31 July 1931, NAACP Papers, Manuscript Division, Library of Congress, Washington, D.C.

2. "New Colored Church for Santa Fe," *SFNM*, 8 August 1933, 1.

3. *Santa Fe City Directory*, 1934, no listing for Robert Smith; and Rita Younis, "Who Killed Angelina?" *La Herencia del Norte* (spring 1998): 39.

4. *Santa Fe City Directory*, 1934. No listing in 1936 edition.

5. Gravestone of Carlos Smith, Rosario Cemetery, Santa Fe, N.Mex.

6. "Cutting Killed," "Nation Grieves at Death of Cutting," and "Obituary," *SFNM*, 6 May 1935, 1, 6.

7. Walter White to Olivia Cutting, 11 May 1935, NAACP Papers, Manuscript Division, Library of Congress, Washington, D.C.

8. Walter White to Olivia Cutting, 17 May 1935, NAACP Papers, Manuscript Division, Library of Congress, Washington, D.C.

9. Lowitt, *Bronson M. Cutting*, 305.

10. Bronson M. Cutting, Probate Record, Santa Fe County Clerk, Santa Fe, N.Mex.; and Lowitt, *Bronson M. Cutting*, 320.

11. "E. Dana Johnson," *SFNM*, 11 December 1936, 1.

12. "E. Dana Johnson," E. Dana Johnson Papers, History Library, Museum of New Mexico, Santa Fe, N.Mex.

13. "Jesus Baca Funeral to Be Held Probably Thursday," *SFNM*, 28 August 1944, 1, 4.

14. "Noted Criminal Lawyer Dies Today," *SFNM*, 26 April 1935, 1; and Jacob H. Crist, Probate Record, Santa Fe County Clerk, Santa Fe, N.Mex.

15. "Judge Otero Dies at Age 85," *SFNM*, 3 November 1977, A12.

16. Jaramillo, *Romance*, 163–64.

17. *Santa Fe City Directory*, 1932.

18. Cleofas Jaramillo, "Founder Offers Factual History of Folklorica," *SFNM*, 26 February 1954; and Getz, *Schools of Their Own*, 111. Cleofas Jaramillo published the following books during her lifetime: *Cuentos del hogar (Spanish Fairy Stories)* (El Campo, Tex.: Citizen Press, 1939); *The Genuine New Mexico Tasty Recipes (Portajes Sabrosos)* (n.p., 1939); *Shadows of the Past (Sombras del Pasado)* (Santa Fe, N.Mex.: Seton Village, 1941); and *Romance of a Little Village Girl* (San Antonio: Naylor, 1955). (Several have since been reprinted.)

19. Quoted in Steve Terrell, "A Tale of Murder, Race, Media and Justice," *SFNM*, 29 October 1995, A-6. At the time of this later murder, reference was made to the Johnson case (William McNulty, "Twin Clues Spur Police in Search for Maniac Slayer," *SFNM*, 20 November 1945, 1).

20. Obituary of Cleofas Jaramillo, *SFNM*, 3 December 1956.

21. Cleofas M. Jaramillo, Probate Record, 18 December 1956, Santa Fe County Clerk, Santa Fe, N.Mex.

22. Jaramillo, *Romance*, 162.

23. Anita Thomas, note dated March 1976, History File #103, Thomas Johnson, New Mexico State Archives, Santa Fe, N.Mex.

24. "The Romance of Cleofas Jaramillo," *The Santa Fe Scene*, 23 August 1958, 6.

25. Jerry Montgomery, "Silent Walls Know History of Old House," *SFNM*, 10 March 1977. Mention of the murder was recently published in a local community newsletter, *La Herencia del Norte* (spring 1998), in an article by Rita Younis titled, "Who Killed Angelina?" In it, the writer states that "those who know what really happened won't talk, so to this day the murder of Angelina Jaramillo remains a mystery" (39).

Bibliography

Manuscript Sources

1910 U.S. Census, National Archives, Washington, D.C.

Appeals records, the Supreme Court of the State of New Mexico, Santa Fe, N.Mex.

Arthur Seligman Papers, State Records and Archives, State of New Mexico, Santa Fe, N.Mex.

Baptismal records, St. Antoine Church, National Archives, Montreal, Quebec, Canada.

Bronson Cutting Papers, Library of Congress, Washington, D.C.

Criminal Complaints, District Court of Santa Fe County, Santa Fe, N.Mex.

Divorce records, District Court of Santa Fe County, Santa Fe, N.Mex.

E. Dana Johnson Papers, History Library, Museum of New Mexico, Santa Fe, N.Mex.

Kansas Penitentiary, Prisoner Ledger, Kansas State Historical Society, Topeka, Kans.

Marriage and property records, Department of Records, Santa Fe County, Santa Fe, N.Mex.

Marriage records, Archives of the Archdiocese of Santa Fe, Santa Fe, N.Mex.

Michigan State Penitentiary Register, Michigan Department of State, Michigan History Center, State Archives, Lansing, Mich.

NAACP Papers, Library of Congress, Washington, D.C.

Prince Papers, State Records Center and Archives, State of New Mexico, Santa Fe, N.Mex.

Probate records, Santa Fe County Clerk's Office, Santa Fe, N.Mex.

Bibliography

Register of Statistics of Arrests, Wright State University, Paul Lawrence Dunbar Library, Archives and Special Collections, Dayton, Ohio.

Thomas Johnson, State Records Center and Archives, State of New Mexico, Santa Fe, N.Mex.

WPA Files, History Library, Museum of New Mexico, Santa Fe, N.Mex.

Books and Journals

"Appeal From the District Court of Santa Fe County, *The State of New Mexico, Appellee, v. Thomas Johnson, Appellant,* No. 3814." *Pacific Reporter,* second series, vol. 21, May–June 1933. St. Paul: West Publishing, 1933.

Austin, Mary. "Life at Santa Fe." *South Atlantic Quarterly* 31 (July 1932): 263–71.

Bardolph, Richard. *The Civil Rights Record: Black Americans and the Law, 1849–1970.* New York: Thomas Y. Crowell, 1970.

Bowers, William J. *Legal Homicide: Death as Punishment in America, 1864–1982.* Boston: Northeastern University Press, M., 1984.

Burrows, Dan. "The Clue of the Lipstick." *The Master Detective* (March 1935): 42–49, 83.

Cole, David. *No Equal Justice: Race and Class in the American Criminal Justice System.* New York: New Press, 1998.

Coleman, Anita Scott. "Arizona and New Mexico." *Messenger* 8 (September 1926): 275–76.

"Color Caste in the United States." *The Crisis* 40 (March 1933): 60, 70.

Deutsch, Sarah. *No Separate Refuge: Culture, Class, and Gender on an Anglo-Hispanic Frontier in the American Southwest, 1880–1940.* New York: Oxford University Press, 1987.

Dittmer, John. *Black Georgia in the Progressive Era, 1900–1920.* Urbana: University of Illinois Press, 1977.

DuBois, W. E. B. "Scottsboro." *The Crisis* 38 (July 1931): 241.

El Paso Directory, 1932–1933. El Paso, Tex.: Hudspeth Publishing, 1932.

"Far West." *The Crisis* 38 (August 1931): 275.

Getz, Lynne Marie. *Schools of Their Own: The Education of Hispanos in New Mexico, 1850–1940.* Albuquerque: University of New Mexico Press, 1997.

Goette, H. A. *Goette's Savannah City Directory for 1902.* Savannah, Ga.: Savannah Morning News, 1902.

———. *Goette's Savannah City Directory for 1910.* Savannah, Ga.: Savannah Morning News, 1910.

———. *Goette's Savannah City Directory for 1921* (Savannah, Ga.: Savannah Morning News, 1921.

"Grace Mott Johnson." In *Contemporary American Sculpture.* San Francisco: National Sculpture Society, 1929, 129.

Grant, Donald L. *The Way It Was in the South: The Black Experience in Georgia.* New York: Carol Publishing Group, 1993.

Hale, Grace Elizabeth. *Making Whiteness: The Culture of Segregation in the South, 1890–1940*. New York: Pantheon Books, 1998.

Henderson, Alice Corbin. "E. Dana Johnson." *New Mexico Historical Review* (January 1938): 120–28.

Henry, Charles P. "Blacks and Competing Groups in American Society." *Western Journal of Black Studies* 4 (winter 1980): 222–30.

Higginbotham, A. Leon. *Shades of Freedom: Racial Politics and Presumptions of the American Legal Process*. New York: Oxford University Press, 1996.

Jaramillo, Cleofas. *Romance of a Little Village Girl*. San Antonio, Tex.: Naylor, 1955.

———. *Shadows of the Past*. Santa Fe, N.Mex.: Seton Village, 1941.

"Johnson, Grace Mott." In *Who's Who in American Art*, vol. I, edited by Alice Coe McGlauflin. Washington, D.C.: American Federation of Arts, 1935, 224.

"Johnson, Grace Mott." In *Who's Who in American Art*, edited by Dorothy Gilbert. New York: Bowker, 1962, 308.

Johnson, Grey. "The Negro and Crime." *Annals of the American Academy of Political Science* 217 (September 1941): 93–105.

Johnson, Judith. "A Mighty Fortress Is Our Pen." In *Essays in Twentieth Century New Mexico History*, edited by Judith Boyce DeMark. Albuquerque: University of New Mexico Press, 1994, 120–26.

Knowlton, Clark S. "Causes of Land Loss Among the Spanish-Americans in Northern New Mexico." In *The Chicanos: Life and Struggles of the Mexican Minority in the United States*, edited by Lopes Y. Rivas. New York: Monthly Review, 1973, 111–21.

Langain, Esther F., ed. *A Mary Austin Reader*. Tucson: University of Arizona Press, 1996.

Lewis, David Levering. *W. E. B. DuBois: The Fight for Equality and the American Century, 1919–1963*. New York: Henry Holt, 2000.

Litwack, Leon. *Trouble in Mind: Black Southerners in the Age of Jim Crow*. New York: Alfred A. Knopf, 1998.

Lowitt, Richard D. *Bronson M. Cutting: Progressive Politician*. Albuquerque: University of New Mexico Press, 1992.

Mann, Coramae Richey. "The Sexualization of Racism: The Black as Rapist and White Justice." *Western Journal of Black Studies* 3 (fall 1979): 168–75.

Meier, Matt. *Mexican Americans–American Mexicans: From Conquistadors to Chicanos*. New York: Hill and Wang, 1993.

Murray, Pauli. *States' Laws on Race and Color*. Cincinnati: Women's Division of Christian Services of the Methodist Church, 1950.

"Opinion on Scottsboro." *The Crisis* 40 (June 1933): 135.

Paulin, Charles O. "Cutting, Bronson Murray." *Dictionary of American Biography*, vol. XI. New York: Charles Scribner's Sons, 1944, 215–16.

Raper, Arthur. *The Tragedy of Lynching*. Chapel Hill: University of North Carolina Press, 1933.

Rebolledo, Tey Diana. "Cleofas Martinez Jaramillo." In *Notable Hispanic American Women*, edited by Diane Telgren. Detroit: Gale Research, 219–20.

Bibliography

Richardson, Barbara. *Black Directory of New Mexico: Black Pioneers of New Mexico, a Documentary and Pictorial History.* Rio Rancho, N.Mex.: Panorama Press, 1976.

"The Romance of Cleofas Jaramillo." *The Santa Fe Scene* (23 August 1958): 4–6.

Rosenfeld, Albert. "New Mexico's Fading Color Line." *Commentary* 20 (September 1955): 203–11.

Russell, John C. "Racial Groups in the New Mexico Legislature." *Annals of the American Academy of Political Science* 195 (January 1938): 63–71.

Sanchez, Ramon. "Cleofas M. Jaramillo." In *Dictionary of Literary Biography,* vol. 122. Detroit: Gale Research, 1992, 154–58.

Savage, W. Sherman. *Blacks in the West.* Westport, Conn.: Greenwood, 1976.

Sellin, Thorsten. "The Negro and the Problem of Law Observance and Administration in the Light of Social Research." In *The Negro in American Civilization,* edited by Charles S. Johnson. New York: Henry Holt, 1930.

Stark, George. *El Delirio: The Santa Fe World of Elizabeth White.* Santa Fe, N.Mex.: School of American Research, 1998.

Stephenson, Gilbert Thomas. *Race Distinctions in American Law.* London: D. Appleton, 1910.

Stephenson, Richard. "Race in the Cactus State." *The Crisis* 61 (April 1954): 197–202.

Taylor, Quintard. "African Americans in the Enchanted State: Black History in New Mexico, 1539–1990." In *History of Hope: The African American Experience in New Mexico,* edited by Quintard Taylor. Albuquerque, N.Mex.: Albuquerque Museum, 1996, 1–10.

———. *In Search of the Racial Frontier: African Americans in the American West, 1528–1990.* New York: W. W. Norton, 1998.

Tindall, George Brown. *South Carolina Negroes, 1877–1900.* Columbia, S.C.: University of South Carolina Press, 1952.

Torrez, Robert. "Murder, Politics and the Administration of Justice in Frontier New Mexico: The Hanging of Perfecto Padilla." *La Crónica de Nuevo Mexico* 32 (December 1991): n.p.

U.S. Department of Commerce, Bureau of the Census, Historical Statistics of the United States. Washington, D.C.: 1975.

Weber, David, ed. *Foreigners in Their Native Land: Historical Roots of the Mexican Americans.* Albuquerque: University of New Mexico Press, 1973.

Weigle, Marta, ed. *New Mexico in Cameo and Camera: New Deal Documentation of Twentieth-Century Lives.* Albuquerque: University of New Mexico Press, 1985.

"Willie Brown." *The Crisis* 40 (April 1933): 94.

Wilson, Chris. *Myth of Santa Fe: Creating a Modern Regional Tradition.* Albuquerque: University of New Mexico Press, 1997.

Younis, Rita. "Who Killed Angelina?" *La Herencia del Norte* (spring 1998): 39.

Index

Abiquiu, New Mexico, 20

African Americans in New Mexico, 20, 47–52, 201; following Johnson trial, 156–58, 186, 188, 194. *See also* "Negro Crime"

Alarid, Ike, 1, 3, 32

Albuquerque, New Mexico: Thomas Johnson in 1–3, 10, 13, 36, 116–18, 125–28; police station and arrest, 1–3, 10, 78–82, 84; Kimo Theater, 25; Spanish quarter, 179–80

Albuquerque Journal, 37, 144; attacks Dana Johnson editorial, 55; Cleofas Jaramillo at trial of Thomas Johnson, 68; Crist at trial of Thomas Johnson, 114; post–Johnson trial reporting, 157; reports on Johnson appeal, 163

Alexander, Bill, 36, 133

Andrew's Garage, 4–5, 19; testimony involving, 78–80, 108–10, 116, 121–24, 133, 138–42

Arroyo Hondo, New Mexico, 19–20, 22–23

Austin, Mary, xiii–xiv, 17

Baca, Jesus, 1, 3–6, 13, 32, 36, 38; death of, 190–91; disturbance at trial of Thomas Johnson, 115; friendship with Bronson Cutting, 57, 190–91; inherits *Santa Fe New Mexican,* 190; jury selection, 60; post–trial theory of Johnson's guilt, 154; testimony at trial of Thomas Johnson, 83–85, 143; uncuffs Johnson at trial, 141, 143

Barnes, Alec, 132–33; testimony at trial of Thomas Johnson, 88–90

Beaufort, South Carolina, 9–10

Bishop, Henry, 9

Bishop, Magdalene, 9

Bishop, Silvena, 9

Bishop, Thomas, 9

Bishop, Thomas, Jr. *See* Johnson, Thomas

Blodgett, George, xiii–xiv, 192

Borchard, Edwin, 172

Brunk, R. E.: testimony at trial of

Index

154; testimony about, 117–18,
136–37, 143
Gonzales, Marie: alerts neighbor to
cousin Angelina Jaramillo's murder,
3, 29, 31; helps gather evidence, 71;
testimony at trial of Thomas
Johnson, 92–94; testimony disputed
on appeal, 166
Guardano, Santiago, 182–83

Hanna, Thomas, urges execution, 171
Henderson, Alice Corbin, 46–47
Holmes, Oliver, 1, 40; testimony about,
134; testimony at trial of Thomas
Johnson, 85–87, 143
Hyde, Hazel, xiii, 192

Jaramillo, Angelina: boarding school in
Albuquerque, 24–25; coroner's
report, 14–15; dancer, aspirations as,
24–25, 28; description, 7–8; first
love, 24; funeral service and burial,
32–34; Loretto Academy, 24–26, 30;
rape and murder, xiv–xv, 3–4, 7–9,
30–33, 43, 176–78; relationship with
aunt, Mae Smith, 26, 28; relationship
with mother, Cleofas Jaramillo, 17-
20, 23–30; relationship with uncle,
Robert Smith, 15, 176–78
Jaramillo, Cleofas: Angelina's murder
allegations, 13–14; Anglo culture,
opposition to, 21–24, 49, 192–93;
death of, 193; discovered by, 31–33;
early life, 19, 22–23; meets and weds
Venceslao Jaramillo, 20–22, 68;
partially rescinds testimony, 192–93;
racial consciousness, 49–51; recovery
from assault, 37, 43; relationship
with daughter, Angelina Jaramillo,
17–20, 23–30; testimony at Johnson
trial,68-69; testimony disputed on
appeal, 165; views daughter's body,
33-34

Jaramillo, Venceslao: death, 23; early
life, 20; meets and weds Cleofas
Martinez, 20–22, 68; political life,
23–24; precarious finances, 23, 25
Jim Crow, 9–11, 49–51, 202
Johnson, E. Dana: attacks "Negro
Crime," 47–49, 53; becomes editor
of Santa Fe New Mexican, 46;
comments on Thomas Johnson
execution, 187; defended by Bronson
Cutting, 55; early life, 46; eulogizes
Bronson Cutting, 189 modifies
editorial stance, 55–56
Johnson, Grace Mott: appeals to Walter
White, 167–70, 175–77; disputes H.
C. Martin's account, 167, 169; final
effort to save Johnson, 179; sends
reports to NAACP, 186, 188
Johnson, Thomas: alibi, 1–3, 36–38,
117–25, 136–38; alleged rape and
murder, xiv–xv, 3, 9, 13–15, 127,
132, 140; appeal process, 152, 155,
158, 160–67, 170, 172–74; body
displayed, 186; burial, 187; capture,
1–3, 125–28, 142; Churchill assault,
2–3, 127, 129, 138–42; early years,
9–13, 116; execution, 182–85;
formally accused, 37; innocence later
discussed, 192, 194 preliminary
hearing, 38–42; previous crimes,
alleged and real, 3, 10–13; receives
news of final appeal denial, 174;
returned to Santa Fe, 6; sentencing,
149–50; time in Albuquerque, 1–3,
10, 13, 116–18, 135; trial, 61–151;
trial date, 43–44; trial testimony,
116–43; verdict, 147–49,
154–55

Kahnt, Beulah, 24–25, 28
Kansas State Penitentiary, 12
Kenney, John J., 1, 3, 6; coroner's
inquest, 13–16; execution, 174;
gathers evidence, 37, 39; jury